Contents

Cambri

Co

IE

Bands 4–5

Student's Book *without Answers*

Guy Brook-Hart and Vanessa Jakeman

CAMBRIDGE UNIVERSITY PRESS
Cambridge, New York, Melbourne, Madrid, Cape Town,
Singapore, São Paulo, Delhi, Tokyo, Mexico City

Cambridge University Press
The Edinburgh Building, Cambridge CB2 8RU, UK

www.cambridge.org
Information on this title: www.cambridge.org/9780521179577

© Cambridge University Press 2012

First published 2012

Printed in the United Kingdom at the University Press, Cambridge

A catalogue record for this publication is available from the British Library.

ISBN 978-0-521-17956-0 Student's Book with Answers with CD-ROM
ISBN 978-0-521-17957-7 Student's Book without Answers with CD-ROM
ISBN 978-0-521-18515-8 Teacher's Book
ISBN 978-0-521-17958-4 Class Audio CDs (2)
ISBN 978-0-521-17960-7 Student's Pack (Student's Book with Answers with CD-ROM and Class Audio CDs (2))
ISBN 978-1-107-60245-8 Workbook with Answers with Audio CD
ISBN 978-1-107-60244-1 Workbook without Answers with Audio CD

Writing	Vocabulary and Spelling	Pronunciation	Key grammar
Writing Task 1 • Describing pie charts and bar charts • Selecting key features • Using accurate data	• Collocations and prepositional phrases • *percent* v. *percentage* • Spelling: Making nouns plural	Sentence stress 1 • Stressing the words which answer the question or give new information	Present simple and present continuous
Writing Task 2 • Discussing advantages and disadvantages • Analysing the task • Planning an answer • Writing an introduction • Opening paragraphs • Using linkers: *also*, *and*, *but* and *however*	• Working out the meanings of words • Spelling: Changes when adding –*ed*	Verbs + –*ed*	Past simple
Writing Task 1 • Describing tables and charts • Comparing data and selecting key points • Writing in paragraphs • Writing an overview	• Topic vocabulary: *renewable energy*, *zero emissions*, *vehicle*, etc.; *commuter*, *congestion*, *smog*, etc. • *make* and *cause* • Spelling: Changes when adding –*er* and –*est* to adjectives	Word stress 1 • Using a dictionary	Making comparisons
Writing Task 2 • To what extent do you agree or disagree? • Brainstorming ideas • Avoiding irrelevance • Organising your ideas	• Topic vocabulary: *design*, *device*, *output*, etc.; *attempt*, *assemble*, *experiment*, etc. • What type of word is it? 1 • Spelling: Using and misusing double letters	Chunking 1 • Using natural pauses to help the listener	Present perfect
Writing Task 1 • Summarising two charts • Comparing bar charts • Grouping information • Analysing the task and planning an answer	• Topic vocabulary: *diet*, *prey*, *breed*, etc. • What type of word is it? 2 • Prepositions in time phrases • Words that give directions • Spelling: Small words often misspelled	Sentence stress 2 • Stressing words which carry meaning or express feeling	Countable and uncountable nouns
Writing Task 2 • Answering a single question • Analysing the task and brainstorming ideas • Planning an answer	• Topic vocabulary: *conventional*, *novelty*, *donate*, etc. • Word building • Expressing opinions and feelings • Word formation and spelling changes • Spelling: Suffixes	Intonation 1 • Indicating that you have or haven't finished your answer	Zero and first conditionals (*if*/*unless*)
Writing Task 1 • Describing trends • Using verb and noun phrases • Using the correct tense • Writing an overview	• *raise* or *rise*? • Spelling: Forming adverbs from adjectives	Word stress 2 • Stressing the correct syllable	Prepositions to describe graphs
Writing Task 2 • Answering two questions • Analysing the task • Planning and writing about both parts • Writing a conclusion	• *tourism* or *tourist*? • Spelling: Introductory and linking phrases	Chunking 2 • Improving overall fluency	Relative pronouns: *who*, *which*, *that*, *where*
Writing Task 1 • Summarising a diagram • Planning an answer • Ordering the information and using time markers: *when*, *after*, *next*, *then* • Comparing two diagrams • Beginning and ending an answer and writing an overview	• Topic vocabulary: *filter*, *pressure*, *marine*, etc. • *effect*, *benefit*, *advantage* and *disadvantage* • Spelling: Some common mistakes	Intonation 2 • Showing that information is new or interesting • Ending a point	The passive
Writing Task 2 • Discussing opposing views and giving your opinion • Analysing the task and brainstorming ideas • Deciding on your own view • Structuring an answer • Proofreading an answer for spelling and punctuation mistakes	• Topic vocabulary: *traditional*, *features*, *construct*, etc. • Word choice • Guessing the meaning of words • Improving vocabulary use • Spelling: Proofreading your essay for common spelling mistakes	Sentence stress 3 • Showing a contrast	Modal verbs

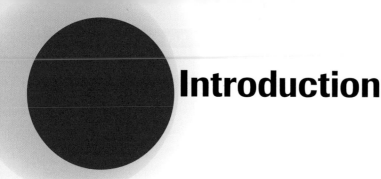

Introduction

Who this book is for

Complete IELTS Bands 4–5 is a short course of 50–60 classroom hours for students who wish to take the Academic module of the International English Language Testing System (IELTS). It teaches you the reading, writing, listening and speaking skills that you need for the exam. It covers all the exam question types, as well as key grammar and vocabulary which, from research into the Cambridge Learner Corpus, are known to be useful to candidates doing the test. If you are not planning to take the exam in the near future, the book teaches you the skills and language you need to reach an intermediate level of English (Common European Framework (CEF) level B1).

What the book contains

In the **Student's Book** there are:

- **ten units for classroom study**, each containing:

  - sections on each of the four papers in the IELTS exam. The units provide language input and skills practice to help you to deal successfully with the tasks in each section.

  - a range of enjoyable and stimulating speaking activities designed to enable you to perform to the best of your ability in each part of the test and to increase your fluency and your ability to express yourself.

  - a step-by-step approach to doing IELTS Writing tasks.

  - key grammar exercises relevant to the exam. When you are doing grammar exercises, you will sometimes see this symbol: ⊙. These exercises are based on research from the Cambridge Learner Corpus and they deal with the areas which cause problems for students in the exam.

  - vocabulary related to IELTS topics and spelling exercises. When you see this symbol ⊙ by an exercise, the exercise focuses on words which IELTS candidates often confuse or use wrongly in the exam.

  - a unit review. These contain exercises which revise the grammar and vocabulary that you have studied in each unit.

- **Speaking and Writing reference sections** which explain the tasks you will have to do in the Speaking and Writing papers. They give you examples, together with additional exercises and advice on how best to approach these two IELTS papers.

- a **Language reference section** which clearly explains all the areas of grammar covered in the book and which will help you in the IELTS exam.

- a complete **IELTS practice test**

- ten **photocopiable word lists** (one for each unit) containing vocabulary found in the units. Each vocabulary item in the word list is accompanied by a definition from the *Cambridge Learner's Dictionary (CLD)*.

- complete **recording scripts** for all the listening material

- a **CD-ROM** which provides you with many interactive exercises, including further listening practice exclusive to the CD-ROM. All these extra exercises are linked to the topics in the Student's Book.

Also available are:

- two **audio CDs** containing listening material for the ten units of the Student's Book plus the Listening Test in the IELTS practice test. The listening material is indicated by different-coloured icons in the Student's Book as follows: ⌒ CD1, ⌒ CD2.

- a **Teacher's Book** containing:

  - **step-by-step guidance** for handling all the activities in the Student's Book

  - a large number of suggestions for **alternative treatments** of activities in the Student's Book and suggestions for **extension activities**

  - advice on the test and task types for teachers to pass on to students

  - **extra photocopiable materials** for each unit of the Student's Book, to practise and extend language

  - complete **answer keys**, including sample answers to Writing tasks

  - complete **recording scripts** for all the listening material

  - five **photocopiable progress tests**, one for every two units of the book

  - a topic-based **word list** of words/phrases and their definitions taken from each unit.

- a **Workbook** containing:

  - ten **units for homework and self-study**. Each unit contains **full exam practice** in one part of the IELTS Reading and Listening papers.

  - further practice of the **grammar** and **vocabulary** taught in the Student's Book

  - an **audio CD** containing all the listening material for the Workbook.

IELTS Academic Module: content and overview

part/timing	content	test focus
LISTENING approximately 30 minutes	• **four sections** • **40 questions** • **a range of question types** • **Section 1:** a conversation on a social topic, e.g. someone making a booking • **Section 2:** a monologue about a social topic, e.g. a radio report • **Section 3:** a conversation on a study-based topic, e.g. a discussion between students • **Section 4:** a monologue on a study-based topic, e.g. a lecture Students have ten minutes at the end of the test to transfer their answers onto an answer sheet. The recording is heard ONCE.	• Candidates are expected to listen for specific information, main ideas and opinions. • There is a range of task types which include completion, matching, labelling and multiple choice. • Each question scores 1 mark; candidates receive a band score from 1 to 9.
READING 1 hour	• **three sections** • **40 questions** • **a range of question types** • **Section 1:** a passage with 13 questions • **Section 2:** a passage divided into paragraphs with 13 questions • **Section 3:** a passage with 14 questions At least one passage contains arguments and/or views. This is usually Section 3.	• Candidates are expected to read for / understand specific information, main ideas, gist and opinions. • Each section contains more than one task type. They include completion, matching, paragraph headings, True / False / Not Given and multiple choice. • Each question scores 1 mark; candidates receive a band score from 1 to 9.
WRITING 1 hour	• **two compulsory tasks** • **Task 1:** a 150-word summary of information presented in graphic or diagrammatic form • **Task 2:** a 250-word essay presenting an argument on a given topic Candidates are advised to spend 20 minutes on Task 1 and 40 minutes on Task 2, which is worth twice as many marks as Task 1.	• Candidates are expected to write a factual summary and a discursive essay. • Candidates are assessed on a nine-band scale for content, coherence, vocabulary and grammar.
SPEAKING 11–14 minutes	• **three parts** • **one examiner + one candidate** • **Part 1:** The examiner asks a number of questions about familiar topics such as the candidate's studies/work, hobbies, interests, etc. *4–5 minutes* • **Part 2:** After a minute's preparation, the candidate speaks for two minutes on a familiar topic provided by the examiner. *3–4 minutes* • **Part 3:** The examiner and the candidate discuss some general questions based on the theme of the Part 2 topic. *4–5 minutes*	• Candidates are expected to be able to respond to questions on familiar and unfamiliar topics and to speak at length. • Candidates are assessed on a nine-band scale for fluency, vocabulary, grammar and pronunciation.

All candidates who take the test receive an Overall Band Score between 1 and 9 that is an average of the four scores for each part of the test. For information on courses, required band scores and interpreting band scores, see www.ielts.org.

Unit 1 Great places to be

1 ....

2 ....

3 ....

4 ....

5 ....

6 ....

Starting off

❶ **Work in pairs. Write the names of the cities beside the photos.**

Amsterdam	Dubai	New York
Rio de Janeiro	Shanghai	Sydney

❷ **Which of the cities would you like to visit? Why? Use these ideas to help you.**

excellent shopping	friendly people	great food	lots to do
unusual buildings	lively festivals	spectacular scenery	

Reading 1
Table completion

❶ **Work in pairs. You are going to read a passage about cities around the world. Before you read, decide if these are good or bad aspects of cities. Write G (good) or B (bad).**

1 friendly inhabitants ☐ G
2 fast public transport ☐
3 crowded streets ☐
4 a high crime rate ☐
5 people in a hurry ☐
6 a relaxed lifestyle ☐

❷ **Work in pairs. Write two more aspects of cities which are good and two more which are bad.**

❸ **Read the passage on page 9 quickly.**

1 Which four cities are mentioned?
2 Which is the friendliest?

The world's friendliest city

A team of social psychologists from California has spent six years studying the reactions of people in cities around the world to different situations. The results show that cities where people *have less* money generally have friendlier *populations*. Rio de Janeiro in Brazil, which *is often known for* its crime, comes out top, and the capital of Malawi, Lilongwe, comes third.

But what makes one city friendlier than another? The psychologists from California State University say it has got more to do with environment than culture or nationality.

They carried out a study into the way locals treated strangers in 23 cities around the world. The team conducted their research through a series of tests, where they dropped pens or pretended they were blind and needed help crossing the street.

The study concludes that people are more helpful in cities with a more relaxed *way of life* such as Rio. While they were there, researchers received help in 93 percent of cases, and the percentage in Lilongwe was only a little lower. However, richer cities such as Amsterdam and New York are considered the least friendly. Inhabitants of Amsterdam helped the researchers in 53 percent of cases and in New York just 44 percent. The psychologists found that, in these cities, people tend to *be short of* time, so they hurry and often *ignore* strangers.

adapted from an article by Victoria Harrison, BBC News

❹ Read the passage quickly again. Which of the good and bad aspects in Exercise 1 are mentioned?

❺ Match the words and phrases in *italics* in this table with the words and phrases in *italics* in the passage.

city	positive aspects	negative aspects	% of help received
Rio de Janeiro	• friendly *inhabitants* • more 1 .... *lifestyle*	• People *don't have so much* 2 .... • *Has reputation for* 3	93%
Amsterdam and New York	• *richer*	People ... • *have little* 4 .... • *don't pay attention to* 5	Amsterdam: 53% New York: 44%

Exam advice   *Table completion*

- Quickly look for words and phrases in the passage which mean the same as words and phrases in the table (for example: *not many – few; well-known – famous*), then read around those words carefully.

- Copy the words from the passage into the table exactly as you see them.

❻ Now complete the table. Choose ONE word from the passage for each answer.

❼ Work in small groups.

1 Are you surprised that people in cities with less money are friendlier? Why? / Why not?
2 What is the friendliest place you have ever visited?
3 How friendly are people in your town or city to visitors? Give examples.

Listening
Form completion

❶ (01) In the IELTS test, you are often asked to complete part of a form by writing a number or a name which is spelled for you. Listen to eight speakers and decide if each name or number is written correctly (✓) or incorrectly (✗).

1 Romney	✓	5 Fawcett	☐
2 Cairns	☐	6 15 cents	☐
3 Bragg	☐	7 0726 05791	☐
4 Jeckyll	☐	8 30 Lower Road	☐

❷ (02) Work in pairs. Spell out these names and read these numbers to each other. Then listen to check your answers.

1 Bracken	5 Vernon
2 Gower	6 17
3 Jeremy	7 01950 674236
4 Pollard	8 31st

❸ Work in small groups. You are going to hear a man phoning to ask about a holiday apartment. Before you listen, answer these questions.

1 What are the advantages and disadvantages of staying in an apartment when you're on holiday?
2 What sort of holiday accommodation do you prefer?

❹ Work in pairs. Look at the form below.

1 In which gaps do you think you will have to:
a write a number only?
b understand words which are spelled out?
c write a number and a word?
2 What sort of information do you need for the other gaps?

Dubai Palm Apartments

Enquiry taken by:	*Amanda*
Name:	**1** ....
Address:	*37* **2** ....
	Vienna
Telephone number:	**3** ....
Number of people:	*four*
Starting date:	**4** .... *January*
Length of stay:	**5** ....
Price per day:	*maximum* **6** .... *euros*

Other requirements:
- fully equipped **7** ....
- view of **8** ....
- air conditioning must be **9** ....
- **10** .... for car

❺ (03) Now listen and complete the form. Write no more than TWO WORDS AND/OR A NUMBER for each answer.

Exam advice   *Form completion*
- Before you listen, think what information you need for each gap.
- Do not write more words than the instructions tell you to.
- Write words or numbers you hear.

❻ Work in pairs. Take turns to talk about a place you have stayed at. Say why you stayed there, who you stayed with, and what you did while you were there.

Reading 2
Note completion

❶ Work in small groups. You are going to read a passage about Costa Rica. Before you read, look at the photos of Costa Rica on the right. What do they tell you about the country?

❷ Read the passage below quickly. Who are:

1 Mariano Rojas?   2 Saamah Abdallah?

The happiest country in the world

Children growing up in Costa Rica are surrounded by some of the most beautiful and diverse landscapes in the world. Preserving tropical rainforests isn't Costa Rica's only success, because the government also makes sure everyone has access to health-care and education. So when the New Economics Foundation released its second Happy Planet Index, Costa Rica came out number one. The index is a ranking of countries based on their impact on the environment and the health and happiness of their citizens.

According to Mariano Rojas, a Costa Rican economics professor, Costa Rica is a mid-income country where citizens have plenty of time for themselves and for their relationships with others. 'A mid-income level allows most citizens to satisfy their basic needs. The government makes sure that all Costa Ricans have access to education, health and nutrition services.' Costa Ricans, he believes, are not interested in status or spending money to show how successful they are.

Created in 2008, the Happy Planet Index examines happiness on a national level and ranks 143 countries according to three measurements: their citizens' happiness, how long they live (which reflects their health), and how much of the planet's resources each country consumes. According to researcher Saamah Abdallah, the Index also measures the outcomes that are most important, and those are happy, healthy lives for everyone.

adapted from *Yes! Magazine*

❸ Look at the notes below.

1 What are the notes about? Find which sentences in the passage deal with this.

2 Find words in the passage which mean the same as the words in *italics*.

The Happy Planet Index

Year *started*: **1** ....

Number of countries it *lists*: **2** ....

Measures each country's happiness according to:

- its *effect* on the **3** .... (i.e. *the quantity* of the Earth's **4** .... that it *uses*);
- the **5** .... of the *population* (i.e. how long people live);
- how happy its **6** .... are.

❹ Now complete the notes. Choose ONE WORD OR A NUMBER from the passage for each gap.

Exam advice   *Note completion*

- Read the title of the notes first and find the right place(s) in the passage.
- Carefully read the parts of the passage which deal with the key ideas in the questions – the answers may not come in passage order.

❺ Work in small groups.

1 Which of these things do you think are important in making people happy, and which are not so important? Why?

- being healthy
- earning a lot of money
- having a good education
- having good relationships
- living in a beautiful place

2 What other things are important?

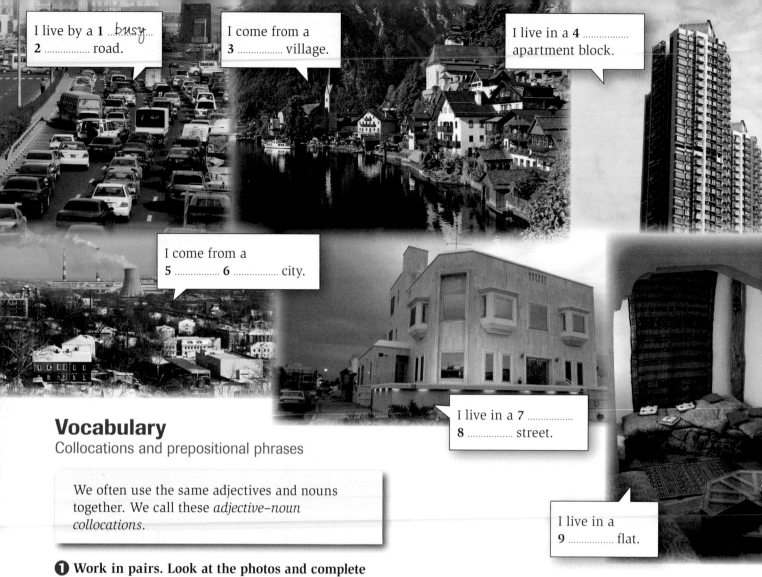

I live by a **1** ..busy.. **2** .... road.

I come from a **3** .... village.

I live in a **4** .... apartment block.

I come from a **5** .... **6** .... city.

I live in a **7** .... **8** .... street.

I live in a **9** .... flat.

Vocabulary
Collocations and prepositional phrases

> We often use the same adjectives and nouns together. We call these *adjective–noun collocations*.

❶ **Work in pairs. Look at the photos and complete the captions by writing an adjective from the box below in each gap. If you need more than one adjective, put the more general one first.**

busy	industrial	large	main	pretty
quiet	suburban	tall	tiny	

❷ **Complete the phrases below describing places where people can live by writing a preposition from the box in each gap. In several cases, more than one answer is possible.**

by	in	near	on

1 ..by.. a river
2 ..in.. the city centre
3 ..on.. the country
4 ..on.. the desert
5 ..in.. the mountains
6 ..on.. the outskirts   by/near
7 by/near the sea
8 ..in.. the suburbs

❸ **Work in small groups. Look at this sentence.**

I live in a pretty village in the mountains.

Take turns to talk about:

- where you live;
- where you would prefer to live, and why.

Speaking
Part 1

❶ (04) **Listen to two students answering these questions and complete the notes in the table below.**

- Can you tell me what you do?
- Where do you come from?
- Can you describe your city/village to me?

name	occupation	where from	where located	words used to describe place
Hanan		Muttrah, Oman		large, ...
Kwan			near Chonju, ...	

▶ Pronunciation: *Sentence stress 1*

❷ Think how you could answer the questions in Exercise 1. Then work in pairs and take turns to ask and answer the questions.

❸ Look at these questions (a–b) and the phrases below (1–8). Which phrases can be used to answer question a, and which phrases can be used to answer question b?

a What do you like about the area where you live?
b What things in your town/city do you not like?

1 Another good thing is …
2 I enjoy …
3 I really dislike …
4 I really like …
5 … is something I don't like.
6 I'm not very keen on …
7 I find … very enjoyable.
8 I find … unpleasant.

❹ 🔊05 Now listen to Hanan and Kwan answering questions a and b. Which phrases are used by Hanan, and which by Kwan?

❺ 🔊05 Listen again and complete this table.

name	likes	dislikes	how changing?
Hanan		the hot weather, …	
Kwan	walking in the mountains, …		

▶ page 14 Key grammar: *Present simple and present continuous*

❻ Think about how you could answer these questions and make notes. Then work with a different partner and take turns to ask and answer the questions.

- Can you tell me what you do? Do you work, or are you a student?
- Where do you come from?
- Can you describe your town or city to me?
- What do you like about the area where you live?
- What things in your town or city do you not like?
- How is the area changing?
- What do people in your area do in their free time?
- What do you think visitors to your town or region should see? Why?

Exam advice Speaking Part 1
- Don't answer questions with just one or two words – use longer sentences.
- Stress the words which answer the question.
- Give some extra information when you can.

Pronunciation
Sentence stress 1

We normally stress the main information in a sentence. When we answer a question, we usually stress the words which give the answer, or give new information.

❶ <u>Underline</u> the words you think Hanan and Kwan should stress in their answers.

Examiner:	Can you tell me what you do, Hanan? Do you work, or are you a student?
Hanan:	Yes, I'm a <u>student</u>. I'm studying medicine because I want to be a doctor.
Examiner:	And where do you come from?
Hanan:	I come from Muttrah in Oman.
Examiner:	Can you tell me what you do, Kwan? Do you work, or are you a student?
Kwan:	I'm a student. I'm studying economics at Chonju University at the moment.
Examiner:	And where do you come from, Kwan?
Kwan:	I come from a small village near Chonju in Korea.

❷ 🔊06 Listen to check your answers.

❸ Work in pairs. Take turns to read the parts of the Examiner, Hanan and Kwan in Exercise 1.

❹ Work alone. Write your own answers to the Examiner's questions in Exercise 1. <u>Underline</u> the words which you should stress.

❺ Work in pairs. Take turns to ask and answer the questions.

Key grammar
Present simple and present continuous

❶ Underline the verbs in these four extracts from the Speaking section and say whether they are present simple or present continuous.

1 At the moment, I'm studying English as well.
   present continuous
2 I come from Muttrah in Oman.
3 I find the traffic very unpleasant.
4 Young people are leaving the village.

❷ Look at the extracts in Exercise 1 again and complete this table.

name of tense	use	example
present continuous	to talk about something happening now	*At the moment, I'm studying English as well.*
pr. simp.	to express what someone feels or thinks	
pr. cont.	to talk about something which is changing	
pr. simp.	to talk about something which is always true	

▶ page 120 *Present simple and present continuous*

❸ Complete these sentences by putting the verb in brackets into the present simple or present continuous.

1 Hassan ...*lives*... (*live*) in Qatar, but right now he *is visiting* (*visit*) friends in Bahrain.
2 I *'m studying* (*study*) geology because I *want* (*want*) to work in the oil industry.
3 He *doesn't like* (*not like*) living in Manchester because it *rains* (*rain*) too much.
4 Transport in my city *is improving* (*improve*) because the government *is building* (*build*) more roads.
5 People in my area *do* (*do*) a lot of sport in their free time because they *like* (*like*) to keep fit.

❹ ⊙ IELTS candidates often make mistakes with the present simple and present continuous. Find and correct the mistakes in these sentences.

1 At the present time, most people ~~are thinking~~ money is important for their lifestyle. *think*
2 I think most children are influenced by their parents while they grow up.
3 Lots of people argue that international tourism ~~bringing~~ us advantages. *brings*
4 Most countries are encourage tourism.
5 Nowadays, more and more cities around the world become bigger and bigger. *are becoming*
6 People in most cities are believing that traffic is one of the most important problems. *believe*

Writing
Task 1

> ### Exam information
> For Writing Task 1, you write a summary of information from graphs, tables, charts or diagrams. You should spend about 20 minutes on this task.

❶ Work in pairs. Look at this pie chart and answer the questions below.

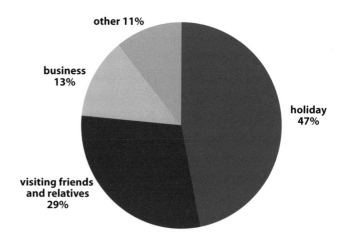

International visitors to New Zealand: reason for visit

- other 11%
- business 13%
- holiday 47%
- visiting friends and relatives 29%

1 What is the main reason for visiting New Zealand?
2 What percentage of visitors go to New Zealand to see friends and family?
3 What does the figure 13% refer to?
4 What is meant by *other* on the chart?
5 In general, do more people visit New Zealand for work or pleasure?

❷ Complete the short summary below with phrases from the box.

> thirteen percent   go to New Zealand
> other reasons   see friends and family
> the largest percentage   for pleasure

The chart shows why people from other countries
1 ....
2 .... , 47 percent, go there on holiday.
Twenty-nine percent visit New Zealand in order to
3 .... **4** .... go there on business, and just
11 percent visit for **5** ....
Overall, the majority of visitors go **6** .... , not
for work.

[handwritten: largest]

❸ Work in pairs. Look at this pie chart and discuss the questions below.

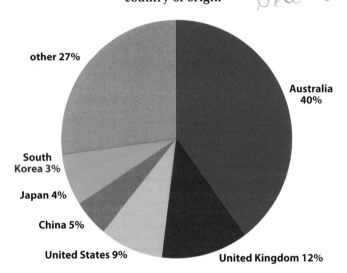

International visitors to New Zealand: country of origin

[handwritten: from which pit where -z.]

other 27%

Australia 40%

South Korea 3%

Japan 4%

China 5%

United States 9%

United Kingdom 12%

1 What does the chart give information about?
2 What nationality is the largest group of visitors?
3 What percentage of visitors come from the United Kingdom, and what percentage from the United States?
4 What percentage of visitors comes from the three countries in East Asia which are mentioned?
5 Are there visitors from countries not mentioned on the chart?
6 What do visitors from Australia, the United Kingdom and the United States have in common?

❹ Read this summary of the pie chart in Exercise 3. It contains five false facts. Rewrite the summary to correct the information.

The chart gives information about ~~the number of people travelling to New Zealand~~. *where people who travel to New Zealand come from*
The percentage of visitors from Australia is the highest, at 40 percent. The third largest group, 12 percent, comes from the United Kingdom, and 9 percent ~~go to~~ the United States. The East Asian countries, China, Japan and South Korea, send 5 percent, 4 percent and 3 percent each. However, 27 percent come from other European countries. Overall, more than 70 percent of visitors come from English-speaking countries. *the*

❺ IELTS candidates often confuse *percent* and *percentage*. Look at this sentence from Exercise 4 and answer the questions below.

The percentage of visitors from Australia is the highest, at 40 percent.

1 Which word (*percent* or *percentage*) is used with a number? *4. percent*
2 Which word is used with *the*? *the percentage*

❻ ⊙ Each of these sentences contains one mistake made by IELTS candidates. Find and correct the mistakes.

1 The ~~percent~~ of teenagers who ride bicycles is higher than for any other age group. *percentage*
2 In the cities, the number of people living alone is 28 percentage.
3 The percent *age* of people over 50 is the lowest in this group.
4 Just over 50 percent~~age~~ of the city's inhabitants are female.
5 ~~The~~ ten percent of females have a university qualification.
6 As can be seen from the table, 60 percent *of the* population live in cities.
7 Australia's share of the Japanese tourist market has increased from 2 percent~~age~~ to nearly 5 percent~~age~~.
8 This chart shows the percent *age of* people attending the cinema in Australia.

7 Work alone. Look at this bar chart and complete the summary below by writing your own words in the gaps. When you finish, compare your ideas with your partner's.

International visitors to New Zealand: reason for visit

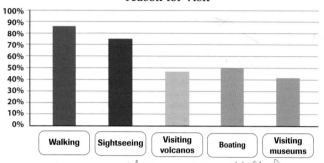

The chart shows 1 _the reason why it plus -z._
The most popular activity is walking, which 2 .... of people on holiday do. Seventy-five percent of visitors 3 .... and 4 .... go to see volcanoes. Another popular activity is boating, which 5 .... of holidaymakers do. Just over 6 .... of visitors also like 7 ....

Overall, 8 .... enjoy doing outdoor activities more than indoor activities.

8 Work in pairs. Look at this chart and discuss the questions below.

International visitors to New Zealand: transport used during visit

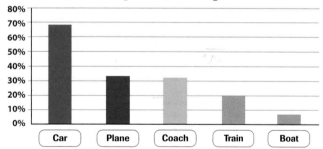

1 What does the chart provide information about?
2 What is the commonest means of transport? What percentage of visitors use it?
3 Which two means of transport are used almost the same amount? What percentage of visitors use them?
4 What is the fourth most popular means of transport? What percentage of visitors use it?
5 Which means of transport is used least? What percentage of visitors use it?
6 Overall, which is more popular: private transport or public transport?

9 Now work alone and write a summary of the information in the chart in Exercise 8.

When you write:
• include all the information you used to answer the questions in Exercise 8;
• use language from the summaries in Exercises 2, 4 and 7 to help you.

Exam advice   *Chart summary*
• Study the chart(s) carefully and look for the most important features.
• Write an introductory sentence which says what the chart(s) show(s).
• Make sure the facts you write are correct.

Spelling
Making nouns plural

1 IELTS candidates often make spelling mistakes when writing nouns in the plural. Write the plural form of these words. Then check your answers by reading the Language reference (page 120).

1 visitor *visitors*   5 man
2 boss   6 match
3 boy   7 party
4 foot   8 wife

▶ page 120 *Spelling changes when we make nouns plural*

2 Write the plural form of each of these words.

1 person *people*   6 family
2 child   7 watch
3 country   8 potato
4 city   9 activity
5 life   10 crash

Unit 2 People's lives

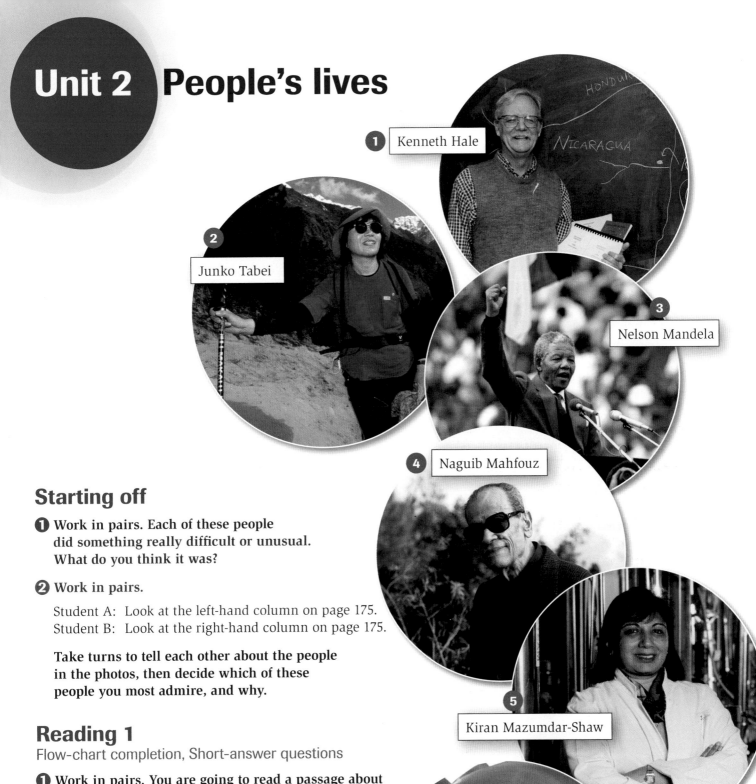

1 Kenneth Hale

2 Junko Tabei

3 Nelson Mandela

4 Naguib Mahfouz

5 Kiran Mazumdar-Shaw

6 Yang Liwei

Starting off

❶ Work in pairs. Each of these people did something really difficult or unusual. What do you think it was?

❷ Work in pairs.

Student A: Look at the left-hand column on page 175.
Student B: Look at the right-hand column on page 175.

Take turns to tell each other about the people in the photos, then decide which of these people you most admire, and why.

Reading 1

Flow-chart completion, Short-answer questions

❶ Work in pairs. You are going to read a passage about Freya Stark, a woman who travelled a lot. Before you read, answer these questions.

1 Do you like travelling? Why? / Why not?
2 Do you think it's better to travel alone or with friends? Why?

❷ Read the passage on page 18 quickly. Is it about Freya Stark's life or her opinions?

❸ Read the passage quickly again and <u>underline</u> all the languages Freya could speak.

Freya Stark, explorer and writer

Freya Stark travelled to many areas of the Middle East, often alone.

Freya Stark was an explorer who lived during a time when explorers were regarded as heroes. She travelled to distant areas of the Middle East, where few Europeans – especially women – had travelled before. She also travelled extensively in Turkey, Greece, Italy, Nepal and Afghanistan.

Stark was born in Paris in 1893. Although she had no formal education as a child, she moved about with her artist parents and learned French, German and Italian. She entered London University in 1912, but at the start of World War I, she joined the nurse corps and was sent to Italy. After the war, she returned to London and attended the School of Oriental Studies. Her studies there led to extensive travel in the Middle East, enabling her to eventually become fluent in Persian, Russian and Turkish.

Stark became well known as a traveller and explorer in the Middle East. She travelled to the Lebanon in 1927 at the age of 33 when she had saved enough money, and while

there, she studied Arabic. In 1928, she travelled by donkey to the Jebel Druze, a mountainous area in Syria. During another trip, she went to a distant region of the Elburz, a mountain range in Iran, where she made a map. She was searching for information about an ancient Muslim sect known as the Assassins, which she wrote about in *Valley of the Assassins* (1934), a classic for which she was awarded a Gold Medal by the Royal Geographic Society. For the next 12 years, she continued her career as a traveller and writer, establishing a style which combined an account of her journeys with personal commentary on the people, places, customs, history and politics of the Middle East.

adapted from Science and its times, 2000

4 Work in pairs. Look at this flow chart. What type of information do you need for each gap?

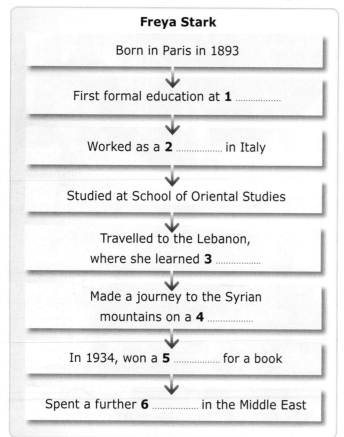

Freya Stark

Born in Paris in 1893

↓

First formal education at **1** ....

↓

Worked as a **2** .... in Italy

↓

Studied at School of Oriental Studies

↓

Travelled to the Lebanon, where she learned **3** ....

↓

Made a journey to the Syrian mountains on a **4** ....

↓

In 1934, won a **5** .... for a book

↓

Spent a further **6** .... in the Middle East

5 Read the passage again and complete the flow chart. Choose NO MORE THAN TWO WORDS AND/OR A NUMBER from the passage for each answer.

Exam advice   *Flow-chart completion*

• Decide what information you need in each gap.
• Spell your answers correctly.

6 Work in pairs. Read these questions and <u>underline</u> the key ideas.

1 <u>What word</u> did people use <u>to describe explorers</u> when Stark was alive?
2 What historical event interrupted Stark's university education?
3 What did Stark produce while travelling in Iran, in addition to a book?
4 What group of people did Stark research in Iran?

7 Now answer the questions in Exercise 6. Choose NO MORE THAN TWO WORDS AND/OR A NUMBER from the passage for each answer.

- <u>Underline</u> the key ideas in each question.
- Read the passage quickly to find where each key idea is dealt with, then read carefully.
- Copy the words and/or numbers you need from the passage exactly.

❽ Work in small groups.

1 Which places would you like to travel to? Why?
2 Do you think it's important to speak the language of places you travel to? Why?

Listening
Note completion

❶ Work in pairs. Match the questions (1–8) with the gapped answers (a–h).

1 Could you read the long number to me, please?
2 Could you give me a contact number, please?
3 How much is the flight to Madrid?
4 What date's your birthday?
5 What time shall we meet?
6 Can you tell me what you do?
7 How far is it to your office?
8 I wonder if you could tell me the address?

a 12th
b Visa card no: ....
c occupation: ....
d .... Street
e about .... km
f at .... p.m.
g price: $ ....
h mobile: ....

❷ Which answers in Exercise 1 need:

1 words only?
2 numbers only?
3 words and numbers?

❸ 🔊 7-10 Listen to four conversations and complete four of the answers to the questions in Exercise 1 (a–h).

❹ Work in small groups. You are going to hear a conversation between a man and a woman who are looking for someone to travel with them to some distant mountains. Before you listen, write down five things you think someone who is going on a difficult journey should know how to do.

Example: He/She should know how to cook.

❺ Look at the notes below. For which question(s) will you have to:

a write a number?
b spell a word?
c write the name of a place?
d write a subject of study or a language?
e write an activity which people do in their spare time?
f write the name of a job?

> Name: *Sanjay* **1** ....
> Age: **2** ....
> Occupation: **3** ....
> Other expeditions:
> • has crossed **4** ....
> • has climbed Mount **5** ....
> Special skills:
> • has done a **6** .... course
> • can speak **7** ....
> Qualifications:
> • degree in **8** ....
> Free-time activities:
> • **9** ....
> • keeping **10** ....

❻ When you listen to the recording, you will often hear a phrase which signals the answer to a question. Match each of these phrases (a–i) with one of the gaps (1–10) in Exercise 5. You will need the same phrase for both gap 9 and gap 10.

a a trip he made ... across
b been to university
c like doing in his spare time
d he can hold conversations in
e he's called
f he's done a course in
g how old he is
h they went up a mountain
i what does he do

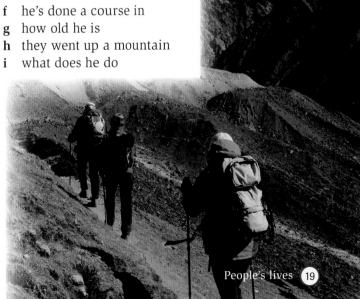

7 (11) Listen and complete the notes in Exercise 5. Write NO MORE THAN TWO WORDS AND/OR A NUMBER for each answer.

8 Match these phrases to make sentences.

1 I can operate   a the guitar.
2 I'd like to be able to play   b a car.
3 I want to learn how to cook   c a computer.
4 I know how to drive   d simple meals.

9 Work in pairs. Look at these two questions. Which sentences from Exercise 8 answer question 1, and which answer question 2?

1 What skills do you have?
2 What skills would you like to have? Why?

10 Work in pairs. Take turns to ask and answer the questions in Exercise 9.

Speaking
Part 1

1 Work in pairs. Which of these suggestions are good advice for Speaking Part 1? Why? Tick (✓) the good advice in first column.

		Hussein
1 Give short answers of just two or three words.	☐	☐
2 Give some extra details when you answer.	✓	☐
3 Correct your mistakes when you can.	☐	☐
4 Give an answer, even when you don't understand the question.	☐	☐
5 Use easy words so that you don't make mistakes.	☐	☐
6 Give reasons for your answers.	☐	☐

2 (12) Now listen to Hussein answering some Part 1 questions and tick the things he does in Exercise 1.

3 (13) Listen again to Hussein answering the first question.

1 What does he say when he doesn't understand the question?
2 What two mistakes does he make?
3 What word does he use when he corrects a mistake?

4 (14) Listen again to Hussein answering the other questions and complete these sentences with the words he uses.

1 I started to play more with friends I made at school because .... things.
2 We went swimming and we played tennis and football because ....
3 We didn't do sports at school, so .... time.
4 I think, perhaps, my chemistry teacher .... very clearly.
5 She made us do tests, I mean experiments, in the laboratories, ...

5 Which sentences in Exercise 4:

1 give reasons?
2 explain results or consequences?

▶ Key grammar: *Past simple*

▶ Pronunciation: *Verbs + –ed*

6 Work alone. Look at these questions and think about how to answer them. Use the good advice from Exercise 1 to help you prepare your answers.

1 Do you come from a large family or a small family?
2 As a child, who did you spend more time with: your family or your friends? Why?
3 When you were a child, how did you spend your weekends?
4 What did you enjoy most about school?
5 When you were at school, who did you think was your best teacher? Why?

7 Now work in pairs and take turns to ask and answer the questions in Exercise 6.

Key grammar
Past simple

❶ The past simple is used to talk about things which happened at a time before now or things which are finished. Complete these tables.

infinitive	past
be	was/were
spend	
look	
play	
start	
make	
enjoy	

infinitive	past
go	went
watch	
do	
like	
explain	
learn	
miss	

❷ 🎧12 Check your answers by listening to Hussein again.

▶ page 121 *Past simple*

❸ Complete these sentences with the past tense of the verbs in brackets.

1 Shuwe ....*lost*.... (*lose*) her dictionary because she ....*left*.... (*leave*) it on the train.
2 My teacher ....*got*.... (*get*) angry with me when I ....*forgot*.... (*forget*) to do my homework.
3 When I was seven, my parents ....*gave*.... (*give*) me a bicycle, which I ....*rode*.... (*ride*) everywhere.
4 I ....*drove*.... (*drive*) the car my father ....*bought*.... (*buy*).
5 Ivan just ....*caught*.... (*catch*) the train in time.
6 Ali ....*wrote*.... (*write*) the number on a piece of paper and ....*put*.... (*put*) it in his pocket.

❹ ⊙ IELTS candidates often make mistakes when writing about the past. Correct the mistake in each of these sentences.

1 The number of females aged 100 or more is 76 in 1911 and then nearly doubled in 1941 to 141. *was*
2 In the past, when we want to go somewhere, we had to walk or ride a horse.
3 This chart informs us about how many people were reached the age of 100 or more in the UK between 1911 and 2011.
4 The amount of leisure time that people spent watching television has dropped to 3% in 2010.
5 The cinema attendance of 25–34-year-olds was risen from 60 percent to 80 percent in 2001. *raised*

Pronunciation
Verbs + –ed

There are three possible ways of pronouncing –ed.

❶ 🎧15 Listen and match how –ed is pronounced for these verbs (1–3) with the symbols (a–c).

1 asked   a /d/
2 mended   b /t/
3 called   c /ɪd/

❷ 🎧16 Listen and write each of these verbs in the correct column of the table below, according to how –ed is pronounced.

appeared asked ended enjoyed finished hoped improved invented liked looked needed occurred played remembered started wanted watched wished

/t/	/ɪd/	/d/
		appeared

▶ page 121 *Pronunciation of verbs + –ed*

❸ Work in pairs. Take turns to say the verbs in Exercise 2.

❹ Work in pairs. Take turns to read these sentences aloud. Then say if they are true or false for you. If they are false, make a sentence about the topic which is true.

1 I never watched television when I was a child.
2 My parents wanted me to study medicine.
3 I started studying English when I was 11.
4 I usually enjoyed myself at school.
5 I never worked hard for exams when I was a child. I just studied a little the night before.
6 At school, when I got high marks, I was surprised.
7 When I couldn't do homework, I asked my parents to help me.
8 When the school holidays came, I felt excited.

Reading 2
True / False / Not Given

❶ **Work in small groups. You are going to read a passage about a man who sailed a boat across the Pacific Ocean. Before you read, what problems do you think sailors might have when they cross oceans in small boats?**

❷ **Read the passage quickly.**

1 What question did Mau want to answer by making his voyage?
2 How did the voyage change Mau's life?

❸ **Read these statements and find the words in *italics* in the first three sentences of the passage.**

1 The *purpose* of Mau's voyage was to find the quickest route between Hawaii and Tahiti.
2 The *purpose* of Mau's voyage was to find out if navigating between islands had been possible in the past.
3 Mau's *boat* belonged to the *Polynesian Voyaging Society*.

❹ **Now decide if the statements above are TRUE, FALSE or NOT GIVEN according to information in the passage. Choose:**

TRUE if the statement agrees with the information
FALSE if the statement contradicts the information
NOT GIVEN if there is no information on this

❺ **Read statements 1–7 below and:**

1 find the words or phrases in *italics* in the passage;
2 decide if the statements are *TRUE, FALSE* or *NOT GIVEN*.

---

1 *At the time* of his voyage, Mau had unique navigational skills.
2 Mau was familiar with the sea around *Tahiti*.
3 Mau thought it would be difficult to use *a compass* and *charts*.
4 Mau's *grandfather* was his only teacher.
5 Mau used *stones* to learn where each star was situated in the sky.
6 The *first inhabitants* of Hawaii could read and write.
7 Mau expected his *students* to memorise the *positions of the stars*.

Mau Piailug, ocean navigator

Mau sailed from Hawaii to Tahiti using traditional methods.

In early 1976, Mau Piailug, a fisherman, led an expedition in which he sailed a traditional Polynesian boat across 2,500 miles of ocean from Hawaii to Tahiti. The Polynesian Voyaging Society had organised the expedition. Its purpose was to find out if seafarers in the distant past could have found their way from one island to the other without navigational instruments, or whether the islands had been populated by accident. At the time, Mau was the only man alive who knew how to navigate just by observing the stars, the wind and the sea.

He had never before sailed to Tahiti, which was a long way to the south. However, he understood how the wind and the sea behave around islands, so he was confident he could find his way. The voyage took him and his crew a month to complete and he did it without a compass or charts.

His grandfather began the task of teaching him how to navigate when he was still a baby. He showed him pools of water on the beach to teach him how the behaviour of the waves and wind changed in different places. Later, Mau used a circle of stones to memorise the positions of the stars. Each stone was laid out in the sand to represent a star.

The voyage proved that Hawaii's first inhabitants came in small boats and navigated by reading the sea and the stars. Mau himself became a keen teacher, passing on his traditional secrets to people of other cultures so that his knowledge would not be lost. He explained the positions of the stars to his students, but he allowed them to write things down because he knew they would never be able to remember everything as he had done.

- Find words and phrases in the passage which are the same as or similar to words and phrases in the statements.
- Choose TRUE if the question says the same as the passage.
- Choose FALSE if the question says something which is the opposite of information in the passage.
- Choose NOT GIVEN if you cannot find anything in the passage about the information in the question.

❻ Work in small groups.

1 What traditional skills and knowledge do people in your family have?
2 Do you think it's important to preserve traditional skills and knowledge? Why? / Why not?

Vocabulary
Working out the meanings of words

❶ When you answer questions on IELTS reading passages, you often have to guess the meanings of words you don't know from the context. Find these words and phrases in the passage. Then work with a partner and say what you think each of them means.

1 seafarers
2 confident
3 charts
4 pools
5 laid out
6 represent

❷ Now choose the best option (a or b) for each word and phrase in Exercise 1.

1 a people who live on islands
  b people who travel by sea
2 a certain about your ability to do things well
  b worried about your ability to do something
3 a diagrams
  b maps of the sea or the sky
4 a small areas of water
  b beds for babies
5 a arranged in a pattern
  b found
6 a look like
  b be a sign or symbol for something

❸ Work in pairs. Look at this example and then say what you think the words (1–4) below mean.

seafarer   connected with sea

  –*er* or –*or* on the end means 'someone/something which does a thing'

= someone/something who 'seafares'
= someone/something who does something connected with the sea – perhaps a sailor?

1 researcher   3 bystander
2 bottle opener   4 communicator

▶ page 121 *Some meanings of affixes*

❹ Work in pairs. Discuss what the words and phrases in *italics* mean.

1 *Cyclists* tend to have more accidents than *motorists*.
2 Studies show that open, extrovert people are more *likeable* than quiet, reserved types.
3 Moreover, *liquefying* gas makes it safer and easier to transport.
4 The islands were *undoubtedly* visited by *prehistoric voyagers.*
5 In ancient times, the river was *navigable* for nearly one thousand miles.
6 The film 'Titanic' has been *remade* several times.
7 *Informants* in different countries have helped to *simplify* the process.
8 The roads are often *impassable* in winter due to snow.

Writing
Task 2

Exam information

In Writing Task 2, you write an essay discussing a topic and giving your opinion. You have about 40 minutes for this task.

❶ Work in pairs. When you do IELTS Writing tasks, you must answer all parts of the question exactly. Look at this Writing task and decide whether the statements below are true (T) or false (F).

> Write about the following topic.
>
> *In many parts of the world, families were larger in the past because people had more children.*
>
> *Do you think there were more advantages or disadvantages to being part of a large family in the past?*
>
> Give reasons for your answer and include any relevant examples from your own knowledge and experience.
>
> Write at least 250 words.

In this essay, you must:
1 write about the past. T
2 discuss whether families were larger in the past.
3 compare families today with families in the past.
4 write about the advantages and disadvantages of having a lot of people in the family.
5 give your opinion and explain why.
6 write 250 words or more.

❷ Work in pairs. Read the sample answer in the next column. Ignore the words in *italics* for now.

1 What advantages and disadvantages does the writer mention?
2 Do you agree with the writer?

Family life in the modern world is not the same experience as in the past, because families are smaller. In the past, there were advantages and disadvantages to being members of a big family.

I believe there were three main benefits. Firstly, children always had other children to play with in the same house, so they learned social skills. **1** *They also / And they* quarrelled, **2** *but / however* when they quarrelled, they learned to defend themselves. Secondly, children helped in the house **3** *and / also* as a consequence they became more responsible. **4** *Also / However,* different generations lived together, so grandparents looked after young children **5** *and / also* younger brothers learned many things from their elder brothers.

I think many of the disadvantages were financial. Firstly, one of the parents could not work, because he or she had to stay at home to look after the children and the grandparents. This meant the family earned less. As a result, parents had less money to pay for their children's education and other activities. **6** *But / However,* in my view, the biggest problem was that parents could not pay so much attention to individual children. As a result, children with problems sometimes suffered.

In my opinion, the advantages of large families were greater than the disadvantages. The family had less money, **7** *but / however* family members formed a stronger relationship and they supported and helped each other when they had problems. **8** *Also, / And* people were always surrounded by their relatives, so they were never lonely.

❸ Read the sample answer again and complete this essay plan by writing phrases a–h in gaps 1–8.

> **Para. 1:** Introduction: families smaller, so **1** ....c....
>
> **Para. 2:** Advantages:
> - played, so **2** ....
> - **3** .... , so more responsible
> - grandparents **4** ....
>
> **Para. 3:** Disadvantages:
> - one parent **5** .... – less money
> - less money for kids' education
> - less **6** .... for each child
>
> **Para. 4:** My opinion: more advantages because
> - family gave **7** ....
> - people never **8** ....

a attention   **e** looked after younger kids
b didn't work   **f** learned social skills
c ~~different experience~~   **g** lonely
d helped in house   **h** support and help

❹ Read the sample answer again and ⟨circle⟩ the correct words and phrases 1–8 in *italics*.

❺ Now answer these questions.

1 Which of these words can be used to begin sentences: *also, and, but, however*?
2 Which words join two sentences?

▶ page 121 *also, and, but and* however

❻ Work in pairs.

1 Look at paragraph 1 of the sample answer and answer these questions.
   a How many sentences does it have?
   b Which sentence says how the world has changed?
   c Which sentence says what the writer is going to talk about in the rest of the essay?
   d Does the writer repeat the words from the Writing task in Exercise 1 exactly? Why? / Why not?
   e What word does he use which means *large*?
   f What phrase does he use which means *part of*?
2 Read the sentences which begin paragraphs 2, 3 and 4. What is their function?
3 Find three phrases in the essay which mean *In my opinion*.

❼ Work in small groups. Read the Writing task below and:

1 underline the key ideas in the task.
2 make a list of advantages and disadvantages.
3 discuss which is better: living in a large city or a small community?

Write about the following topic.

In the past, most people lived in small villages where everyone knew everyone else. Nowadays, most people live in large cities where they only know a few people in their area.

What do you think were the advantages and disadvantages of living in a small community?

Give reasons for your answer and include any relevant examples from your own knowledge and experience.

---

❽ Work in pairs and write a plan for your essay using ideas from Exercise 7.

1 Use the plan in Exercise 3 to help you.
2 Decide how many paragraphs you need and what you will say in each paragraph.

❾ Work alone and write your answer to the task in Exercise 7. Write at least 250 words.

When you write:
• start your paragraphs with a short introductory sentence like the ones in the sample answer;
• use *also, and, but* and *however* to link ideas;
• make your own opinion clear: use *I think, I believe, In my opinion, In my view.*

When you have finished writing, read your answer and check your spelling.

Exam advice   *Writing Task 2*

• Read the question carefully first and make sure you know what you must write about.
• Brainstorm ideas before you start and make a plan.
• Write your essay following your plan.

Spelling
Changes when adding *-ed*

❶ Write these verbs in the past simple by adding *-ed* and a double letter where necessary. Then check your answers by reading the Language reference (page 121).

1 admit *admitted*   5 open
2 appear   6 play
3 carry   7 save
4 end   8 stop

▶ page 121 *Spelling changes when adding* –ed *to verbs*

❷ ⊙ IELTS candidates often make mistakes with these words. Work in pairs. Decide which word in each pair is spelled correctly.

1 occured   ⟨occurred⟩
2 remembered   rememberred
3 prefered   preferred
4 dropped   droped
5 developed   developped
6 happenned   happened
7 staied   stayed
8 studied   studed
9 destroyed   destroied
10 remained   remainded

Vocabulary and grammar review Unit 1

Vocabulary

❶ Complete the sentences below with words and phrases from the box.

city centre	country	~~mountains~~	outskirts	sea	suburbs

1 Feodor is keen on climbing and he would love to live in the
mountains .

2 Khaled lives in the .... , just near the main square and next to the central station.

3 Leila takes a bus to get to college from her home on the .... of the city.

4 Hua was born and brought up in the .... , surrounded by fields and farms.

5 I don't really live in the city; I live in a village nearby, so I suppose I live in the ....

6 Piau's father was a fisherman, so he has always lived by the ....

❷ Match the phrases on the left (1–8) with phrases on the right (a–h) which express similar ideas.

1 crowded streets
2 fast public transport
3 friendly inhabitants
4 lots to do
5 people in a hurry
6 spectacular scenery
7 has a reputation for
8 a relaxed lifestyle

a Everyone is in a rush.
b The local population is very welcoming.
c The pavements are full of people.
d quiet way of life
e is known for
f There are wonderful views from the hotel.
g The underground will take you rapidly where you want to go.
h There are plenty of interesting places to visit.

❸ Complete the sentences using adjectives that fit the crossword grid.

1 Students in this city tend to share ....tiny.... flats, so their living conditions are very crowded.

2 Fatma comes from a large, ... city with lots of factories and smoke.

3 Neighbours who live by the .... main road often complain about the traffic noise.

4 It's such a .... village that it attracts plenty of tourists.

5 Raul's house is in a .... suburb with a low crime rate.

6 Chen lives on the 15th floor of a .... apartment block.

Grammar

❹ Complete these sentences with the correct form of the verb in brackets: present simple or present continuous.

1 The number of medical students at my university _is rising_ (rise).

2 Sayed .... (enjoy) playing football when he .... (have) time.

3 Walid .... (live) in Qatar, where he was born, but he .... (work) in Dubai almost every day.

4 Nowadays, more and more people .... (leave) the villages to work in the city.

5 Katya .... (study) English because she .... (want) to be a flight attendant.

6 People's reading habits .... (change) because they .... (read) more on the Internet and fewer books.

Vocabulary and grammar review **Unit 2**

Vocabulary

1 Complete the sentences below with the words in the box.

able | ~~can~~ | how | know | learn

1 I ...*can*... swim quite well.
2 I'd like to be .... to fly a plane.
3 I don't .... how to cook well.
4 I want to .... to paint.
5 Once you've learned, you never forget .... to ride a bicycle.

2 Match the words in *italics* in sentences 1–8 with their definitions (a–h).

1 His friends found his behaviour *unacceptable*. *g*
2 The examiners were *satisfied* that he had a good knowledge of the subject.
3 Scientists decided to *re-examine* the evidence, as it did not completely match their theory.
4 The Moon approaches *exceptionally* close to the Earth every 19 years.
5 Although he's highly intelligent, his behaviour is *inexplicable*.
6 The colours were *indistinguishable* at such a great distance.
7 It was impossible to *quantify* how many people used the new service.
8 Paganini was perhaps the best *violinist* of all time.

a impossible to see as different or separate
b look again very carefully, especially to try to discover something
c measure the amount of something
d pleased because something happened in the way that they wanted
e so strange or unusual that you cannot understand or explain it
f someone who plays a violin
g ~~too bad to be allowed to continue~~
h very unusually

Grammar

3 Complete these sentences with the past simple of the verbs in brackets.

1 The town council ...*built*... (*build*) a bridge across the river to the island.
2 Mahfouz .... (*write*) more than 15 books during his life.
3 In my country, many people .... (*stop*) smoking when the price of cigarettes .... (*go*) up.
4 In this region, most people .... (*speak*) the local language a hundred years ago.
5 In 2004, the company .... (*develop*) a new technique using digital technology.
6 The change .... (*happen*) because more immigrants .... (*arrive*) in the country.
7 The storm which .... (*occur*) at the end of January .... (*destroy*) several houses.
8 The number of students in higher education .... (*rise*) until 2003 and then .... (*fall*) the following year.

4 Complete these sentences with *also, and, but* or *however*.

1 The journey was long ...*and*... complicated.
2 Few students look forward to doing exams, ... they realise they are necessary.
3 Many people travel to see new places. They .... want to experience other cultures.
4 Marco Polo travelled to Persia .... then he travelled to China.
5 Visitors to this region are often surprised that the inhabitants are poor .... happy.
6 Working with children can be very challenging. .... , it can be very satisfying as well.

Unit 3 Getting from A to B

Starting off

1 Work in small groups. Look at the photos. Which of these forms of transport do you think is the:

- cleanest?
- healthiest?
- noisiest?
- most exciting?
- fastest?
- most comfortable?
- most dangerous?
- quietest?

2 What types of transport do you use regularly? Why?

Reading 1
Labelling a diagram

1 Work in pairs. You are going to read a passage about cars.

1 Read the title and subtitle of the passage on page 29 and look at the diagram. What do you think the passage will be about?
2 Read the passage quickly and find the advantages of electric cars which are mentioned.

2 Quickly <u>underline</u> these words (1–8) in the passage on page 29. Then match them with their definitions from the *Cambridge Learner's Dictionary* (*CLD*) (a–h).

1 existing
2 urban
3 vehicle
4 renewable energy
5 zero emissions
6 efficiency
7 link
8 ensure

a belonging or relating to a town or city
b make a connection between two or more people, things or ideas
c make certain that something is done or happens
d something such as a car or bus that takes people from one place to another, especially using roads
e when someone or something uses time and energy well
f which exist or are used at the present time
g when the power that comes from electricity, etc. can be produced as quickly as it is used
h when no gas is sent out into the air

The electric revolution

Your next car may be electric. We look at the technologies that will bring the revolution.

The main reasons why electric cars are not more popular at present are their price and their relatively small range. Existing battery systems only allow electric cars to travel a distance of between 100 and 160 km. However, this distance may not be a problem for urban drivers. A recent Sydney study reported that 70 percent of journeys were 30 km or less, and recent data from the US suggests that 77 percent of trips taken there are 48 km or less.

An innovative company called Better Place is aiming to make electric cars an option for all drivers. It wants to see existing vehicles replaced by electric vehicles which, it says, offer a number of benefits. Firstly, they can be powered by renewable energy which produces zero emissions. What is more, electric motors are more efficient and can convert more than 90 percent of power into movement, whereas the efficiency of diesel or petrol engines is less than 20 percent. To achieve its aim, Better Place plans to use technology which is already available.

The plan is simple but revolutionary. It starts with the installation of a home charge point, and through this, the vehicle will be plugged into the electricity grid whenever it is in the garage, typically at night. In the morning, with a fully charged battery, the car is capable of as much as 160 km in urban motoring conditions. In addition to the home charge point, the battery can be topped up by charge points at work and at supermarkets.

The battery is linked to a control centre by smart technology inside the vehicle. Better Place can then ensure that the car is charged with electricity from renewable sources at the cheapest price. For longer trips, a navigation system directs the driver to the nearest switch station, where the depleted battery can be replaced with a charged one by a robot within a couple of minutes.

by Tim Thwaites, issue 29 of *Cosmos*, October 2009

---

3 Work in pairs. Look at the diagram on the right. What information do you need for each gap?

4 Complete the labels on the diagram on the right. Choose NO MORE THAN TWO WORDS AND/OR A NUMBER from the passage for each answer.

> **Exam advice** — *Labelling a diagram*
>
> - Find where the picture(s) is/are dealt with in the passage.
> - Find words in the passage that mean the same as the words already on the diagram.
> - Decide what type(s) of word you need for each gap.
> - <u>Underline</u> the word(s) you need in the passage and copy it/them exactly.

5 Work in pairs.

1 Do you think electric cars will replace diesel or petrol cars? Why? / Why not?

2 Would you like to have an electric car? Why? / Why not?

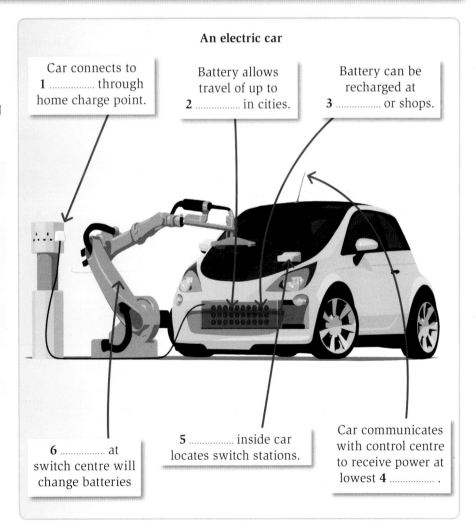

An electric car

Car connects to 1 .... through home charge point.

Battery allows travel of up to 2 .... in cities.

Battery can be recharged at 3 .... or shops.

6 .... at switch centre will change batteries

5 .... inside car locates switch stations.

Car communicates with control centre to receive power at lowest 4 ....

Listening

Labelling a diagram, Multiple choice

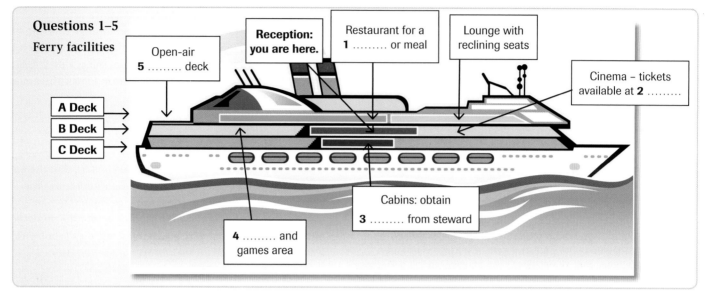

Questions 1–5

Ferry facilities

Open-air
5 .... deck

**Reception:
you are here.**

Restaurant for a
1 .... or meal

Lounge with
reclining seats

Cinema – tickets
available at **2** ....

A Deck →

B Deck →

C Deck →

Cabins: obtain
3 .... from steward

4 .... and
games area

❶ **Work in pairs. You are going to hear an information announcement for passengers on a ship. Before you listen, look at the diagram above and answer these questions.**

1 Where are you on the plan?
2 Which places are on A Deck?
3 Which places are next to reception?
4 What places are below reception?
5 Which questions may need the name of a place on the ship?
6 Which question may need the name of something you can eat or drink?
7 Which question may need the name of something you can take to your cabin?

❷ **Each of these extracts from the announcement is related to one of the gaps on the diagram. Write the number of the gap by each extract.**

a ... people who want a bit of fresh air ... ☐ 5
b On this deck, that is B Deck, you'll also find an area where you can either play games ... ☐
c To access your cabin, ... ☐
d ... just next door ... is a 40-seat cinema ... ☐
e ... go up the stairs to A Deck, where you'll find the restaurant. ☐

> *Exam advice*   *Labelling a diagram*
>
> • Look at the diagram and decide what type(s) of word you need.
>
> • Look at the words on the diagram and listen for similar words and phrases to tell you the answer is coming.

❸ 🔊 **Now listen and label the diagram. Write ONE WORD ONLY for each answer.**

❹ **Read Questions 6–10 and <u>underline</u> the key ideas in each question.**

> **Questions 6–10**
>
> 6 At approximately <u>what time</u> will the ship <u>arrive</u>?
>
>   **A** at 7 a.m.   **B** at 8 a.m.   **C** at 9 a.m.
>
> 7 Which of these can children have in the restaurant?
>
>   **A** a children's menu
>
>   **B** earlier mealtimes
>
>   **C** a children's party
>
> 8 What are available at a reduced price?
>
>   **A** souvenirs of the ship
>
>   **B** first-class cabins
>
>   **C** train tickets
>
> 9 Which of these is situated in the lounge?
>
>   **A** a computer
>
>   **B** a coffee machine
>
>   **C** a television
>
> 10 What special event will happen during the voyage?
>
>   **A** a fashion show
>
>   **B** a concert
>
>   **C** a competition

5 Each of these phrases from the recording will help you to focus on the correct question when you listen. Write the number of the question (6–10) by each phrase.

a a unique feature on this crossing only `10`
b for those using the lounge ☐
c for 20 percent off ☐
d passengers with children ☐
e reaching our destination ☐

6 🎧(18) Now listen and answer Questions 6–10. Choose the correct letter: A, B or C.

> **Exam advice** *Multiple choice*
> • Underline the key idea in each question to help you focus on the meaning.
> • Listen for a phrase which means the same as one of the options.

Speaking
Part 2

> **Exam information**
> • You speak for between one and two minutes on a topic the examiner gives you.
> • You have one minute to think and write some notes before you speak.

1 Work in pairs. Read the task below.

1 Underline the key ideas.
2 Decide what tenses you will need.

> Describe a journey you made in the past that you remember well.
>
> You should say:
>
> what forms of transport you used and why
>
> who you travelled with
>
> what was good and bad about it
>
> and explain why you remember the trip so well.

2 🎧(19) Complete the notes in the next column, which Kyung-Soon made for the points in the task in Exercise 1, by writing words from the box in the gaps. Then listen to check your answers.

| Chinese | difficult | free |
| ~~new~~ | powerful | public |

Transport:
• motorbike – not 1 …..new….
• not 2 ……….. transport
Travelled with:
• 3 ………….. friend
Good/bad:
• met people
• saw places – 4 …………. to reach
• trip was cheap
• 5 ………….. engine
• rain/heat
Remember trip because
I felt 6 …………..

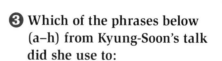

3 Which of the phrases below (a–h) from Kyung-Soon's talk did she use to:

1 introduce the talk? g
2 introduce new points?
3 finish the talk?

a I have great memories of the trip because …
b I made the trip with …
c I bought it because …
d In all, I think …
e The bad things were …
f The good thing about the journey was …
g ~~Well, I'm going to talk about …~~
h The transport I used was …

▶ page 32 Pronunciation: *Word stress 1*

4 Work alone. Make notes for the Speaking task in Exercise 1. Think about how you can use phrases similar to the ones in Exercise 3 to introduce your talk, introduce new points and finish the talk.

5 Work in pairs and take turns to give your talks. You should each try to speak for two minutes.

❻ Work alone. Read this task and make notes.

> Describe a journey you made where you learned something new.
>
> You should say:
>
>   what happened on the journey
>
>   what forms of transport you used
>
>   how you felt
>
> and explain what you learned which was new.

❼ Work in pairs. Which of the phrases below (a–f) can you use to:

1 introduce the talk?   b
2 introduce new points?
3 finish the talk?

a During the trip, I …
b I'm going to talk about a trip I made …
c Generally, I felt …
d I learned a lot from the experience, especially …
e Finally, I'd like to say that …
f I travelled by …

❽ Work in pairs. Take turns to give your talks. Use phrases from either Exercise 3 or Exercise 7 to structure your talk.

Exam advice   *Speaking Part 2*

• Use your minute of preparation to note down ideas, words and phrases you want to use.

• Look at your notes, but also look at the examiner when you speak.

• Continue speaking until the examiner says *Thank you.*

Pronunciation

Word stress 1

> In words with more than one syllable, we stress one syllable more than the others.

❶ ⟨20⟩ The word *motorbike* contains three syllables:

• • •

mo-tor-bike

Which syllable is stressed? Listen to check your answer.

> When you look in a dictionary, the main stress in the word will usually be shown with this sign '. So you will see *motorbike* also written like this: /ˈməʊtəbaɪk/. This shows the main stress and the pronunciation in phonetics.

❷ Write ' before each of the syllables you think is stressed in these words.

transport studying independent
holiday university powerful exciting
expensive memories interesting

❸ ⟨21⟩ Listen and check your answers.

❹ Work in pairs. Take turns to practise saying the words in Exercise 2.

Reading 2
Matching headings

❶ Work in pairs. You are going to read a passage about traffic.

1 How bad are traffic jams where you come from?
2 What problems do traffic jams cause?
3 What solutions to the problem can you think of?

❷ Read the passage on page 33 quickly. How many solutions to traffic congestion are mentioned?

❸ Quickly underline these words in the passage (1–8). Then match them with their definitions from the *CLD* and the *CALD* (a–h).

1 congestion
2 smog
3 developed
4 developing
5 commuter
6 toll
7 rush hour
8 off-peak

a air pollution in a city that is a mixture of smoke, gases and chemicals
b situation when something is full or blocked, especially with traffic
c describes a country or area of the world which is poorer and has less-advanced industries
d describes a country with an advanced level of technology, industry, etc.
e money that you pay to use a bridge, road, etc.
f not at the most popular and expensive time
g someone who travels regularly between work and home
h the time when a lot of people are travelling to or from work and so roads and trains are very busy

4 Work in pairs. Read this list of headings and discuss what you think each one means.

> **List of Headings**
>
> i   A solution which is no solution
> ii   Changing working practices
> iii   Closing city centres to traffic
> iv   Making cars more environmentally friendly
> v   Not doing enough
> vi   Paying to get in
> vii   A global problem

5 The reading passage has five paragraphs, A–E.

1 The correct heading for paragraph A is vii. Can you say why?
2 The correct heading for paragraph B is either iii or vi. Which heading is correct? Why?
3 Now read paragraphs C–E one by one and choose the correct heading for each.

> *Exam advice*   *Matching headings*
>
> • <u>Underline</u> the key ideas in the headings before you read the passage.
> • Read the paragraphs one by one to choose the correct headings.

Traffic jams – no end in sight

There are no easy answers to the problems of traffic congestion.

A Traffic congestion affects people throughout the world. Traffic jams cause smog in dozens of cities across both the developed and developing world. In the US, commuters spend an average of a full working week each year sitting in traffic jams, according to the Texas Transportation Institute. While alternative ways of getting around are available, most people still choose their cars because they are looking for convenience, comfort and privacy.

B The most promising technique for reducing city traffic is called congestion pricing, whereby cities charge a toll to enter certain parts of town at certain times of day. In theory, if the toll is high enough, some drivers will cancel their trips or go by bus or train. And in practice it seems to work: Singapore, London and Stockholm have reduced traffic and pollution in city centres thanks to congestion pricing.

C Another way to reduce rush-hour traffic is for employers to implement flexitime, which lets employees travel to and from work at off-peak traffic times to avoid the rush hour. Those who have to travel during busy times can do their part by sharing cars. Employers can also allow more staff to telecommute (work from home) so as to keep more cars off the road altogether.

D Some urban planners still believe that the best way to ease traffic congestion is to build more roads, especially roads that can take drivers around or over crowded city streets. But such techniques do not really keep cars off the road; they only accommodate more of them.

E Other, more forward-thinking, planners know that more and more drivers and cars are taking to the roads every day, and they are unwilling to encourage more private automobiles when public transport is so much better both for people and the environment. For this reason, the American government has decided to spend some $7 billion on helping to increase capacity on public-transport systems and upgrade them with more efficient technologies. But environmentalists complain that such funding is tiny compared to the $50 billion being spent on roads and bridges.

adapted from ©*The Environmental Magazine*, Earthtalk®

Vocabulary

make and *cause*

❶ IELTS candidates often confuse *make* and *cause*. Which verb in *italics* is correct in each of these sentences?

1 Traffic jams *cause / make* smog in dozens of cities across both the developed and developing world.
2 Traffic jams *cause / make* people angry.

❷ Read these extracts from the *CLD*. Then answer the questions below.

> • **cause:** to make something happen:
> *The hurricane caused widespread damage.*
>
> • **make somebody/something happy/sad/difficult, etc.:** to cause someone or something to become happy, sad, difficult, etc.:
> *You've made me very happy.*

1 Which verb is followed by a noun/adjective + noun?
2 Which verb is followed by a noun/pronoun + adjective?

❸ Complete these sentences by writing the correct form of *cause* or *make* in each gap.

1 The bad weather .... the accident yesterday.
2 The heavy traffic .... it impossible to arrive at work on time this morning.
3 Road works .... a traffic jam last week.
4 Driving .... people tired.

❹ ⊙ IELTS candidates often use *make* when they should use *cause*. Find and correct the mistakes in three of these sentences. One sentence is correct.

1 Cars make serious pollution.
2 The number of vehicles is increasing, and this can make a lot of traffic congestion.
3 Pollution makes cities unhealthy.
4 However, using planes makes other problems.

Writing

Task 1

❶ Work in small groups. Find out who:

- travels furthest to class;
- has the shortest journey to class;
- spends the most time travelling.

❷ Work in pairs. Look at this Writing task and answer the questions below.

> *The table below shows information about travelling to work in one US city.*
>
> *Summarise the information by selecting and reporting the main features, and make comparisons where relevant.*
>
> | | average distance (miles) | average time (minutes) | average speed (mph) |
> |---|---|---|---|
> | car (1 person) | 17 | 33 | 31 |
> | car (more than 1 person) | 24 | 42 | 34 |
> | cycle/walk | 4 | 20 | 10 (cycle) 3 (walk) |
> | train/bus | 23 | 49 | 28 |

Which ways of travelling:

1 do people use for the longest journeys?
2 do people use for the shortest journeys?
3 take the most/least time?
4 are fastest/slowest?

▶ page 36 Key grammar: *Making comparisons*

❸ Complete this sample answer to the Writing task in Exercise 2 by writing the correct form of the adjective in brackets in each gap.

> The table gives information about different means of transport which people use to reach their work in one city in the US. People who use public transport or share a car travel the **1** *greatest* (*great*) distance, on average 23 or 24 miles, while cyclists and pedestrians have the **2** .... (*short*) journey – just 4 miles. By comparison, car drivers without passengers travel an average of 17 miles. People travelling on trains and buses spend the **3** .... (*long*) time commuting to work because it takes them 49 minutes on average. Walkers and cyclists take the **4** .... (*little*) time, because they get to work in about 20 minutes. Cars tend to be the **5** .... (*fast*) way of travelling. People going together by car have an average speed of 34 mph and people driving alone have an average of 31 mph. Walking is the **6** .... (*slow*) at 3 mph. Overall, for long distances, the **7** .... (*quick*) way to travel is to share a car, but for short distances, walking or cycling is the **8** .... (*good*).

4 **Work in pairs. The sample answer in Exercise 3 needs to be divided into five paragraphs.**

1 Write // to show where you think a paragraph should end and a new one should begin.
2 Match the paragraphs (1–5) with their purpose (a–e).

Paragraph **1**   **a** compares distances
Paragraph **2**   **b** compares speed
Paragraph **3**   **c** compares time taken
Paragraph **4**   **d** gives an overview of the information
Paragraph **5**   **e** says what the table shows

5 **Work in pairs. Look at this Writing task and answer the questions at the top of the next column.**

> *The table and the bar chart below give information about travelling to work in Houston, Texas.*
>
> *Summarise the information by selecting and reporting the main features, and make comparisons where relevant.*
>
> | | % of travellers per form of transport | average age of traveller |
> |---|---|---|
> | car (1 person) | 48 | 43 |
> | car (more than 1 person) | 11 | 44 |
> | cycle/walk | 4 | 39 |
> | train/bus | 37 | 47 |
>
> **CO₂ emissions from different forms of transport**
>
>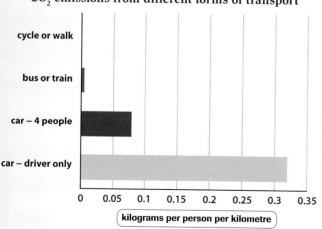
>
> kilograms per person per kilometre

1 What does the table show?
2 Which is the most common means of transport?
3 Which is the least common?
4 Which group of travellers has the highest average age?
5 Which group of travellers has the lowest average age?
6 What does the chart show?
7 Which forms of transport cause little or no pollution?
8 Which form of transport causes the most pollution?

6 **Read this sentence giving an overview of the information and choose the correct options in *italics*.**

Overall, cars with just the driver are the *most / least* common means of transport to work and cause *more / less* pollution than all the other means of transport combined.

7 **Work alone. Write your answer to the Writing task in Exercise 5. When you write:**

- use your answers to the questions in Exercise 5;
- use these paragraphs to structure your answer:
  - an introduction saying what the table and chart show
  - the percentage of people using each type of transport
  - the average age of people travelling by each type of transport
  - the CO₂ emissions for each form of transport
  - an overview (if you wish, you can use the overview from Exercise 6);
- use language from the sample answer in Exercise 3 which you think is useful;
- make sure you compare information in the table and the chart.

Exam advice   *Writing Task 1*

- Think about and analyse the information in the chart(s) and table(s) before you write.
- Organise the information into paragraphs and include a general overview.
- Make sure that you compare information in the chart(s) and table(s).

Key grammar
Making comparisons

❶ Complete this table. Then check your answers by reading the Language reference.

adjective	comparative	superlative
fast	1 *faster*	2 *the fastest*
high	3	4
expensive	5	6
healthy	7	8
steadily	9	10

▷ page 122 *Making comparisons*

❷ Complete these sentences by putting the adjective or adverb in brackets into the correct form.

1 Riding a motorcycle is *more economical* (*economical*) than driving a car.
2 It's .... (*easy*) to walk than to catch a bus.
3 Trains have .... (*low*) CO_2 emissions than buses.
4 Riding a bicycle is the .... (*healthy*) means of transport because you get some exercise.
5 Bicycles are probably also the .... (*dangerous*) means of transport.
6 You can get to work .... (*quickly*) by private transport than by public transport.

❸ Write sentences of your own about different means of transport using the correct form of these words.

- cheap
- comfortable
- enjoyable
- quickly
- slow

❹ Complete these sentences by putting the irregular adjectives and adverbs in brackets into the correct form.

1 I need to buy a .... (*good*) car than the one I have now.
2 Generally, people who take the train to work live .... (*far*) away than people who cycle.
3 Traffic problems in the city are getting .... (*bad*).
4 There are .... (*many*) cars on the road now than in the past.
5 It takes .... (*little*) time to cycle to work than to walk.

❺ ⊙ IELTS candidates often make mistakes with comparison of adjectives and adverbs. Find and correct the mistakes in each of these sentences.

1 International tourism brings many benefits such as ~~more better~~ transport systems. *better*
2 Private cars produced the most great amount of pollution.
3 Driving a car is more easier on motorways than in cities.
4 It was the second large category of travellers.
5 In many parts of the world, animals are still the better means of transport.
6 Sharing cars is the second common way of travelling to work.

Spelling
Changes when adding –er and –est to adjectives

❶ IELTS candidates often make spelling mistakes when they add –er and –est to adjectives. Add –er to each of these words. Then check your answers by looking at the Language reference.

1 clean *cleaner*
2 fit
3 friendly
4 happy
5 big
6 new

▷ page 123 *Spelling changes when adding –er and –est to adjectives*

❷ ⊙ Find and correct the spelling mistakes in these sentences written by IELTS candidates.

1 One of the ~~greattest~~ inventions, the car, gives us a better life. *greatest*
2 Auckland had the lowest population, but it had the hightest percentage of motor vehicles.
3 This is the bigest problem related to traffic all over the world.
4 The lowwest temperature is in the middle of July.
5 November was the hotest month of the year.
6 Motorcycles tend to be noisyer than cars.

Unit 4 It was all new once

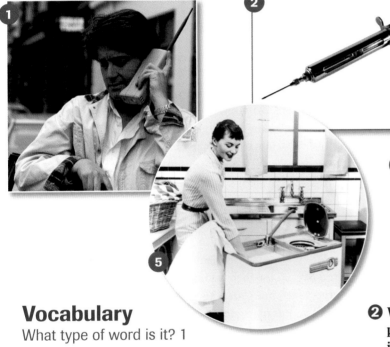

Starting off

Work in small groups.

1 Name each of the inventions in the photos.
2 How has each of them changed people's lives?

Vocabulary
What type of word is it? 1

When dealing with a difficult word in a passage, it helps to decide what type of word it is: noun, verb or adjective.

❶ Work in pairs.

1 Find and <u>underline</u> these two words in the reading passage on page 38 and decide what type of word each is. What helped you decide?

moisture   cited

2 Match them with these definitions from the *CLD*.

a very small drops of water in the air or on a surface
b to mention something as an example or proof of something else

▶ page 123 *Deciding the type of word*

❷ Work in pairs. <u>Underline</u> these words (1–6) in the passage. Then decide what type of word each one is and match them with their definitions from the *CLD* (a–f).

		type of word		definition
1	design	*verb*	a	large factory where an industrial process happens
2	plant		b	piece of equipment that is used for a particular purpose
3	device			
4	spread		c	one of the things that has an effect on a particular situation
5	output			
6	factor		d	the amount of something that is produced
			e	draw or plan something before making it
			f	increase to cover a larger area

Reading 1
Multiple choice

❶ Work in small groups. You are going to read a passage about air conditioning.

1 How important is air conditioning in your country?
2 Why is it important to have comfortable places to work and study?

❷ Read the passage quickly. Who is/was:

1 Willis Carrier?   2 Jed Brown?

Air conditioning

The history of an invention that makes life more pleasant

Willis Carrier designed the first air-conditioning unit in 1902, just a year after graduating from Cornell University with a Masters in Engineering. At a Brooklyn printing plant, fluctuations in heat and moisture were causing the size of the printing paper to keep changing slightly, making it hard to align different colours. Carrier's invention made it possible to control temperature and humidity levels and so align the colours. The invention also allowed industries such as film, processed food, textiles and pharmaceuticals to improve the quality of their products.

In 1914, the first air-conditioning device was installed in a private house. However, its size, similar to that of an early computer, meant it took up too much space to come into widespread use, and later models, such as the Weathermaker, which Carrier brought out in the 1920s, cost too much for most people. Cooling for human comfort, rather than industrial need, really took off when three air conditioners were installed in the J.L. Hudson Department Store in Detroit, Michigan. People crowded into the shop to experience the new invention. The fashion spread from department stores to cinemas, whose income rose steeply as a result of the comfort they provided.

To start with, money-conscious employers regarded air conditioning as a luxury. They considered that if they were paying people to work, they should not be paying for them to be comfortable as well. So in the 1940s and '50s, the industry started putting out a different message about its product: according to their research, installing air conditioning increased productivity amongst employees. They found that typists increased their output by 24% when transferred from a regular office to a cooled one. Another study into office working conditions, which was carried out in the late '50s, showed that the majority of companies cited air conditioning as the single most important contributor to efficiency in offices.

However, air conditioning has its critics. Jed Brown, an environmentalist, complains that air conditioning is a factor in global warming. Unfortunately, he adds, because air conditioning leads to higher temperatures, people have to use it even more. However, he admits that it provides a healthier environment for many people in the heat of summer.

❸ Read Questions 1–5 and <u>underline</u> the key ideas. Do not read the options yet.

Questions 1–5

1 When Willis Carrier invented air conditioning, <u>his aim</u> was to

  A make workers feel cooler.

  B produce more attractive paper.

  C set up a new business.

  D solve problems in a factory.

2 Home air conditioners were not popular at first because they were

  A too big and expensive.

  B not considered necessary.

  C too inefficient.

  D complicated to use.

3 Employers refused to put air conditioning in workplaces at first because they

  A could not afford to pay for it.

  B thought it was more suitable for cinemas.

  C did not want to spend money improving working conditions.

  D thought people would not work so hard in comfortable conditions.

4 What was the purpose of the research done in the 1940s and '50s?

  A to make office workers produce more

  B to compare different types of air conditioner

  C to persuade businesses to buy air conditioners

  D to encourage employees to change offices

5 What does Jed Brown say about air conditioning?

  A In future, everyone will need it.

  B Turning it off will not reduce global warming.

  C It can seriously damage people's health.

  D It is good for people, but bad for the environment.

---

❹ Now read the passage and find where each question is dealt with. Then read that part carefully and choose the correct option: A, B, C or D.

Exam advice   *Multiple choice*

- <u>Underline</u> the key idea in the question.
- Find the part of the passage which deals with the key idea and read it carefully.
- Choose the option which matches the information in the passage.

❺ Work in small groups. Apart from air conditioning, what other inventions have made your life more comfortable? In what ways?

Listening

Sentence completion, Pick from a list

❶ Work in pairs. You are going to listen to a woman, Irina, talking to a man at the ticket desk at an exhibition.

1 Have you ever been to an exhibition? If so, what did it show, and what did you like and dislike about it?

2 What sort of exhibitions might interest you? Why?

❷ Look at Questions 1–6 below.

1 How many sections are mentioned?

2 Which questions relate to which sections?

3 <u>Underline</u> the key ideas in each sentence.

Questions 1–6

Electronics exhibition

1 The <u>first section</u> deals with electronics designed to .... <u>the environment</u>.

2 One new device is for checking .... temperatures at different levels.

3 The theme of the second section is children and their ....

4 There are a number of inventions to avoid an .... in the home.

5 They demonstrate a device for checking if older children are at ....

6 The third section contains devices for dealing with ....

---

3 (22) **Listen and complete Questions 1–6 in Exercise 2. Write ONE WORD for each answer.**

Exam advice   *Sentence completion*

- Underline the key idea(s) in each sentence and think what information you need to complete the sentences.
- Listen and write the words when you hear them.

4 **Look at Questions 7–10 below. Underline the key ideas in each question.**

Questions 7–10

7 Which <u>TWO reasons</u> does Irina give for <u>visiting the exhibition</u>?
  A to meet a friend
  B to improve her knowledge
  C to buy something
  D to check prices
  E to entertain her child

8 Which TWO devices has Irina bought recently?
  A a calculator
  B a computer
  C a camera
  D a phone
  E a digital recorder

9 What TWO things does Irina like about the building?
  A the electric lights
  B the space
  C the activity
  D the ceiling
  E the entrance

10 Which TWO problems did Irina have coming to the exhibition?
  A driving in heavy traffic
  B finding the car park
  C parking the car
  D waiting to enter the exhibition
  E standing outside in the rain

5 (23) **Now listen. Choose TWO letters A–E for each question (7–10) in Exercise 4.**

Exam advice   *Pick from a list*

- Underline the key idea in each question.
- Listen carefully: you may hear something about the wrong answers as well as the correct answers, and the speakers may not use the same words as in the questions.

6 **Work in pairs.**

1 What electronic devices interest you? Why?
2 What electronic devices would you like to buy in the future?

Speaking
Part 2

1 **Work in pairs. Look at this Speaking task and decide which device each of you will find it easiest to speak about for two minutes.**

Describe an electronic device you use often.
You should say:
> how long you have had it
> how often you have used it
> what you have used it for
and explain why you use it so often.

2 (24) Work in pairs. You are going to hear a student, Amani, doing the Speaking task in Exercise 1. Before you listen, match the beginnings and endings of these sentences. Then check your answers by listening to Amani.

1 Actually, I've got it here **because** …
2 Everything is automatic, **so** …
3 I didn't ask for a camera, **so** …
4 I've carried it with me everywhere I've gone on holiday. **For example**, …
5 I've taken lots of photos of special occasions. **For instance** …
6 I use it to remember things, **so** …
7 Then I upload them onto Facebook, **so** …
8 I've used the camera so often **because** …

a I just point it and press the button.
b I put all the photos on my computer.
c in July I went on holiday to Denmark and Sweden.
d it was a complete surprise.
e it's easy to use and I carry it everywhere.
f it's very small and fits in my bag.
g my friends can see them.
h when my grandmother was 70, I took photos of her party.

3 Which words in bold in sentence beginnings 1–8 in Exercise 2 introduce:

1 a reason?   2 an example?   3 a consequence?

▶ Pronunciation: *Chunking 1*

▶ page 42 Key grammar: *Present perfect*

4 Work alone. Make notes for the Speaking task in Exercise 1. Then work in pairs. Take turns to give your talks.

5 Work alone. Make notes for this Speaking task.

> **Describe something you own which has improved your life.**
>
> **You should say:**
>
> > **how long you have had it**
> >
> > **when you use it**
> >
> > **what it looks like**
>
> **and explain how it has improved your life.**

6 Work in pairs and take turns to give your talks for the task in Exercise 5.

Exam advice   *Speaking Part 2*

• To keep speaking for two minutes, you have to add extra information, so give reasons and examples, explain consequences and describe things.

• Use your own words: don't just repeat the words in the task.

Pronunciation
Chunking 1

> We say words in groups and we pause or hesitate between these groups. Forming groups of words when we speak is called *chunking*. There are no rules about when to pause, but some places are more natural than others. Chunking makes you easier to understand.

1 (25) Listen to part of Amani's answer again. Mark with / where the speaker pauses.

I've had this camera / for two years. My parents gave it to me for my birthday when I was 18. I didn't ask for a camera, so it was a complete surprise, but it's been really useful.

2 (26) Work in pairs. Read this extract from Amani's answer and decide where she should pause. Then listen and check your answer.

Since I got the camera, I've carried it with me everywhere I've gone on holiday. For example, in July I went on holiday to Denmark and Sweden. They're lovely places, and in summer it's still light at midnight, so I got some great photos there.

3 Work in pairs. Take turns to read the extracts from Exercises 1 and 2 aloud with pauses.

4 Work alone. Write three or four sentences about an electronic device you have used often and put / where you should pause.

5 Work in pairs and take turns to read your sentences.

Key grammar
Present perfect

> The present perfect is formed with *have* + past participle (*done, opened, eaten,* etc.):
> *I've had this camera for two years.*

1 Look at the extract in blue from Amani's talk in the recording script on page 163 and underline the verbs in the present perfect.

2 Match these uses of the present perfect with the examples you underlined in Exercise 1.

We use the present perfect for something which:
1 started in the past and continues in the present.
2 happened in the past, but we don't say an exact time in the past.

▶ page 124 *Present perfect*

3 Complete these sentences by putting the verbs in brackets into the present perfect.

1 The number of people using mobile phones *has risen* (*rise*) by 500 percent since 2003.
2 The invention of electronic books .... (*change*) the way many people read.
3 Since I started using email, I .... (*not write*) a traditional letter.
4 I .... (*forget*) the word which means 'in the middle of the night'.
5 The library .... (*become*) much more comfortable since they installed air conditioning.
6 It is a device to help people find keys which they .... (*lose*).

4 ⊙ IELTS candidates often make mistakes with the present perfect. Find and correct the mistakes in these sentences.

1 In recent years, life ~~changed~~ and it's not like it was in the past. *has changed*
2 In the last few years, new technologies has brought enormous benefits.
3 In recent years, there are many problems arising regarding things you can find on the Internet.
4 With the rapid progress of science and technology, there are a lot of changes in the world.
5 During the last few years, money become more important as a way of satisfying our needs.

5 Look at these two sentences from Amani's talk and answer the questions below.

I've had this camera for two years.
I've taken more than a thousand photos since July.

Which preposition (*for* or *since*) is used to say:
1 the length of time (a number of days or weeks or years, etc.)?
2 from a specific time in the past (a day, a month, etc.) until now?

▶ page 124 for *and* since

6 Complete these sentences by writing *for* or *since* in each gap.

1 I've had this mobile phone *for* six months.
2 I was given this touchscreen computer for my birthday, so I've had it .... March.
3 He's been in Australia .... almost a year.
4 She hasn't taken any photos .... last summer.
5 She hasn't phoned me .... the meeting.
6 Ali hasn't done any homework .... three weeks.

Reading 2
Summary completion

1 You are going read a passage about Rubik's Cube. Before you read, work in small groups.

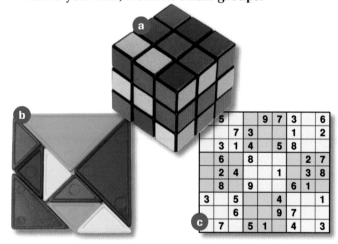

1 Match the puzzles above (a–c) with their names (1–3).
   1 Chinese tangram   2 sudoku   3 Rubik's Cube
2 What do you have to do in each puzzle?
3 Are any of these puzzles popular in your country?
4 Do you enjoy doing any of these puzzles? Why? / Why not?

❷ **Read the passage below quickly.**

1 When did Rubik start working on his Cube?
2 When did it become a success?

❸ <u>Underline</u> **these words (1–6) in the passage. Then decide what type of word each is and match them with their definitions from the** *CLD* **(a–f).**

1 preliminary *adjective*   **a** break into pieces
2 fall apart   **b** build something by joining parts together
3 attempt   **c** done or happening in order to prepare for the main event or activity
4 assemble   **d** the purpose of something
5 experiment   **e** try something in order to discover what it is like
6 object   **f** try to do something, especially something difficult

Rubik's Cube
How the puzzle achieved success

Erno Rubik first studied sculpture and then later architecture in Budapest, where he went on to become a teacher of interior design. It was while he was working as a teacher that he began the preliminary work on an invention that he called the 'Magic Cube'.

Rubik was inspired by geometric puzzles such as the Chinese tangram, a puzzle consisting of various triangles, a square and a parallelogram which can be combined to create different shapes and figures. However, unlike the tangram, which is two-dimensional, Rubik was more interested in investigating how three-dimensional forms, such as the cube, could be moved and combined to produce other forms.

His design consisted of a cube made up of layers of individual smaller cubes, and each smaller cube could be turned in any direction except diagonally. To ensure that the cubes could move independently, without falling apart, Rubik first attempted to join them together using elastic bands. However, this proved to be impossible, so Rubik then solved the problem by assembling them using a rounded interior. This permitted them to move smoothly and easily. He experimented with different ways of marking the smaller cubes, but ended up with the simple solution of giving a different colour to each side. The object was to twist the layers of small cubes so that each side of the large cube was an identical colour.

Rubik took out a patent for the Cube in 1977 and started manufacturing it in the same year. The Cube came to the attention of a Hungarian businessman, Tibor Laczi, who then demonstrated it at the Nuremberg Toy Fair. When British toy expert Tom Kremer saw it, he thought it was amazing and he persuaded a manufacturer, Ideal Toys, to produce 1 million of them in 1979. Ideal Toys renamed the Cube after the toy's inventor, and in 1980, Rubik's Cube was shown at toy fairs all over the world. It won that year's prize in Germany for Best Puzzle. Rubik's Cube is believed to be the world's best-selling puzzle; since its invention, more than 300 million Cubes have been sold worldwide.

❹ **Work in pairs. Look at the summary below. Read around the gaps and decide what type of word and what information you might need for each gap.**

Rubik's Cube

Originally named the **1** ...., Rubik's Cube consists of a number of smaller cubes organised in **2** .... The smaller cubes can be twisted in almost any way, though not **3** .... The Cube's **4** .... is shaped in a way that allows the smaller cubes to move smoothly. Each side of the smaller cubes has a different colour, and the aim of the puzzle is to organise the cubes so that the colours on the sides of the large cube are **5** ....

The manufacturers of the puzzle changed the name of the Cube to the name of its **6** .... It has now sold more than any other **7** .... in the world.

❺ **Now complete the summary. Choose NO MORE THAN TWO WORDS from the passage for each answer.**

Exam advice   *Summary completion*

• Read the summary carefully first: decide what information and what type(s) of word you need for each gap.

• When you have completed the summary, read it again to check it makes sense.

Writing
Task 2

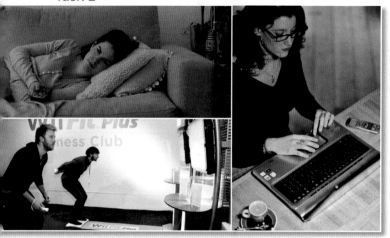

1 Work in small groups. Read this Writing task and <u>underline</u> the key ideas. Then discuss the questions below.

> Write about the following topic.
>
> *As a result of electronic inventions such as the computer and television, people do less physical activity, and this is having a negative effect on their health.*
>
> *To what extent do you agree or disagree?*
>
> Give reasons for your answer and include any relevant examples from your own knowledge or experience.

1 Do you agree that people do less physical activity than in the past? Why? / Why not?
2 What areas of people's lives have modern inventions affected in this way?
3 If you agree that people do less physical activity, do you agree that this has had a negative effect on their health?
4 Do you think people who do physical work or do a sport have better health than other people?
5 How might working with computers or watching television affect people's health? Think about these things: eyes, weight, heart and muscles.

2 Work in pairs. These sentences were written by different IELTS students as part of their answers to the Writing task in Exercise 1. Which sentences do you think are relevant (R) and which are irrelevant (I)? Why?

1 For young people, computers have become a more popular form of entertainment than television.
 I (It's not related to people's health.)

2 As far as work is concerned, office employees have always worked sitting down and the introduction of computers has not changed that.
3 Generally, people like working with computers, so they find their work more enjoyable.
4 However, people have also put on weight because they eat more food than in the past, so we should not blame modern inventions for everything.
5 For example, lifestyles have become more hygienic, people do not catch so many infections and they live longer.
6 As a result, sportspeople have become fitter and they continue to break records.

3 Read this sample answer to the Writing task in Exercise 1. Then answer the questions on page 45.

> There is no doubt that modern electronic inventions have transformed people's jobs and their leisure time, so that many people spend less time taking exercise. However, it is not so certain that this has damaged their health.
>
> As far as work is concerned, office employees have always worked sitting down, and computers have not changed that. Computers have not affected physical jobs such as farming or building either, and people still do physical work like they did in the past. In fact, other machines such as washing machines and tractors, not computers, have reduced the amount of physical work people do.
>
> On the other hand, the way people spend their spare time has changed greatly. People spend many hours watching television and playing with their computers, so they do not do so much physical exercise. This is one of the things which has made more people overweight, and this affects their health when they are older.
>
> However, people have also put on weight because they eat more food than in the past, so we should not blame modern inventions for everything. What is more, new technologies have led to better medicine, and as a result people live longer.
>
> In conclusion, I believe that generally people live more healthily now. In my view, it is difficult to argue that modern inventions have had a harmful influence on our health. On the other hand, we need to make sure that we still take a reasonable amount of exercise.

Which paragraph:

1 summarises the writer's opinions?

2 introduces the subject and says what the writer agrees with and what she disagrees with?

3 mentions other factors which affect people's health?

4 says to what extent the writer agrees with the idea that computers have changed the way people work?

5 says to what extent the writer agrees that computers and television have changed the way people spend their free time, and how this has affected their health?

④ Work in pairs. <u>Underline</u> the key ideas in this Writing task. Then answer the questions below.

Write about the following topic.

Modern forms of communication such as email and messaging have reduced the amount of time people spend seeing their friends. This has had a negative effect on their social lives.

To what extent do you agree or disagree?

Give reasons for your answer and include any relevant examples from your own knowledge or experience.

1 How did people communicate with friends in the past? How do they communicate now? Has this changed?

2 Do you agree that people don't see their friends so much? If so, do you agree that things like email and messaging have caused this, or has something else caused it?

3 Do you think that people's social lives have got better or worse than in the past? If you think their social lives have got worse, is this a result of modern forms of communication?

4 Do you use these methods of communication? How do they affect your social life?

Now change partners and compare your ideas.

⑤ Work alone.

1 Decide how many paragraphs your answer to the Writing task in Exercise 4 will have.

2 Write down the purpose of each paragraph (as in Exercise 3).

When you have finished, compare your ideas with a partner's.

⑥ Work alone and write your answer. You should write at least 250 words.

Exam advice | Writing Task 2

• Think through the question carefully before you make your plan.

• Make sure that everything you write is relevant to the question.

Spelling
Using and misusing double letters

① IELTS candidates often use single and double letters wrongly. Work in pairs and correct the spelling of these words.

1 ofice 2 siting 3 afected 4 physicall
5 beter 6 generaly 7 dificult 8 harmfull

Check your answers by looking at the sample answer in Writing Exercise 3.

② Work in pairs. Choose the correct spelling of each of these words from this unit.

1 (efficiency)	eficiency
2 instaled	installed
3 anoyed	annoyed
4 atractive	attractive
5 atention	attention
6 apart	appart
7 sucessfuly	successfully
8 diferent	different
9 benefit	benefitt
10 attempted	atempted
11 apearrance	appearance
12 comunicate	communicate

Vocabulary and grammar review **Unit 3**

Vocabulary

❶ Find nine more words and phrases in the grid connected with transport and travel. You can find the remaining words horizontally.

A	I	X	F	T	B	U	F	J	O	U	R	N	E	Y
T	P	P	S	T	R	A	F	F	I	C	J	A	M	P
C	X	C	O	M	M	U	T	E	R	L	A	L	V	Y
T	D	E	S	T	I	N	A	T	I	O	N	J	H	T
W	E	K	J	W	F	W	Y	J	N	M	O	J	R	F
L	M	E	K	M	R	U	B	O	E	J	P	C	J	O
M	B	D	V	W	K	O	I	D	J	O	Z	A	J	P
P	U	B	L	I	C	T	R	A	N	S	P	O	R	T
X	O	A	B	H	S	X	Q	B	C	J	S	G	O	B
B	Q	M	B	E	C	P	A	S	S	E	N	G	E	R
T	I	Y	G	T	R	M	V	B	R	R	G	H	F	S
B	N	N	O	F	F	P	E	A	K	K	H	K	A	H
J	O	H	Y	F	B	P	R	A	O	D	W	I	F	J
C	U	M	V	E	H	I	C	L	E	F	J	B	E	C
H	G	D	R	U	S	H	H	O	U	R	O	K	Y	P

❷ Complete these sentences with the correct form of *cause* or *make*.

1 I've just eaten some food which has made me ill.
2 The cold weather .... many problems on the railways in recent weeks.
3 Traffic jams .... people late for work and as a result, they feel stressed.
4 Recent increases in petrol prices .... public transport more popular.
5 The bad condition of this road .... three accidents this year.
6 According to the study, private transport .... 60% more pollution than public transport.

Grammar

❸ Complete these sentences using the correct form of the adjective in brackets.

1 Aeroplanes are one of the ...safest.. (*safe*) forms of transport.
2 Cars use less fuel because their engines are becoming .... (*efficient*).
3 I have never travelled .... (*far*) than Delhi.
4 Traffic pollution is probably the .... (*great*) problem facing the modern world.
5 The .... (*hot*) month of the year in Khartoum is June.
6 I think Saheh needs to see an optician because his driving is getting .... (*bad*).
7 Overall, the .... (*high*) number of commuters travel to work by car.
8 Atmospheric pollution was .... (*low*) two years ago than it is now.

❹ Complete the sentences below describing this chart. Use words from the box in the correct form.

cloudy	cold	dry	hot	sunny	wet

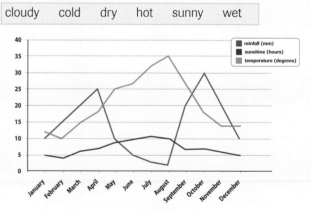

1 February is the coldest month, with an average temperature of 10 degrees.
2 August is the .... month, when the average daily temperature is 35 degrees.
3 October is the .... month, with 30 mm of rainfall per day.
4 August is the .... month, with less than 3 mm of rainfall per day.
5 July is the .... month, with 11 hours of sunshine per day.
6 February is the .... month, with fewer than five hours of sunshine per day.

Vocabulary and grammar review **Unit 4**

Vocabulary

❶ **Choose the correct option in *italics* in each sentence.**

1 The *plant* / *device* produces more than 500 cars a day.
2 *Factor* / *Output* increased by 20% after they installed air conditioning.
3 Scientists have *designed* / *spread* a new type of motor which runs on ethanol.
4 Biologists have been *attempting* / *experimenting* with bacteria which will eat plastic.
5 The cars are *demonstrated* / *assembled* at a factory outside Beijing.
6 The *object* / *layer* of the puzzle is to make each side of the cube the same colour.

❷ **Find and correct one spelling mistake in each of these sentences.**

1 New technologies allow people to ~~comunicate~~ more easily. *communicate*
2 The machine was installed sucessfully.
3 She works in an ofice with three other employees.
4 Teachers get annoyed when students don't pay atention.
5 Appart from university students, few people are affected by the new regulations.
6 If you improve your appearance, you will feel better and benefitt in other ways also.
7 The new building is certainly attractive and looks diferent from the others.
8 Studies show that physicall fitness improves mental fitness.

Grammar

❸ **Complete these sentences with *because, so, for example* or *for instance*. In some cases, more than one answer is possible.**

1 I couldn't afford an expensive computer, ...*so*...... I bought a cheaper one.
2 Several of the components, ... the microchips, are produced in Japan.
3 At first, air conditioners were not installed in private homes .... they were too large.
4 The heat made employees uncomfortable, ... employers decided to install air conditioning.
5 Employees' output increased .... their working conditions improved.
6 Domestic appliances have improved the way people live. .... , washing machines save people several hours of hard work each week.

❹ **Complete these sentences with the present perfect of the verb in brackets.**

1 Scientists *have thought* (*think*) of a way of removing carbon dioxide from the atmosphere.
2 My tutor .... (*just write*) a paper for a scientific journal.
3 The cost of these machines .... (*rise*) by 16% in the last three years.
4 Our neighbours .... (*buy*) a new car.
5 They .... (*do*) a number of experiments and now they think they .... (*find*) a solution to the problem.
6 We .... (*finish*) the work, but they .... (*not pay*) us yet.

❺ **Complete these sentences with *for* or *since*.**

1 The exhibition has been open ...*since*... last week.
2 He studied at Wuhan University .... five years.
3 The department has been open .... 1993.
4 Anwar visited Kuwait .... a week.
5 I haven't spoken to her .... we were children.

Unit 5 Animal world

Starting off

1 Work in pairs. Match the names of these animals with the photos (1–7).

cow	crocodile	penguin	scorpion
tree frog	whale	zebra	

2 What are typical habitats for each of the animals in Exercise 1? Choose from the following.

1 grassland   2 farmland   3 rivers and lakes
4 on the coast and in the sea   5 oceans
6 desert   7 rainforest

3 Which of these animals have you seen? When and where?

Reading 1

Sentence completion

1 Work in pairs. You are going to read about a colourful species of bird. Before you read the whole passage, look at the title and subheading of the passage on page 49. What do you expect the passage to contain?

2 Read the passage quickly.

1   What is the bee-eater's habitat?
2   How long do they live?

3 <u>Underline</u> these words (1–7) in the passage, decide what type of word each one is, then match it with its definition from the *CLD* (a–g).

		type of word	definition
1	diet	*noun*	**a** group of birds
2	prey		**b** home built by birds for their eggs
3	breed		**c** animal that kills and eats other animals
4	flock		**d** produce a young animal
5	migration		**e** journey from one place to another at the same time each year
6	predator		**f** the type of food that a person or animal usually eats
7	nest		**g** an animal that is hunted and killed by another animal

The life of the European bee-eater

A brilliant movement of colour as it catches its food in the air, the European bee-eater moves between three continents.

True to their name, bee-eaters eat bees (though their diet includes just about any flying insect). When the bird catches a bee, it returns to its tree to get rid of the bee's poison, which it does very efficiently. It hits the insect's head on one side of the branch, then rubs its body on the other. The rubbing makes its prey harmless.

European bee-eaters (*Merops apiaster*) form families that breed in the spring and summer across an area that extends from Spain to Kazakhstan. Farmland and river valleys provide huge numbers of insects. Flocks of bee-eaters follow tractors as they work fields. When the birds come upon a beehive, they eat well – a researcher once found a hundred bees in the stomach of a bee-eater near a hive.

European bees pass the winter by sleeping in their hives, which cuts off the bee-eater's main source of food. So, in late summer, bee-eaters begin a long, dangerous journey. Massive flocks from Spain, France and northern Italy cross the Sahara desert to their wintering grounds in West Africa. Bee-eaters from Hungary and other parts of Central and Eastern Europe cross the Mediterranean Sea and Arabian Desert to winter in southern Africa. 'It's an extremely risky stratagem, this migration,' says C. Hilary Fry, a British ornithologist who has studied European bee-eaters for more than 45 years. 'At least 30 percent of the birds will be killed by predators before they make it back to Europe the following spring.'

In April, they return to Europe. Birds build nests by digging tunnels in riverbanks. They work for up to 20 days. By the end of the job, they've moved 15 to 26 pounds of soil – more than 80 times their weight.

The nesting season is a time when families help each other, and sons or uncles help feed their father's or brother's chicks as soon as they come out of their eggs. The helpers benefit, too: parents with helpers can provide more food for chicks to continue the family line.

It's a short, spectacular life. European bee-eaters live for five to six years. The difficulties of migration and avoiding predators along the way affect every bird. Bee-eaters today also find it harder to find food, as there are fewer insects around as a result of pesticides. Breeding sites are also disappearing, as rivers are turned into concrete-walled canals.

by Bruce Barcott, *National Geographic* magazine, 2008

❹ **Read Questions 1–8 below.**

1 <u>Underline</u> the key ideas.
2 Decide what type of information you need for each gap.

Questions 1–8

1 Bee-eaters' prey are bees and other ....
2 Bee-eaters need to remove the .... from bees before eating them.
3 There is plenty of food for bee-eaters on agricultural land and in ....
4 Bee-eaters migrate to spend the winter in different parts of ....
5 Because of .... , almost one-third of bee-eaters do not survive migration.
6 Bee-eaters make nests in .... , which they build themselves.
7 When nesting, the .... receive food from different family members.
8 One problem for bee-eaters is .... , which have reduced the amount of food available.

❺ **Now complete Questions 1–8 in Exercise 4. Write NO MORE THAN TWO WORDS from the passage for each answer.**

> *Exam advice*   *Sentence completion*
>
> • <u>Underline</u> the key idea in each question.
> • Decide what type of information you need to complete the sentence.
> • Read the section of the passage which deals with the key idea and choose your answer.
> • Read the completed sentence to make sure it is grammatically correct.

❻ **Work in small groups.**

1 Are there any animals in your country which are in danger of disappearing?
2 Is this because their habitat or food is disappearing, or is there another cause?

Listening

Table completion, Labelling a map or plan

❶ You are going to hear an information officer at a zoo talking to a group of visitors. Before you listen, work in pairs.

1 Do you think it is a good idea to keep animals in zoos? Why? / Why not?
2 What can children and adults learn from zoos?

❷ Look at this table. What information do you need for each gap?

Animal World – today's events			
name of event	location	type of event	time
The World of Ants	the **1**	**2**	11 a.m.
The **3**	**4**	film	12 noon
Encouraging **5**	Exhibition Room	demonstration	2.30 p.m.
Birds of Prey	the lawn	**6**	**7** .... p.m.

❸ ⟨27⟩ Now listen and complete the table above. Write NO MORE THAN TWO WORDS OR A NUMBER for each answer.

> *Exam advice*　*Table completion*
>
> • Before you listen, read the table to see what information you are given and what information you need.
> • You hear the answers in the same order as the questions in the table.

❹ Work in pairs. You are going to hear the information officer saying where things are in the zoo. Before you listen, look at the map below and answer these questions. For some of the questions, you must answer with a letter, e.g. A.

1 Where are you on the plan?
2 If you take the left-hand path when you come to the lake, what is on your left?
3 If you take the right-hand path when you come to the lake, what is on your left?
4 What animals are next to the lake on your right?
5 What is between D and the penguins?
6 Which two places are opposite D?
7 What is over the crossroad on your right?
8 If you turn left at the crossroad and continue walking past B, what is on your left?

▶ page 124 *Directions and prepositions of place*

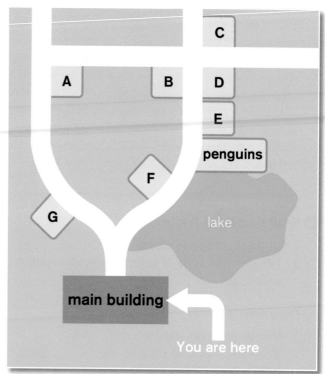

❺ ⟨28⟩ Now listen and write the correct letter (A–G), next to these questions (1–3).

1 gift shop　2 restaurant　3 picnic area

> *Exam advice*　*Labelling a map or plan*
>
> Before you listen, check where each of the options is in relation to where:
> • you are on the map/plan;
> • the things are which are already labelled.

Speaking
Parts 1 and 2

1 Work in pairs. Look at Part 1 questions a–d below.

1 Which question(s) ask(s) you to express your feelings or opinions?

2 Which question(s) ask(s) you for information?

---

a Which are your favourite animals? Why?

b Which animals don't you like? Why?

c Where are the best places in your country to see wildlife?

d How popular is watching wildlife in your country?

---

2 Work alone. Think how you could answer questions a–d in Exercise 1 with two or three sentences. If you like, note down some ideas.

3 (29) Listen to Suchin. What are her answers to the questions?

4 (29) Complete these phrases by writing one or two words in each gap. Then listen to Suchin again to check your answers.

1 I .... my cat ...

2 I'm not sure .... you say this, but ...

3 I'm quite .... on birds ...

4 I .... insects in the summer.

5 I don't know .... their name is in English.

6 I'm not .... keen on flies, either.

7 .... a difficult question. I'm not sure.

8 It's .... to say.

9 What is the activity .... ?

5 Which phrases from Exercise 4 does Suchin use:

a when she doesn't know a word?

b when she's not sure of the answer?

c to express strong feelings?

d to express feelings which are not so strong?

▶ Pronunciation: *Sentence stress 2*

6 Work in pairs. Take turns to ask and answer questions a–d from Exercise 1. Use phrases from Exercise 4 where necessary.

7 Work alone. Take a minute to read this prompt card for Speaking Part 2 and make notes.

Describe a place you have visited where you can see interesting animals.

You should say:

why you went there

what the place looked like

what you did there

and say which animals you found particularly interesting.

---

8 Work in pairs. Take turns to do the Speaking task.

Pronunciation
Sentence stress 2

We stress the words in the sentence which carry the most meaning, or which express our feelings.

---

1 Work in pairs. Underline the word(s) you should stress in these sentences.

1 I'm not <u>sure</u> how you <u>say</u> this, but when he's <u>there</u>, I'm not <u>alone</u>.

2 I don't know what their name is in English.

3 That's a difficult question. I'm not sure.

4 It's hard to say.

5 What is the activity called?

2 (30) Work in pairs. Listen and check your answers, then say the sentences in Exercise 1.

3 Which words in these sentences do you think should be stressed?

1 I've had him for nearly a year now and I love him. He's so beautiful.

2 I hate insects in the summer. They're horrible!

4 (31) Work in pairs. Listen and check your answers to Exercise 3, then say the sentences.

5 Work alone. Write your answers to these questions and <u>underline</u> the words you would stress.

1 Which are your favourite animals? Why?

2 Which animals don't you like? Why not?

6 Work in pairs. Ask and answer the questions.

Writing
Task 1

❶ Work in pairs. Look at the Writing task below and say whether the sentences in the next column are true (T) or false (F). If a sentence is false, correct it.

The charts below show information about animals and rainfall at the Nboro Nature Reserve.

Summarise the information by selecting and reporting the main features and make comparisons where relevant.

Numbers of animals, Nboro Nature Reserve

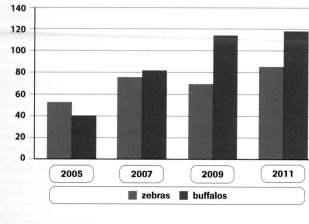

Annual rainfall, Nboro Nature Reserve

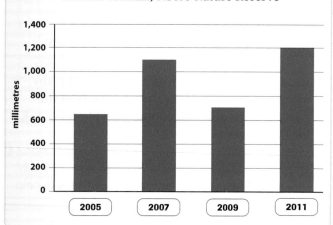

1 The charts give information about the number of zebras and buffalos and the amount of rain at theNboro Nature Reserve **between** 2005 and 2011. T

2 **In** 2005, there were fewer zebras than buffalos, with 40 zebras and 50 buffalos.
   F (There were 50 zebras and 40 buffalos.)

3 **From** 2005 **to** 2011, the number of buffalos rose each year till it reached just under 120.

4 On the other hand, the number of zebras fell to 75 in 2007 and then went up to 70 animals in 2009.

5 The zebra population then increased again to reach about 85 in 2011.

6 **During** the same period, there were 1,000 millimetres of rain in 2005.

7 The amount rose to 1,100 millimetres in 2007 and dropped to 700 millimetres in 2009, when there was little rain.

8 However, in 2011, 1,200 millimetres of rain fell.

9 Overall, numbers of both animals have decreased **over** the six-year period, but the amount of rain appears to affect the number of zebras.

10 When there is more rain, there are more zebras.

❷ Read the corrected sentences in Exercise 1 again and group them so that they form paragraphs with these topics.

a an introduction to the information in the charts
b a summary and comparison of information about the animals
c a summary of the information about rainfall
d a general overview of all the information in the charts

▶ page 56 Key grammar: *Countable and uncountable nouns*

❸ Find words and phrases in the sentences in Exercise 1 which mean *rose* and *fell*.

❹ Look at the prepositions in bold in the sentences in Exercise 1. Then choose the correct preposition in *italics* in each of the sentences below.

1 They started the research *in / on* 2002.
2 The number of animals increased *from / between* 2004 and 2008.
3 Average temperatures decreased *from / between* 2006 to 2010.
4 Animal numbers increased by 20% *during / from* this period.
5 Rainfall went up *between / over* the six-month period.

▶ page 126 *Prepositions in time phrases*

Speaking
Parts 1 and 2

❶ Work in pairs. Look at Part 1 questions a–d below.

1 Which question(s) ask(s) you to express your feelings or opinions?
2 Which question(s) ask(s) you for information?

> a Which are your favourite animals? Why?
> b Which animals don't you like? Why?
> c Where are the best places in your country to see wildlife?
> d How popular is watching wildlife in your country?

❷ Work alone. Think how you could answer questions a–d in Exercise 1 with two or three sentences. If you like, note down some ideas.

❸ 🔊29 Listen to Suchin. What are her answers to the questions?

❹ 🔊29 Complete these phrases by writing one or two words in each gap. Then listen to Suchin again to check your answers.

1 I .... my cat ...
2 I'm not sure .... you say this, but ...
3 I'm quite .... on birds ...
4 I .... insects in the summer.
5 I don't know .... their name is in English.
6 I'm not .... keen on flies, either.
7 .... a difficult question. I'm not sure.
8 It's .... to say.
9 What is the activity .... ?

❺ Which phrases from Exercise 4 does Suchin use:

a when she doesn't know a word?
b when she's not sure of the answer?
c to express strong feelings?
d to express feelings which are not so strong?

▶ Pronunciation: *Sentence stress 2*

❻ Work in pairs. Take turns to ask and answer questions a–d from Exercise 1. Use phrases from Exercise 4 where necessary.

❼ Work alone. Take a minute to read this prompt card for Speaking Part 2 and make notes.

> Describe a place you have visited where you can see interesting animals.
>
> You should say:
>
> why you went there
>
> what the place looked like
>
> what you did there
>
> and say which animals you found particularly interesting.

❽ Work in pairs. Take turns to do the Speaking task.

Pronunciation
Sentence stress 2

> We stress the words in the sentence which carry the most meaning, or which express our feelings.

❶ Work in pairs. Underline the word(s) you should stress in these sentences.

1 I'm not <u>sure</u> how you <u>say</u> this, but when he's <u>there</u>, I'm not <u>alone</u>.
2 I don't know what their name is in English.
3 That's a difficult question. I'm not sure.
4 It's hard to say.
5 What is the activity called?

❷ 🔊30 Work in pairs. Listen and check your answers, then say the sentences in Exercise 1.

❸ Which words in these sentences do you think should be stressed?

1 I've had him for nearly a year now and I love him. He's so beautiful.
2 I hate insects in the summer. They're horrible!

❹ 🔊31 Work in pairs. Listen and check your answers to Exercise 3, then say the sentences.

❺ Work alone. Write your answers to these questions and underline the words you would stress.

1 Which are your favourite animals? Why?
2 Which animals don't you like? Why not?

❻ Work in pairs. Ask and answer the questions.

Vocabulary
What type of word is it? 2

When we read a word we don't know, we can often tell what type of word it is by looking at its ending, e.g. a word ending in –*ion* is often, but not always, a noun: *migration*.

❶ Work in pairs. Look at the endings of these words and decide if they are nouns, verbs, adjectives or adverbs.

1 previous *adjective*   2 biologist   3 extensive
4 international   5 distinctive   6 routinely
7 estimate   8 destination   9 oceanographer
10 indicate   11 recover   12 extinction

▶ page 125 *Types of word and word endings*

❷ Underline the words from Exercise 1 in the passage on this page and the next.

❸ Work in pairs. Check your answers to Exercise 1 by looking at the positions of the words in the sentences. Then discuss what you think each word means from the context.

❹ Check your answers by matching the words with their definitions on page 175.

Reading 2
Pick from a list

❶ Work in small groups. You are going to read about an unusual whale. Before you read, decide whether these sentences are true (T) or false (F). If they are false, correct them.

1 Whales are fish. F (*Whales are mammals.*)
2 Whales are the largest living creatures.
3 Many whales are predators.
4 Some whales are never seen because they live deep under the ocean.
5 Some whales sing.
6 There are only ten species of whale.
7 Some species of whale are endangered.

Now look on page 175 to check your answers.

❷ Look at the title and subheading of the passage. What do you think it will be about?

❸ Read the passage quickly. Which of these sentences is the best summary of it?

A Researchers have quite a complete picture of whales' behaviour.
B Researchers have many things to learn about whales' behaviour.

Humpback whale breaks migration record

A whale surprises researchers with her journey.

A lone humpback whale travelled more than 9,800 kilometres from breeding areas in Brazil to those in Madagascar, setting a record for the longest mammal migration ever documented.

Humpback whales (*Megaptera novaeangliae*) are known to have some of the longest migration distances of all mammals, and this huge journey is about 400 kilometres farther than the previous humpback record. The finding was made by Peter Stevick, a biologist at the College of the Atlantic in Bar Harbor, Maine.

The whale's journey was unusual not only for its length, but also because it travelled across almost 90 degrees of longitude from west to east. Typically, humpbacks move in a north–south direction between cold feeding areas and warm breeding grounds – and the longest journeys which have been recorded until now have been between breeding and feeding sites.

The whale, a female, was first spotted off the coast of Brazil, where researchers photographed its tail fluke and took skin samples for chromosome testing to determine the animal's sex. Two years later, a tourist on a whale-watching boat snapped a photo of the humpback near Madagascar.

To match the two sightings, Stevick's team used an extensive international catalogue of photographs of the undersides of tail flukes, which have distinctive markings. Researchers routinely compare the markings in each new photograph to those in the archive.

The scientists then estimated the animal's shortest possible route: an arc skirting the southern tip of South Africa and heading north-east towards Madagascar. The minimum distance

is 9,800 kilometres, says Stevick, but this is likely to be an underestimate, because the whale probably took a detour to feed on krill in the Southern Ocean near Antarctica before reaching its destination.

Most humpback-whale researchers focus their efforts on the Northern Hemisphere because the Southern Ocean near the Antarctic is a hostile environment and it is hard to get to, explains Rochelle Constantine, who studies the ecology of humpback whales at the University of Auckland in New Zealand. But, for whales, oceans in the Southern Hemisphere are wider and easier to travel across, says Constantine. Scientists will probably observe more long-distance migrations in the Southern Hemisphere as satellite tracking becomes increasingly common, she adds.

Daniel Palacios, an oceanographer at the University of Hawaii at Manoa, says that the record-breaking journey could indicate that migration patterns are shifting as populations begin to recover from near-extinction and the population increases. But the reasons why the whale did not follow the usual migration routes remain a mystery. She could have been exploring new habitats, or simply have lost her way. 'We generally think of humpback whales as very well studied, but then they surprise us with things like this,' Palacios says. 'Undoubtedly there are a lot of things we still don't know about whale migration.'

by Janelle Weaver, published online in *Nature*

❹ **Look at Questions 1–7 below. <u>Underline</u> the key ideas in the questions, but not the options.**

Questions 1–7

1   What **TWO** <u>aspects</u> of the <u>whale's journey surprised researchers</u>?

   A the destination   **D** the reason

   B the direction   **E** the season

   C the distance

2   The passage mentions reasons why whales generally migrate.

   What **TWO** reasons are given?

   A to avoid humans   **D** to keep warm

   B to be safe   **E** to produce young

   C to eat

3   What **TWO** methods did researchers use to record the identity of the whale near Brazil?

   A They analysed part of the whale's body.

   B They marked its tail.

   C They made notes of its behaviour.

   D They recorded the sounds it made.

   E They took a picture.

4   The passage mentions places the whale may have passed close to on its journey.

   Which **TWO** places may the whale have passed?

   A Antarctica   **D** New Zealand

   B Hawaii   **E** South Africa

   C Maine

5   The passage says that more research is done in the Northern Hemisphere.

   Which **TWO** reasons are given for this?

   A It contains more whales.

   B It has friendlier surroundings.

   C There are more samples available.

   D It is easier to reach.

   E It contains smaller whales.

6   The passage suggests why the whale made a different journey from usual.

   Which **TWO** reasons does it suggest?

   A She did not know where she was going.

   B She did not want to breed.

   C She wanted to escape a danger.

   D She was looking for a new place to live.

   E She was recovering from an illness.

7   Which **TWO** methods of finding out where whales migrate are mentioned in the passage?

   A attaching radio transmitters

   B comparing pictures taken in different places

   C following them in boats

   D placing cameras in key positions

   E following their movements from space

❺ **Read the passage again to find where the key ideas are mentioned. Read those parts of the passage carefully and choose TWO letters (A–E), for Questions 1–7.**

Exam advice   *Pick from a list*

• <u>Underline</u> the key ideas in the questions to help you find the right place in the passage.

• Match ideas in the passage to the options.

Writing
Task 1

1 Work in pairs. Look at the Writing task below and say whether the sentences in the next column are true (T) or false (F). If a sentence is false, correct it.

The charts below show information about animals and rainfall at the Nboro Nature Reserve.

Summarise the information by selecting and reporting the main features and make comparisons where relevant.

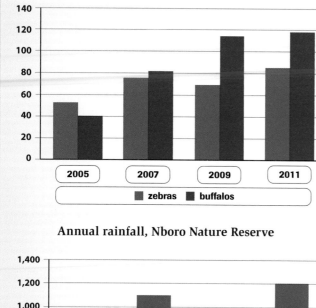

Numbers of animals, Nboro Nature Reserve

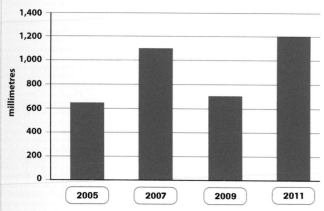

Annual rainfall, Nboro Nature Reserve

1 The charts give information about the number of zebras and buffalos and the amount of rain at theNboro Nature Reserve **between** 2005 and 2011. T

2 **In** 2005, there were fewer zebras than buffalos, with 40 zebras and 50 buffalos.
F (There were 50 zebras and 40 buffalos.)

3 **From** 2005 **to** 2011, the number of buffalos rose each year till it reached just under 120.

4 On the other hand, the number of zebras fell to 75 in 2007 and then went up to 70 animals in 2009.

5 The zebra population then increased again to reach about 85 in 2011.

6 **During** the same period, there were 1,000 millimetres of rain in 2005.

7 The amount rose to 1,100 millimetres in 2007 and dropped to 700 millimetres in 2009, when there was little rain.

8 However, in 2011, 1,200 millimetres of rain fell.

9 Overall, numbers of both animals have decreased **over** the six-year period, but the amount of rain appears to affect the number of zebras.

10 When there is more rain, there are more zebras.

2 Read the corrected sentences in Exercise 1 again and group them so that they form paragraphs with these topics.

a an introduction to the information in the charts
b a summary and comparison of information about the animals
c a summary of the information about rainfall
d a general overview of all the information in the charts

▶ page 56 Key grammar: *Countable and uncountable nouns*

3 Find words and phrases in the sentences in Exercise 1 which mean *rose* and *fell*.

4 Look at the prepositions in bold in the sentences in Exercise 1. Then choose the correct preposition in *italics* in each of the sentences below.

1 They started the research *in / on* 2002.
2 The number of animals increased *from / between* 2004 and 2008.
3 Average temperatures decreased *from / between* 2006 to 2010.
4 Animal numbers increased by 20% *during / from* this period.
5 Rainfall went up *between / over* the six-month period.

▶ page 126 *Prepositions in time phrases*

5 ⊙ **IELTS candidates often make mistakes with prepositions in time phrases. Find and correct a mistake with a preposition in each of these sentences.**

1 The charts compare numbers of elephants ~~across~~ 1981 and 2001. *between*

2 The figures increased during 1950 to 1965.

3 The oldest nature reserve in Spain was established on 1918.

4 The temperature fell from 25° to 15° on July and it recovered slowly.

5 This is information about rainfall in Australia since 1990 to 2010.

6 **Work in pairs. Look at the Writing task below and answer the questions in the next column.**

1 What does each chart show, and what years are covered by the charts?

2 Are these words countable or uncountable?
   a *colony*   **b** *honey*

3 How many honey-bee colonies were there in 1970, and how much honey did they produce?

4 Did these figures rise or fall from 1970 to 1980? What comparison can you make about this period?

5 Did these figures rise or fall from 1980 to 1990? What comparison can you make?

6 Did honey-bee colonies and honey production rise or fall between 1990 and 2010?

7 For your overview, what in general can you say about bee colonies and honey production between 1970 and 2010?

7 **Work in pairs and discuss how you will organise your summary. Make notes while you speak.**

- What information will you put in your introductory paragraph?
- Will you deal with the number of bee colonies and the production of honey together or separately?
- How many paragraphs will you need, and what will be the subject of each of them?

8 **Work alone and write your summary. Write at least 150 words.**

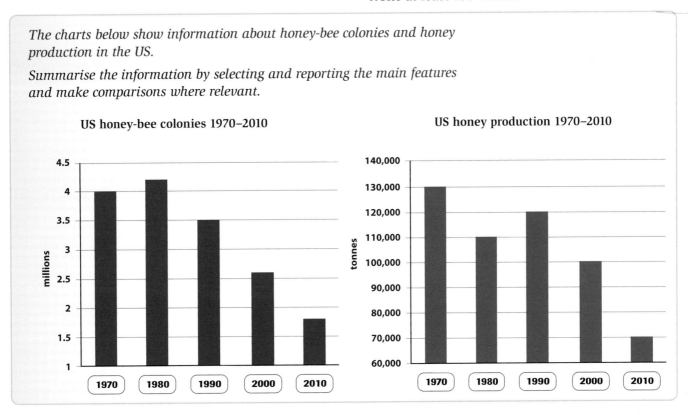

The charts below show information about honey-bee colonies and honey production in the US.

Summarise the information by selecting and reporting the main features and make comparisons where relevant.

US honey-bee colonies 1970–2010

millions

| | 1970 | 1980 | 1990 | 2000 | 2010 |

US honey production 1970–2010

tonnes

| | 1970 | 1980 | 1990 | 2000 | 2010 |

Key grammar
Countable and uncountable nouns

> Nouns are either countable [C] or uncountable [U]. Countable nouns can be made plural; uncountable nouns are always singular.

1 Look at these words from Writing Exercise 1. Which are [C] and which are [U]?

1 zebra 2 buffalo 3 rain

2 Look at these words from Writing Exercise 1. Which words can we use with countable [C] nouns and which with uncountable [U] nouns?

1 amount 2 few 3 little 4 number

▶ page 126 *Countable and uncountable nouns*

3 Are the words in bold in these sentences countable [C] or uncountable [U]?

1 **Zebras** eat **grass** and they need to drink **water** frequently.
2 He discovered a new **species** of frog in a **rainforest** in Indonesia.
3 These **frogs** don't require large **amounts** of **food**, but they only eat **insects**.
4 **Bee-eaters** dig **tunnels** in **mud** to make their **nests**.
5 I enjoy watching **programmes** about **wildlife** and **nature**.

4 ☉ IELTS candidates often make mistakes with the countable and uncountable nouns in the box. Write the nouns in the correct column of the table below.

activity advice behaviour car device education equipment fact information job knowledge machine pollution research study suggestion traffic university work

countable	uncountable
activity	advice

5 Choose the correct option in *italics* for each of these sentences.

1 The *number* / *amount* of humpback whales has increased during the last 20 years.
2 Due to global warming, *fewer* / *less* birds are migrating than 50 years ago.
3 The *number* / *amount* of ice in the Arctic Ocean is decreasing.
4 Scotland produces *fewer* / *less* wool than New Zealand.
5 There are twice as *many* / *much* polar bears as 30 years ago.
6 We have so *many* / *much* information about animals living in rainforests.

6 ☉ IELTS candidates often make mistakes with *amount*, *number*, *few*, *less*, *many* and *much*. Find and correct the mistake in each of these sentences.

1 The chart shows the ~~amount~~ of people visiting wildlife reserves. *number*
2 The five charts illustrate the number of water consumed per person in different countries.
3 From the chart, we could say that women generally work less hours than men.
4 Killing too much animals will cause a lot of environmental problems.
5 Not everybody puts rubbish in the right place, and that is why there is so many rubbish on the ground.
6 The number of oil continued to increase from 3,000 to 3,700 million tonnes at the end of 2010.

Spelling
Small words often misspelled

☉ IELTS candidates often confuse *the* and *they*; *there* and *their*; *than* and *then*; *to* and *too*. Find and correct the spelling mistakes in these sentences.

1 When there is more rain, zebras have more grass to eat, so ~~there~~ numbers rise. *their*
2 Buffalos and zebras occupy the same habitat and the have the same diet.
3 The number of animals on the reserve was higher last year then ten years ago.
4 Whales may have to find new breeding sites, when the ocean where they live becomes to crowded.
5 The number of elephants rose to 80 and than went down to 60.

Unit 6 Being human

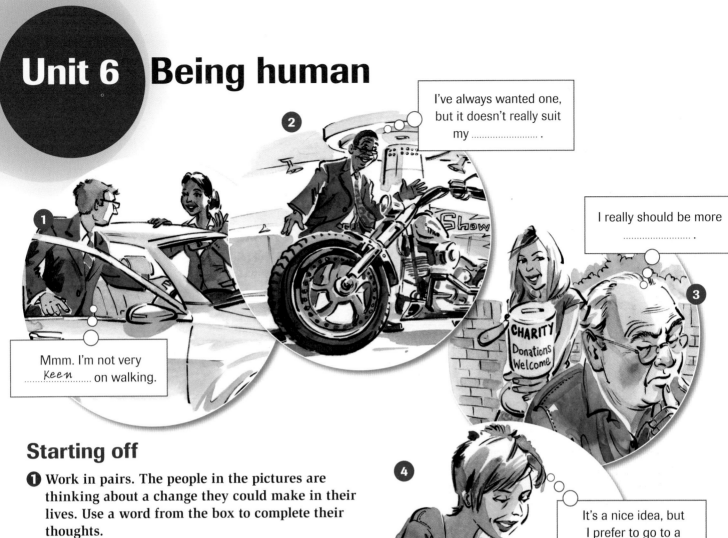

2 I've always wanted one, but it doesn't really suit my ....

1 Mmm. I'm not very ..... *Keen* ..... on walking.

3 I really should be more ....

4 It's a nice idea, but I prefer to go to a .... place.

Starting off

1 Work in pairs. The people in the pictures are thinking about a change they could make in their lives. Use a word from the box to complete their thoughts.

boring	chance	familiar	generous
image	~~keen~~	real	unusual

2 What reasons might they have for changing?

Example: *They need to take more exercise.*

3 Do you think any of the people will change? Why? / Why not?

Reading 1
Yes / No / Not Given

1 Work in pairs. You are going to read a passage about people and change. Read the title and subheading on page 58 first. What do you think the writer is going to say about change?

2 Read the whole passage quickly. Then choose the option (A, B, C or D) which states the writer's main idea.

A People of all ages dislike change.
B People can change if they want to.
C Change gets harder as people grow older.
D Change is easier for people at work than at home.

3 Work in pairs. Find these words (1–6) in the passage, then match them with their correct definition from the *CLD* (a–f).

1 donate
2 consistency
3 insecurity
4 conventional
5 novelty
6 openness (to)

a having no confidence in yourself and what you can do
b the quality of being new or unusual
c willing to consider a discussion, suggestion, experience, etc.
d to give money or goods to a person or organisation that needs help
e traditional and not willing to try new ideas
f when someone always behaves or performs in a similar way

Making a change

How easy is it for us to change our lives – and why?

In 1990, a young American named Christopher McCandless gave up his career plans, left behind everyone he knew, including his family, and went off on an adventure. He was 22 at the time. In an act of kindness, he donated all his savings to the famous charity, Oxfam International, and hitchhiked his way through America to Alaska. His decisions were so unusual for his age that Jon Krakauer wrote a book about them called *Into the Wild*, and Sean Penn directed a film that had the same title.

Of course, this is an unusual story. Most college graduates would not do quite the same thing. However, studies do show that in teenage years, people are more likely to try out new experiences. Instead of following the family career path, for example, and working his way up the same organisation like his grandfather did, a 15-year-old may dream about becoming a traveller – only to find in his early 20s that this fascination with new places is declining and change is less attractive. This age-related trend can be observed in all cultures.

The reason why people all over the world become less keen to change as they get older may be because people's lives generally follow similar patterns and involve similar demands. Most people, wherever they are, aim to find a job and a partner. As they get older, they may have young children to look after and possibly elderly family members. These responsibilities cannot be achieved without some degree of consistency, which means that new experiences and ideas may not have a place in the person's life. New experiences may bring excitement but also insecurity, and so most people prefer to stay with the familiar.

However, not every individual is the same. One toddler may want to play a different game every day and get fed up if nothing changes at the nursery. Another may seek out and play with the same children and toys on every visit. Young children who avoid new experiences will grow up to be more conventional than others. Psychologists argue that those who have more open personalities as children are more open than others might be when they are older. They also suggest that young men have a greater interest in novelty than women, although, as they age, this desire for new experiences fades more quickly than it does in women.

The truth is that, as we get older, we prefer the things we know. We tend to order the same meals in restaurants, sit on the same side of the train when we commute to work, go on holiday to the same places and construct our day in the same way. If you are older than 30, remember that your openness to new experiences is slowly declining. So you are better off making a new start today than postponing it until later.

Unit 6

4

Underline the words in sentences a–c that you think will help you find the right place in the passage. Then **underline** the relevant part of the passage.

a Christopher McCandless was generous to give his money to Oxfam International.

b Many young people make the same decisions as Christopher McCandless.

c *Into the Wild* is a good title for Jon Krakauer's book.

5

Look again at questions a–c in Exercise 4 and answer these questions.

1 Write 'Yes' beside the question that agrees with the writer's views. Which words in the passage give you the answer?

2 Which of the questions is 'No', and which is 'Not Given'? Which words in the passage help you find the 'No' answer? Why is the other answer 'Not Given'?

6

Work in pairs. Read Questions 1–6 below and underline the words that will help you find the right place in the passage.

Questions 1–6

Do the following statements agree with the claims of the writer in the reading passage?

Write

YES	*if the statement agrees with the claims of the writer*
NO	*if the statement contradicts the claims of the writer*
NOT GIVEN	*if it is impossible to say what the writer thinks about this*

1 Teenagers are more ready to have new experiences than young adults.

2 Grandparents usually encourage their grandchildren to get a well-paid job.

3 Life demands are different depending on which country you live in.

4 Some toddlers find repetitive activities boring.

5 Children who dislike new experiences become more adventurous than others as adults.

6 If you want to change something in your life, you should avoid delay.

7 Work alone. Answer Questions 1–6.

- <u>Underline</u> words in the statements to help you find the right places in the passage.
- Look for words in the passage that have the same meaning as or the opposite meaning to the ideas in the statements.
- If there is nothing in the passage about the idea, the answer is 'NOT GIVEN'.

8 **Work in small groups. Take turns to describe a change that you made in your life.**

1 Why did you make it?
2 Did anyone help you?
3 Was it successful? Why? / Why not?

Reading 2
Summary completion with a box

1 **Work in pairs. You are going to read a passage about memory. Look at page 4 of this book and choose a passage you have already read. Work together to remember as much as possible about it.**

2 **Read the title and subheading of the passage on page 60. Then read and complete this sentence.**

I expect this passage to describe a **1** .... into the effect of **2** .... on the number of **3** .... people make when they remember things.

3 **Now quickly read the whole passage and find out which group of people Fenn thinks could benefit most from her work.**

4 **The words in bold in the passage are used to describe academic research. Match each of them to one of these definitions, then check your spelling.**

1 discoveries from a study *findings*
2 organised (e.g. a test)
3 a detailed study of a subject
4 tests done to find something out
5 people who take part in an activity
6 people who work together

5 **Read the title of the summary in Questions 1–5.**

1 Find the paragraph which describes it in the passage.
2 Work in pairs. Read the summary and decide what information you need for each gap.

Questions 1–5

Complete the summary using the list of words and phrases, A–J, below.

Fenn's Memory Experiments

The groups in the study saw or heard lists of words at **1** ....*G*....... times of the day. After **2** .... hours, the groups tried to identify these words correctly in a test. Before the test, one group had **3** .... sleep and chose the words in the evening. The other group had their test in the morning.

In three experiments, the results were **4** .... : the groups that had slept during the experiment remembered **5** .... words correctly than the other groups.

A	more	**F**	ten
B	complex	**G**	different
C	12	**H**	no
D	six	**I**	fewer
E	less	**J**	the same

---

6 **Now answer Questions 2–5 on your own. Check your answers with a partner.**

- Use the title to find the right part of the passage.
- Read the summary and decide what information you need for each gap.
- Read the sentence(s) in the passage carefully and <u>underline</u> words that provide the missing information. Choose the option in the box that means the same.

7 **Work in groups.**

1 Have you ever taken part in a study? When? Why?
2 Have you ever conducted any tests or experiments? What were they, and what did the results show?

Reducing errors in memory

Sleep may reduce mistakes in memory, according to a first-of-its-kind study led by a scientist at Michigan State University.

The **findings**, which appear in the September issue of the journal *Learning & Memory*, have practical implications for many people, from students doing multiple-choice tests to elderly people confusing their medicine, says Kimberly Fenn, principal investigator and assistant professor of psychology.

'It's easy to muddle things in your mind,' Fenn says. 'This **research** suggests that after sleep, you're better able to pick out the incorrect parts of that memory.' Fenn and **colleagues** from the University of Chicago and Washington University in St Louis studied the presence of incorrect or false memory in groups of college students. While previous research has shown that sleep improves memory, this study is the first one that looks at errors in memory, she said.

Study **participants** were 'trained' by being shown or listening to lists of words. Then, twelve hours later, they were shown individual words and asked to identify which words they had seen or heard in the earlier session. One group of students was trained at 10 a.m. and tested at 10 p.m. after the course of a normal sleepless day. Another group was trained at night and tested twelve hours later in the morning, after about six hours of sleep. Three **experiments** were **conducted**. In each experiment, the results showed that students who had slept did not have as many problems with false memory and chose fewer incorrect words.

How does sleep help? The answer isn't known, Fenn said, but she suspects it may be due to sleep strengthening the source of the memory. The source, or context in which the information is acquired, is a vital element of the memory process. In other words, it may be easier to remember something if you can also remember where you first heard or saw it. Or perhaps the people who didn't sleep as much during the study received so much other information during the day that this affected their memory ability, Fenn said.

Further research is needed, she said, adding that she plans to study different population groups, particularly the elderly. 'We know older individuals generally have worse memory performance than younger individuals. We also know from other research that elderly individuals tend to be more prone to false memories,' Fenn said. 'Given the work we've done, it's possible that sleep may actually help them to reject this false information. And potentially this could help to improve their quality of life.'

adapted from *Michigan State University News*
http://news.msu.edu/story/6804

Speaking

Part 3

1 Look at this Part 3 question and Kim's answer. What do you think about the answer? Tick three of the boxes below.

We've been talking about memory … What methods do people use to help themselves remember things?

That's easy. I use a notepad.

1 It is not on the topic. ☐
2 It is personal, not general. ☐
3 It is too short. ☐
4 It only gives one method. ☐
5 It is grammatically inaccurate. ☐

2 Work in pairs. Look at the answer below to the question in Exercise 1. Complete it using the ideas in these pictures.

Well, some people use a **1** .... and others use a **2** .... But I think if you're really busy, you'll make a **3** .... , maybe on your iPhone if you have one. Or sometimes you see a note on the back of someone's **4** .... !

3 🔊 Listen and compare the speaker's answers with your own.

4 *Some people* refers to people in general. <u>Underline</u> other words in the answer in Exercise 2 that refer to people in general.

5 Work in small groups. Discuss these Part 3 questions.

1 What sort of things do people forget?
2 What can people do if they forget something important like meeting a relative for lunch?

6 🔊 Listen to Anna Maria, an IELTS candidate, speaking.

1 Which question in Exercise 5 is she answering?
2 Complete the answer below by writing the things people forget in the gaps.
3 <u>Underline</u> the words she uses to talk about people in general.

I think **1** .... are very easy to forget. You have to write the dates in a diary if you want to remember them! Um – and some older people can't remember where they put their **2** .... or their **3** .... Oh, and, er, if something unexpected happens, you might forget a **4** .... or a **5** .... – there are lots of things …

▶ page 62 Pronunciation: *Intonation 1*

7 Work in pairs. Take turns to ask and answer these questions.

Sleep
1 In what places can people fall asleep?
2 What things can make people fall asleep?
3 Why do some people not get enough sleep?

Memory
4 What sort of things do people need to remember every day?
5 Why do people sometimes forget important things?
6 What activities can help improve people's memory?

Exam advice Speaking Part 3

• Listen carefully to the question so that you know what to include in your answer.

• Talk about people in general.

Pronunciation

Intonation 1

> We use a rising intonation to tell our listener that we haven't finished what we are saying, and a falling intonation to show we're finishing.

1 (03) **Listen to these two extracts from Anna Maria's answer. Does the speaker's voice rise or fall on each underlined word?**

You have to write the dates in a <u>diary</u> if you want to <u>remember</u> them.

… you might forget a <u>lunch date</u> or a <u>meeting</u> …

2 (04) **Work in pairs. Look at these sentences. Underline the words where the speaker's voice might rise to show that they haven't finished speaking. Then listen and check your answers.**

1 Sometimes people forget their dentist or doctor's appointment and things like that.
2 If a friend waits a long time for you, you should say you're sorry and pay next time you go out.
3 People don't usually fall asleep at work unless they're very tired.
4 A boring meeting or a long car journey can make people go to sleep!

3 **Take turns to read sentences 1–4 in Exercise 2 aloud.**

Listening

Matching, Pick from a list

1 **Work in pairs. You are going to hear a conversation about successful people. Before you listen, look at the photos below and discuss these questions.**

1 What do you think has made each person successful?
2 Complete this sentence:
   The key to success is …

2 **Read Questions 1–4 and options A–F. How many extra options are there? What words/ideas do you expect to hear for each option?**

Questions 1–4

What helped each person to become successful?

*Choose **FOUR** answers from the box and write the correct letter, **A–F**, next to Questions **1–4**.*

People

1 the film maker   3 the scientist
2 the ballet dancer   4 the chef

Reasons for success

A a personal style   D an invention
B a lot of money   E a wise decision
C a relative's influence   F a change of job

---

3 (05) **Now listen and answer Questions 1–4.**

4 (05) **Listen to the recording again and when you hear the speakers' questions below, note down a few words that give you the answer. Use these to check your answers to Questions 1–4.**

1 So what made him successful?
   uncle / film student
2 Was she very talented?
3 So why did she do better?
4 Did he make a famous dish?

Exam advice   *Matching*

- Read the questions and options and think about what they mean.
- You hear the answers in the same order as the questions.

❺ Look at Questions 5–10 below and <u>underline</u> the key ideas in each question. Quickly read through the options.

> **Questions 5–10**
>
> *Choose **TWO** letters, A–E.*
>
> **Questions 5–6**
>
> *Which **TWO** criteria will the students use to choose a successful person?*
>
> **A** age
> **B** gender
> **C** individual talent
> **D** fame
> **E** global importance
>
> **Questions 7–8**
>
> *Which **TWO** things do the students agree to do before they meet again?*
>
> **A** write a biography
> **B** conduct more research
> **C** find photographs
> **D** write a talk
> **E** plan a seminar
>
> **Questions 9–10**
>
> *Which **TWO** things do the students agree are linked to success?*
>
> **A** wealth
> **B** experience
> **C** talent
> **D** effort
> **E** location

❻ (06) Now listen and answer Questions 5–10.

> **Exam advice** ▸ *Pick from a list*
>
> • <u>Underline</u> the key idea in each question.
> • Quickly read through the options before you listen.
> • Remember to choose *two* answers for each question.

❼ Work in pairs. Look again at the options in Questions 5–6 and 9–10. Which three of these do you think are most important for success?

Vocabulary
Word building

❶ IELTS candidates often make mistakes in their writing when they change the form of words. Complete this table of words related to the topic of success.

noun (phrase)	adjective	verb	adverb
1 ...*success*...	successful	2	successfully
3	hard-working	work hard	
talent	4		
practice	practical	5	practically
	regular		6 ....
nature	natural		7 ....
8	skilful/skillful		skilfully
achievement		9	
fame	10		famously

❷ Check your answers by looking at the sample answer in Writing Exercise 3 (page 64).

▶ page 127 *Word formation and spelling*

❸ Choose the correct word in these sentences.

1 Teachers praise ⟨hard work⟩/ *hard-working* and ignore laziness.
2 Some people have a *natural / naturally* ability to play music.
3 We had a party to celebrate my uncle's unexpected *fame / famous*.
4 Not all *talent / talented* actors become famous.
5 Winning a sporting competition is a great *achieve / achievement*.
6 If you are determined to *success / succeed*, you will.
7 I *regular / regularly* attend a choir practice.
8 Only people who are *skill / skilful* can do two things at the same time.

Writing
Task 2

> Write about the following topic.
>
> *Some people say that success is '10 percent talent and 90 percent hard work'.*
>
> *Is hard work the key to success, or is talent also important?*
>
> Give reasons for your answer and include any relevant examples from your own knowledge or experience.

❶ Work in pairs. Read the Writing task above.

1 Complete this rephrasing of the quote in the task:
  a ....*little*.... talent and .... hard work
2 Complete this rephrasing of the question in the task:
  Can .... alone bring success, or do you need .... as well?

❷ Work in small groups. Discuss these questions using the Vocabulary exercises on page 63 to help you.

1 Who is the most successful person in your family? Is he/she successful because of hard work or talent? What other things helped him/her to become successful?
2 Can you name someone who is successful in your culture? How have they achieved success?
3 Are talented people always successful? Why? / Why not?
4 Do people usually have to work hard to become successful? Why? / Why not?
5 Are there any other reasons why people become successful?

❸ Work in pairs. Read this sample answer, then answer the questions below.

Many people want to be successful, but it is not easy. However, a few people get to the top. Most of them succeed because of their hard work, but in my view, they also need to be talented and have a natural ability to do something well.

If you want to be good at something, you must practise hard and regularly. For example, international footballers have to train for many hours every day. If a professional footballer does not train, his manager will drop him from the team.

However, talent is important, too. Although some people try hard, they do not achieve much because they are not naturally talented. I like singing, but I will not make money unless I have a good singing voice. Similarly, if someone wants to work in finance, they need to have good number skills.

Talent and hard work are not the only important things. As we can often improve our skills by taking courses, money is useful, too. Luck can also help you achieve success. For example, you can be more successful in business if you meet the right people. So there can be many factors that contribute to success.

In conclusion, I do not think you can do something consistently well if you do not practise and you are not talented. However, some people become famous for other reasons. Everyone is different, so you cannot always say why one person succeeds and another person does not.

1 Underline the main ideas in paragraphs 2 and 3.
2 Does paragraph 4 just focus on the factors for success mentioned in the Writing task?
3 What is the main idea of paragraph 4, and where is it?
4 Note down the writer's opinion in your own words. Where is it? Does the writer stick to his opinion throughout the essay?
5 What examples of people does the writer use to support his views?

❹ Work in small groups. Read the Writing task on page 65 and discuss the questions below it. Make notes of some useful ideas and vocabulary.

Write about the following topic.

Televised talent shows have become popular in many societies today.

Are these shows a good method of finding talented people, or are they just entertainment?

Give reasons for your answer and include any relevant examples from your own knowledge or experience.

1 What talent shows are there where you live? What happens during the shows?
2 Why do people enter talent shows, and why do people watch them?
3 What happens to the people who win/lose? Why?
4 Who profits financially from talent shows?
5 What other methods are there of finding talented people?
6 Which methods are most reliable? Why?

▶ Key grammar: *Zero and first conditionals (if/unless)*

❺ Work in pairs.

1 Write a plan for the Writing task in Exercise 4. Decide how many paragraphs to write and which ideas will go in each paragraph. Also plan your introduction and conclusion.
2 Write your answer in at least 250 words.

> *Exam advice*   Writing Task 2
>
> • Analyse the task and plan your answer.
> • Include a range of relevant vocabulary.
> • Give reasons for your opinions and ideas.
> • Check your answer when you have finished.

Spelling
Suffixes

▶ page 127 *Spelling words with suffixes*

⊙ **IELTS candidates often make mistakes when they change the form of words. Find and correct the mistake in each of these words.**

1	attendence	7	successfull
2	begining	8	developping
3	developement	9	hapenned
4	unecessary	10	realy
5	lazyness	11	carful
6	achivment	12	arguement

Key grammar
Zero and first conditionals (*if/unless*)

❶ Work in pairs. Look at these extracts from the sample answer on page 64. Underline the conditional clauses in each one.

1 If you want to be good at something, you must practise hard and regularly.
2 If a professional footballer does not train, his manager will drop him from the team.
3 I will not make money unless I have a good singing voice.
4 For example, you can be more successful in business if you meet the right people.

❷ Work in pairs.

1 Which sentences in Exercise 1 are about something the writer thinks is generally true?
2 Which sentences are about something that is likely to be true?
3 What verb forms are used in each sentence?

▶ page 128 *Zero and first conditionals*

❸ ⊙ IELTS students often make mistakes using zero and first conditionals. Correct the punctuation and underlined errors in these sentences.

1 If we lost it we'll never find it again.
   If we lose it, we'll never find it again.
2 If children get a good education, they could deal better with problems.
3 If parents didn't help children to learn how to be on their own, they will never feel comfortable taking a role as a leader.
4 People can solve all kinds of problems if they will begin to understand that everyone's view is important.
5 I would say that if you are always depressed you would not be able to do things well.
6 A child cannot communicate well if he wouldn't be given enough attention.

❹ Complete these sentences using your own ideas.

1 I won't go shopping unless …
2 If I do well in my IELTS test, …
3 If children are good at something, …
4 Unless you know how to swim, …
5 I'll give some money to charity if …

Vocabulary and grammar review **Unit 5**

Vocabulary

1 Complete the sentences below using words connected with animals and wildlife that fit the crossword grid.

```
                    1            2
                    n
   3         4      e
                    s
       5            t
           6
```

Down

1 The birds build a ...*nest*... high in a tree and lay their eggs there.
2 On their annual .... , the birds fly from central Asia to southern Africa.
4 A zebra's .... consists of grass and other plants.
5 Lions' .... are usually zebras or antelopes.

Across

3 The birds .... in spring and look after their young for four to five weeks.
5 Lions are .... , which means they hunt and eat other animals.
6 The crocodile's .... is mainly rivers and lakes.

2 Look at the endings of these words and decide what type of word (noun, verb, adjective or adverb) each one is.

1 numerous *adjective*
2 intensive
3 epidemiologist
4 irrational
5 fascinate
6 unsuccessfully
7 distinction
8 rediscover

Grammar

3 Complete the sentences below with the words from the box. You can use each one more than once.

amount	few	little	many	much	~~number~~

1 The ...*number*... of endangered species is increasing.
2 Not much is known about the problem because scientists have done very .... research.
3 We managed to obtain a large .... of information on the subject.
4 There are very .... tigers still alive in the wild, so your best chance of seeing one is in a zoo.
5 We've had so .... rain this spring that the country is looking very green.
6 We have .... knowledge of fish at the bottom of the ocean and we need to investigate more.
7 There is so .... pollution that .... species of fish no longer live in the lake.
8 The project is almost completed and needs very .... work to finish it off.

4 Choose the correct option in *italics* in these sentences.

1 The zoo was opened (*in*)/ *on* June 2002.
2 *In / On* July 1st, more than 3,000 people visited the zoo.
3 The total number of visitors *from / between* January and July was 128,000.
4 The number of animals kept at the zoo went up *during / for* this period.
5 More adults than children visited the zoo *from / between* January to March.
6 *Between / Over* the three-month period April–June, more children than adults visited the zoo.

Vocabulary and grammar review **Unit 6**

Vocabulary

❶ Complete the sentences below with the words in the box.

> backgrounds   colleagues   ~~conduct~~   conventional
> donate   experiences   findings   participants

1 Students must *conduct* some research when they do their project.
2 If you are lucky, work .... can also become good friends.
3 After the flood, the schoolchildren decided to .... their pocket money to the local hospital.
4 The six .... in the study did not know each other.
5 Some people do not like new .... – they prefer their familiar routines.
6 Some people are very adventurous and do not want to have a .... lifestyle.
7 The .... of the study showed that children have more reliable memories than adults.
8 I get on well with my classmates, even though we come from different cultural ....

❷ Complete these sentences using the correct form of the words in brackets.

1 In the past, it was not easy to become a *famous* (fame) female scientist.
2 Most experts agree that .... (happy) is not linked to wealth.
3 .... (safe) is an important aspect of any type of travel.
4 Most children cannot hide their .... (disappoint) if they lose a game.
5 Last week's newspaper article .... (critic) the behaviour of some celebrities.
6 Writing a novel is a great .... (achieve).
7 The students had to explain their .... (absent) to the tutor.
8 We should remember our .... (succeed) and not our failures.

Grammar

❸ Match the sentence halves.

1 If your children don't work hard at school,
2 If our employees work hard,
3 Elderly people often feel anxious
4 Unless workers trust a new system,
5 Toddlers can get bored
6 If staff want to be healthy,
7 You'll feel more comfortable at the meeting
8 Children shouldn't talk to people

a if they have to make a change.
b they can walk to work.
c if you see a familiar face.
d they won't achieve success in their exams.
e unless they know them.
f they won't adapt to it.
g they will get a pay rise.
h if they play with the same toy repeatedly.

❹ Circle the correct option in *italics* in each sentence.

1 If I earn enough money, I *buy* / *will buy* a sports car.
2 I get bored if I *work* / *should work* on the same project for too long.
3 Unless someone complains, we *won't open* / *didn't open* the library during the festival period.
4 Child experts say that if you *want* / *will want* a healthy child, you must encourage them to do exercise from an early age.
5 Academics cannot become well known unless they *publish* / *will publish* their ideas.
6 If I write next week's appointment in my diary, I *couldn't* / *can't* forget it!
7 My tutor says that if I work really hard, I *achieve* / *will achieve* an A grade.
8 Musicians find it hard to make money unless they *are* / *will be* truly talented.

Unit 7 Literacy skills

Starting off

❶ Work in pairs. Match each photo (1–6) with a phrase from the box (a–f).

a attending a lecture	**d** using the library
b talking to a tutor	**e** giving a presentation
c writing an assignment	**f** participating in a seminar

❷ Work in small groups.

1 How often do you do each of the activities in Exercise 1?
2 How much do you enjoy each of them?

Listening
Form completion, Multiple choice

❶ Work in small groups. You are going to hear a student talking to someone on the telephone about doing an online course. Before you listen, discuss these questions.

1 Have you ever done an online course?
2 Are online courses popular in your culture?

❷ Work in pairs. Look at Questions 1–5 below.

1 What type of information do you need for each gap (e.g. a date, a place)?
2 What will you write in each gap (letters, words, numbers or a combination of these)?

Questions 1–5

Complete the form below.

*Write **NO MORE THAN TWO WORDS AND/OR A NUMBER** for each answer.*

Online Writing Course
Request for brochure

Example	
First name:	Alex

Last name:	1 ....
Address:	Flat 4A, **2** 396 .... Road
Town/City:	Preston
Postcode:	**3** ....
Phone number:	**4** ....
Email address:	alex7@ptu.com
Message box:	deliver brochure **5** ....

3 (07) **Now listen to the first part of the conversation and answer Questions 1–5.**

Exam advice   *Form completion*

Exam advice   *Form completion*
- Use the words already on the form to help you listen for the answers you need.
- Check your spelling is correct.

4 **Work in pairs. Read Questions 6–10 quickly. <u>Underline</u> the key ideas in each question.**

Questions 6–10

*Choose the correct letter, **A**, **B** or **C**.*

6   The caller wants to do a <u>writing course to help</u> with
   A his hobby.
   B his job.
   C his children's education.

7   What does the course pack include?
   A multimedia items
   B a list of books to buy
   C lesson and assignment dates

8   How much does the course cost?
   A £340
   B £375
   C £400

9   Alex's first assignment will be about his
   A family life.
   B school experiences.
   C expectations of the course.

10 What does the feedback include?
   A a tutorial
   B an exercise
   C a discussion group

---

5 (08) **Now listen and answer Questions 6–10.**

Exam advice   *Multiple choice*
- <u>Underline</u> the key idea(s) in each question.
- Listen for the same words or words that have the same meaning. This will tell you that the answer is coming.
- Match what you hear to the correct option – you may hear the same words or a paraphrase of the answer.

6 (07) (08) **Now look at the recording script on pages 166–167. Listen again and <u>underline</u> the words in the script which gave you the answers.**

Example: *Q6 advertising agency / like to write better*

7 **Work in pairs. Ask and answer these questions.**

1   What do you write in your own language?
2   How easy do you find it to write in English?

Vocabulary
Raise or *rise*?

1 **IELTS candidates often confuse *raise* and *rise*. Read these extracts from the *CLD*, then choose the correct word in sentences 1–4 from the Listening.**

---

raise 'to lift something to a higher position' or 'to increase an amount or level'. This verb must always be followed by an object*.
*The government has **raised** the price of petrol.*
The government has ~~rised~~ the price of petrol.

---

rise 'to increase or move up'. This verb cannot be followed by an object.
*The price of petrol is **rising**.*
The price of petrol is ~~raising~~.

NB *Raise* is regular, but *rise* is irregular: the noun is *rise*, and the verb forms are *rise*, *rose* and *risen*.

---

* An object is a noun or pronoun which follows a verb.

1   I just want to *raise / rise* the standard of my own writing.
2   I'd like my salary to *raise / rise*.
3   They've just *raised / risen* the prices.
4   Fees *raised / rose* a month ago, I'm afraid.

2 ⊙ **These sentences contain mistakes made by IELTS candidates. Find and correct the mistakes.**

1   In 2008, the number of 35–49-year-olds studying ~~raise~~ dramatically. *rose*
2   The number of internet users in Asia has risen from 1.1 to 1.5 million.
3   For women today, the trend raises a little bit to 41 percent.
4   The government is trying to rise educational standards.
5   In 2010, the figure rised gently from 1.8 to 2 million.

Reading

Matching information, Table completion

❶ **You are going to read a passage about reading techniques. Before you read, work in pairs.**

1 What problems do you have reading in English?
2 What can you do to improve your reading?

❷ **Read the title and the subheading of the passage. What do you expect to read about?**

❸ **Read the passage quickly to find three ways you can improve your reading speed.**

Speed reading

What is speed reading, and why do we need it?

A Speed reading is not just about reading fast. It is also about how much information you can remember when you have finished reading. The World Championship Speed-Reading Competition says that its top competitors average between 1,000 and 2,000 words a minute. But they must remember at least 50 percent of this in order to qualify for the competition.

B Nowadays, speed reading has become an essential skill in any environment where people have to master a large volume of information. Professional workers need reading skills to help them get through many documents every day, while students under pressure to deal with assignments may feel they have to read more and read faster all the time.

C Although there are various methods to increase reading speed, the trick is deciding what information you want first. For example, if you only want a rough outline of an issue, then you can skim the material quickly and extract the key facts. However, if you need to understand every detail in a document, then you must read it slowly enough to understand this.

D Even when you know how to ignore irrelevant detail, there are other improvements you can make to your reading style which will increase your speed. For example, most people can read much faster if they read silently. Reading each word aloud takes time for the information to make a complete circuit in your brain before being pronounced. Some researchers believe that as long as the first and last letters are in place, the brain can still understand the arrangement of the other letters in the word because it logically puts each piece into place.

E Chunking is another important method. Most people learn to read either letter by letter or word by word. As you improve, this changes. You will probably find that you are fixing your eyes on a block of words, then moving your eyes to the next block of words, and so on. You are reading blocks of words at a time, not individual words one by one. You may also notice that you do not always go from one block to the next: sometimes you may move back to a previous block if you are unsure about something.

F A skilled reader will read a lot of words in each block. He or she will only look at each block for an instant and will then move on. Only rarely will the reader's eyes skip back to a previous block of words. This reduces the amount of work that the reader's eyes have to do. It also increases the volume of information that can be taken in over a given period of time.

G On the other hand, a slow reader will spend a lot of time reading small blocks of words. He or she will skip back often, losing the flow and structure of the text, and muddling their overall understanding of the subject. This irregular eye movement quickly makes the reader tired. Poor readers tend to dislike reading because they feel it is difficult to concentrate and comprehend written information.

H The best tip anyone can have to improve their reading speed is to practise. In order to do this effectively, a person must be engaged in the material and want to know more. If you find yourself constantly having to re-read the same paragraph, you may want to switch to reading material that grabs your attention. If you enjoy what you are reading, you will make quicker progress.

adapted from speed-reading-techniques.com

4 Work in pairs. Read the instructions for Questions 1–6 below.

1 How many letters should you write for each answer?
2 Will you use all the letters A–H?
3 Can you use the same letter twice?

5 Underline the key words in each question.

> **Questions 1–6**
>
> The reading passage has seven paragraphs, **A–H**.
>
> Which paragraph contains the following information?
>
> *Write the correct letter, **A–H**.*
>
> **NB** *You may use any letter more than once.*
>
> 1 the <u>types of people</u> who need to <u>read more quickly</u>
> 2 the fastest reading speeds
> 3 how a reader can become confused
> 4 why reading material should be interesting
> 5 a definition of speed reading
> 6 what you should consider before you start reading

6 Now answer Questions 1–6 by reading each paragraph in the passage separately and deciding whether it contains the information in any of the questions.

> **Exam advice**   *Matching information*
>
> • <u>Underline</u> the key ideas in each question.
> • Start with Paragraph A and decide if it matches a question. If there is no match, go on to the next paragraph.

Am I going too fast for you?

7 Read the instructions for Questions 7–13 and the title of the table. Which three paragraphs do you need to read carefully to complete the table?

> **Questions 7–13**
>
> *Complete the table below.*
>
> *Choose **NO MORE THAN TWO WORDS** from the passage for each answer.*
>
> **Chunking**
>
> | type of reader | reading method | effect of method on reader |
> |---|---|---|
> | skilled reader | • many **7** .... in a block
• reader hardly ever goes back | • reader's **8** .... do less work
• more **9** .... is processed |
> | **10** .... | • small blocks
• reader **11** .... goes back | • reader easily gets **12** ....
• finds it hard to **13** .... on passage |

8 Now answer Questions 7–13. Use the words around each question to help you find the answers.

> **Exam advice**   *Table completion*
>
> • Use the heading to find the right place in the passage.
> • Read around each gap to predict the missing words.

9 Work in small groups.

1 Do you think the Reading test is the hardest part of IELTS? Why? / Why not?
2 What techniques have you practised in this book that will help you with the Reading test?
3 Which reading questions do you find most difficult/easy? Why?

Speaking
Parts 2 and 3

❶ Work in small groups. Look at the statements below about reading.

1 Discuss which of these statements are true for you, and why.
2 Write another sentence about reading which is true for you.

> I have to get information from books to help me write my assignments.

> I only read things on the Internet.

> I read journals to help me with my science projects.

> I only read things that I find interesting.

> I prefer magazines to books.

> I don't have time to read.

❷ Work alone. Read this Speaking Part 2 task.

1 Write some brief notes for each part of your talk.
2 Note down some vocabulary you can use.

> Describe a book or article that you enjoyed reading for your studies.
>
> You should say:
>
> what the book or article was about
>
> why you read it
>
> how long it took you to read
>
> and explain why you enjoyed reading it.

❸ Work in pairs. Take turns to give your talk – you should speak for two minutes.

❹ Work in pairs. Look at these questions from Speaking Part 3 and match them with the answers in the speech bubbles (A–B) in the next column.

1 How important is it for children to read books?
2 When do children usually read books?

A

> I think they enjoy doing this with their parents, um, they like to read with their parents, particularly at bedtime, because it helps them relax … small children do a lot of activities during the day, so they need to calm down at night, and reading's good for that.

B

> In my view, it's essential. Um … one reason is that books are good for children's imagination … and another is just that we all need to learn to read – it's part of our education. No one wants to be illiterate when they grow up.

❺ Complete this table with words and phrases speakers A and B use to introduce their opinions and their reasons in Exercise 4.

introducing an opinion	giving a reason
I think	

❻ ⟨09⟩ Listen to Pashta and Haroon answering two more questions on the same topic. As you listen, add phrases they use to the table in Exercise 5.

▶ Pronunciation: *Word stress 2*

❼ Work in pairs. Discuss how to answer these questions, giving your opinions and ideas and supporting them with reasons.

1 Why do some adults dislike reading?
2 What sort of problems do adults have if they can't read or write?
3 How can people be encouraged to read more?

❽ Change partners and take turns to ask and answer the questions in Exercise 7. Use some of the words and phrases from the table in Exercise 5.

Exam advice   *Speaking Part 3*

• Introduce your opinion clearly.

• Use appropriate words and phrases to introduce your reasons.

Pronunciation

Word stress 2

> You will pronounce words more clearly if you stress the correct syllable.

❶ (10) Listen to these words from Speaking Part 3. As you listen, mark the stressed syllable in each one.

par'ticularly	relax	activities
imagination	education	illiterate

❷ (11) Work in pairs. Take turns to read these extracts aloud, then listen and check the pronunciation of the words in *italics*.

1 They like to read with their parents, *particularly* at bedtime.
2 It helps them *relax*.
3 Small children do a lot of *activities* during the day.
4 Books are good for children's *imagination*.
5 It's part of our *education*.
6 No one wants to be *illiterate* when they grow up.

❸ (12) Pronounce the words in this list, stressing the marked syllables. Then listen and check your answers.

'parents	'secondary	dis'cussing	'chatting
im'portant	en'joyed	a'ssignment	pre'fer
com'puters	a'ttractive		

❹ Work in pairs. Take turns to read these sentences aloud.

1 I really *enjoyed* my *secondary*-school education.
2 It's *important* to read the newspaper every day.
3 *Chatting* online is more interesting than *discussing* something face to face.
4 I *prefer* reading magazines to books.
5 My *parents* bought me my first *computer*.

❺ Work in small groups. Say whether the sentences in Exercise 4 are true or false for you and give reasons.

Writing

Task 1

❶ Work in pairs. Complete the phrases that describe the trends on the line graph below with words from the box. Sometimes more than one word is possible.

decrease	fall	increase	peak	rise

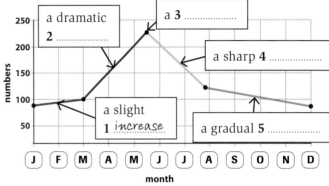

Student enrolment Lees College 2011

a dramatic 2 ....

a 3 ....

a sharp 4 ....

a slight 1 *increase*

a gradual 5 ....

❷ Complete this paragraph about the graph using words and phrases from Exercise 1.

The graph shows the changes in student numbers at Lees College over a one-year period.
Between January and March, there was 1 *a slight increase* in student numbers. This was followed by a 2 .... in numbers over the next three months.
In June, enrolments reached a 3 ....
After that, there was a 4 .... in numbers.
Finally, there was a 5 .... in numbers from August to December.
Over the year, there was a lot of fluctuation in the numbers.

> The second sentence in Exercise 2 uses a noun phrase to describe the trend.
> *Between January and March, there was **a slight increase** in student numbers.*
>
> Trends can also be written using a verb phrase:
> *Student numbers **increased slightly** between January and March.*

❸ Complete these sentences based on Exercise 2 using verb phrases.

1 Over the next three months, numbers ....
2 Enrolments .... in June.
3 After that, numbers ....
4 Finally, numbers .... from August to December.
5 The numbers .... over the year.

④ **Work in pairs. Complete these sentences using** *from, to, of* **or** *at.*

1 Between January and March, student numbers increased slightly ...*from*... 90 ...*to*... to 100.
2 Between January and March, there was a slight increase .... ten students.
3 In June, numbers peaked .... 225 students.
4 From June to August, numbers fell .... 120 students.
5 Numbers fell .... 120 in August .... 90 in December.

▶ page 76 Key grammar: *Prepositions to describe graphs*

⑤ **Complete the description below of the trend in graph A.**

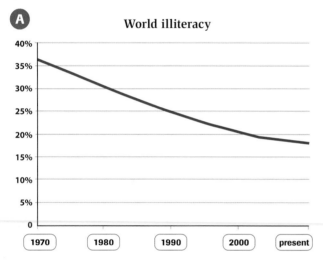

A   **World illiteracy**

The graph shows that the percentage of people in the world who cannot read and write has
1 .... from 37 percent in 1970 to 18 percent now. However, from 1970 to 2002, the decline was 2 .... than it has been between 2002 and the present day.

⑥ **It is important to include an overview of the graph or chart. This usually comes at the end of your answer, though it may fit somewhere else, such as after the introduction. Circle the correct word in** *italics* **to complete this overview of graph A in Exercise 5.**

Overall, there has been *an upward / a downward / a stable* trend in world illiteracy over the past 40 years.

⑦ **Complete the description and overview below of chart B.**

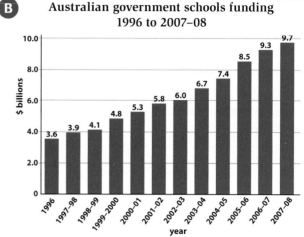

B   **Australian government schools funding 1996 to 2007–08**

According to the chart, the amount of money received by schools in Australia **1** .... from 3.6 to 6 billion dollars between 1996 and 2003. It then **2** .... to 9.7 billion dollars in 2008. There was a general **3** .... trend in government funding between 1996 and 2008.

⑧ **Look at the graph, chart and descriptions in Exercises 5, 6 and 7 again and answer these questions.**

1 Which graph/chart shows a trend that began in the past and goes up to the present?
2 Which graph/chart shows a trend that ended in the past?
3 Which tenses are used in each graph/chart?
4 Why are the tenses different?

▶ pages 121 and 124 *Past simple; Present perfect*

⑨ **Look at this graph and complete the summary on page 75 by putting the verbs in brackets into the correct tense.**

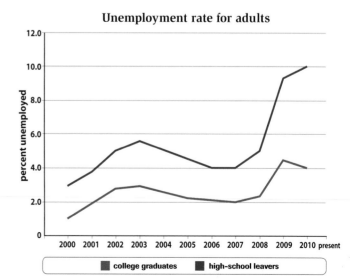

Unemployment rate for adults

college graduates   high-school leavers

The graph 1 ...gives... (give) information about unemployment among college graduates and high-school leavers.

It 2 .... (show) the trends between 2000 and the present day.

These trends 3 .... (follow) a similar pattern since 2000. However, more high-school leavers 4 .... (always be) unemployed than graduates.

In 2000, 1.5 percent of graduates and 3 percent of school leavers 5 .... (not have) a job. Between 2000 and 2003, these percentages 6 .... (rise) to 3 and 5.5 respectively. After that, there was a gradual fall in numbers until 2006, when figures 7 .... (remain) stable for a year.

Since 2007, the percentage of unemployed high-school leavers 8 .... (rise) dramatically and reached 10 percent. Although the figure for graduates is lower, it 9 .... (also increase) to 4 percent.

Overall, there 10 .... (be) an upward trend in unemployment rates for young students. However, the difference between school leavers and graduates 11 .... (become) much greater in recent years.

⑩ Work in pairs. Look at the Writing task below.

1 What does the graph show?
2 Which key trends should you describe?
3 What comparisons will you make?
4 How many paragraphs will you need?
5 What will your overview include?

The graph below shows the number of library books read by boys and girls at Starmouth School from 2006 to the present.

Summarise the information by selecting and reporting the main features, and make comparisons where relevant.

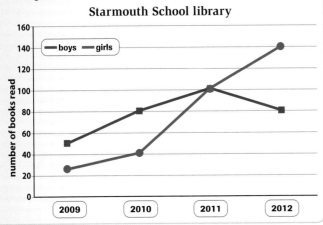

Starmouth School library

⑪ Now work alone and write your summary. You should write at least 150 words.

Spelling
Forming adverbs from adjectives

❶ Match the rules for forming adverbs from adjectives (1–5) with the examples (a–e).

1 In most cases, add –ly.
2 If an adjective ends in –l, the adverb ends –lly.
3 If the adjective ends in –y, the adverb ends –ily.
4 Replace a final –e with –ly.
5 Add –ally if the adjective ends in –ic.

a *happy → happily*
b *terrible → terribly*
c *first → firstly*
d *basic → basically*
e *hopeful → hopefully*

❷ Complete these sentences giving advice on Writing Task 1 by writing the adverb form of the adjective in brackets.

1 Always read the question ..carefully.. (*careful*).
2 The key points in the graph should be .... (*clear*) stated.
3 Your summary must be .... (*factual*) accurate.
4 It is .... (*extreme*) important to include an overview in your answer.
5 Your reader should be able to follow your points .... (*easy*).
6 Paragraphs help to show that the information is .... (*logic*) organised.
7 Avoid using the same vocabulary .... (*repetitive*).
8 Leave time to .... (*thorough*) check your spelling and punctuation.

❸ ⊙ IELTS candidates often make mistakes forming and spelling adverbs and adjectives. Find and the correct the mistakes made by IELTS candidates in these sentences.

1 It then increased ~~gradualy~~ until 1996. *gradually*
2 The trend fell steadly from 1990 to 2010.
3 The graph shows the figures will rise dramaticlly in the future.
4 It has been increasing slighty and will get higher.
5 There was a gentley decrease from 1990 to the present.
6 Spending on equipment rose rapid.

Key grammar
Prepositions to describe graphs

❶ Work in pairs. Look at the graph on ebook sales and the sentences below (a–g) that describe it.

1 Which preposition is used with particular months and years?
2 Which prepositions are used to cover a whole time period?
3 Which prepositions are used with a period of time in months?
4 Which preposition is used with a noun to say what has changed?
5 Which preposition is used to say how much something has risen or fallen?
6 Which prepositions are used to state the figures at the start and end of a trend?

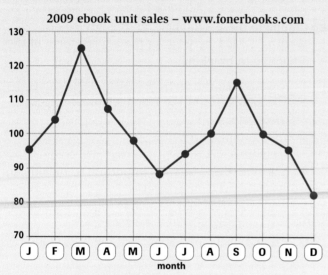

2009 ebook unit sales – www.fonerbooks.com

a The graph shows ebook sales over a one-year period.
b During the year, ebook sales fluctuated.
c Sales rose sharply from 95 units in January to 125 in March.
d Sales peaked in March and in September.
e Sales fell between March and June.
f From June to September, sales rose by 25 units.
g There was a sharp decrease in sales after September.
h Overall, sales fell in 2009.

▶ page 128 *Prepositions to describe trends and changes*

❷ Complete the sentences below describing the graph with the prepositions in the box.

at	between	by	during	~~from~~	in
over	to				

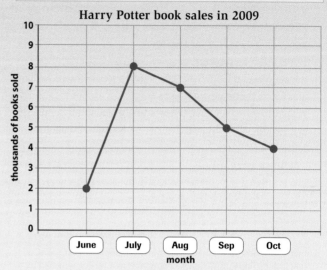

Harry Potter book sales in 2009

The trend for Harry Potter book sales:
1 rose sharply ......*from*...... 2,000 in June .... 8,000 in July.
2 peaked .... 8,000 in July.
3 fell .... 1,000 in August.
4 dropped sharply .... 5,000 .... the next month.
5 fell .... 5,000 to 4,000 in October.
6 fluctuated .... June and October 2009.

❸ ⊙ IELTS candidates often make mistakes using prepositions to describe graphs. Find and correct the mistakes made by IELTS candidates in these sentences.

1 For the 14–24 age group, attendance reached a peak ~~as~~ 95% in 1996. *at*
2 Exam results were high on January and after that month, they fell.
3 In 2050, the percentage will fall down to 0.9 billion again.
4 During 2000 to 2005, profits remained stable at five million dollars.
5 The trend decreases gradually from 2006 and ends at just over 70% 2010.
6 From the chart, we can see there is an increase of years of schooling.

Unit 8 Tourist attractions

Starting off

1 Work in pairs. Match the photos of tourists in different holiday destinations around the world (1–6) with the activities (a–f).

a sightseeing   ☐
b backpacking   ☐
c a safari   ☐

d skiing   ☐
e shopping   ☐
f an Arctic cruise   ☐

2 Work in pairs.

1 Where do you think each photo was taken?
2 What do people find enjoyable about each of these holidays?
3 Which holiday would you enjoy most? Why?

Reading

Summary completion, Matching features

❶ Work in pairs. You are going to read a passage about tourism in the Arctic and in Antarctica. Look at the photo in the passage. Where are the Arctic and Antarctica? What happens there?

❷ Read the title and subheading.

1 What link is there between the title and the phrase *before it's too late*?
2 What do you think the phrase *icy wildernesses* refers to?
3 What do you expect to read about in the passage?

❸ Discuss these questions, then quickly read the passage to find the answers.

1 Do you think the number of tourists going to the polar regions has risen or fallen recently?
2 Do you think the number of tourists going to these regions will rise or fall in the future?

❹ Work in pairs.

1 Read the title of the summary in Questions 1–7 below and find the relevant paragraphs in the passage.
2 Read the summary and decide what type of information you need for each gap.

Questions 1–7

Complete the summary below.

Choose NO MORE THAN TWO WORDS AND/OR A NUMBER *from the passage for each answer.*

Polar tourism – the figures

Tourism in the Arctic began in the **1** .... , and visitor numbers have risen since that time. These days, over **2** .... people travel there, mostly by ship. The country with the greatest increase in visitors is **3** .... Tourism has expanded in the Arctic because the **4** .... lasts longer than it used to.

Travel to the Antarctic has fallen by **5** .... over the past year. However, many more people are using small planes and **6** .... to land on the ice. Aircraft are also taking visitors to huge ships that hold as many as **7** .... tourists.

Here today, gone tomorrow

The Arctic and Antarctica are now within reach of the modern tourist, with many going to see these icy wildernesses before it's too late. Christian Amodeo reports on the growth of polar tourism.

Travel at the North and South Poles has become an expensive leisure activity, suitable for tourists of all ages. The poles may be inhospitable places, but they are seeing increasing numbers of visitors.

Annual figures for the Arctic, where tourism has existed since the 19th century, have increased from about a million in the early 1990s to more than 1.5 million today. This is partly because of the lengthening summer season brought about by climate change.

Most visitors arrive by ship. In 2007, 370,000 cruise passengers visited Norway, twice the number that arrived in 2000. Iceland, a country where tourism is the second-largest industry, has enjoyed an annual growth rate of nine percent since 1990. Meanwhile, Alaska received some 1,029,800 passengers, a rise of 7.3 percent from 2006. Greenland has seen the most rapid growth in marine tourism, with a sharp increase in cruise-ship arrivals of 250 percent since 2004.

The global economic downturn may have affected the annual 20.6 percent rate of increase in visitors to the Antarctic – last season saw a drop of 17 percent to 38,200 – but there has been a 760 percent rise in land-based tourism there since 1997. More people than ever are landing at fragile sites, with light aircraft, helicopters and all-terrain vehicles increasingly used for greater access, while in the past two seasons, 'fly–sail' operations have begun. These deliver tourists by air to ships, so far more groups can enjoy a cruise in a season; large cruise ships capable of carrying up to 800 passengers are not uncommon.

In addition, it seems that a high number of visitors return to the poles. 'Looking at six years' worth of data, of the people who have been to the polar regions, roughly 25 percent go for a second time,' says Louisa Richardson, a senior marketing executive at tour operator Exodus.

In the same period that tourism has exploded, the 'health' of the poles has 'deteriorated'. 'The biggest changes taking place in the

Antarctic are related to climate change,' says Rod Downie, Environmental Manager with the British Antarctic Survey (BAS). Large numbers of visitors increase these problems.

Although polar tourism is widely accepted, there have been few regulations up until recently. At the meeting of the Antarctic Treaty in Baltimore, the 28 member nations adopted proposals for limits to tourist numbers. These included safety codes for tourist vessels in Antarctic waters, and improved environmental protection for the continent. They agreed to prevent ships with more than 500 passengers from landing in Antarctica, as well as limit the number of passengers going ashore to a maximum of 100 at any one time, with a minimum of one guide for every 20 tourists. 'Tourism in Antarctica is not without its risks,' says Downie. 'After all, Antarctica doesn't have a coastguard rescue service.'

'So far, no surveys confirm that people are going quickly to see polar regions before they change,' says Frigg Jørgensen, General Secretary of the Association of Arctic Expedition Cruise Operators (AECO). 'However, Hillary Clinton and many other big names have been to Svalbard in the northernmost part of Norway to see the effects of climate change. The associated media coverage could influence others to do the same.'

These days, rarely a week passes without a negative headline in the newspapers. The suffering polar bear has become a symbol of a warming world, its plight a warning that the clock is ticking. It would seem that this ticking clock is a small but growing factor for some tourists. 'There's an element of "do it now",' acknowledges Prisca Campbell, Marketing Director of Quark Expeditions, which takes 7,000 people to the poles annually. Leaving the trip until later, it seems, may mean leaving it too late.

adapted from *Geographical* magazine

⑤ Now answer Questions 1–7.

> **Exam advice**   *Summary completion*
> - Remember that the answers may not be in passage order.
> - Check that the summary makes sense and is grammatically correct when you have finished.

⑥ Look at Questions 8–12 below.

1   Quickly scan the passage for the names (A–D) and <u>underline</u> them.
2   <u>Underline</u> the key ideas in statements 8–12.
3   Answer the questions by reading around each name carefully and then read the list of statements to find the ones that match.

Questions 8–12

Look at the following statements and the list of people below.

*Match each statement with the correct person, **A–D**.*

NB *You may use any letter more than once.*

8   Some tourists believe they should not delay their trip to the poles.

9   There are some dangers to travelling in Antarctica.

10   Some famous people have travelled to polar regions to look at the impacts of global warming.

11   Some tourists make more than one trip to the poles.

12   There is no evidence that visitors are hurrying to the poles.

> **List of People**
> A   Louisa Richardson
> B   Rod Downie
> C   Frigg Jørgensen
> D   Prisca Campbell

Work in pairs. Which words and phrases in the passage have a similar meaning to these words and phrases from Questions 8–12?

1 not delay *do it now*
2 dangers
3 impacts
4 global warming
5 make more than one trip
6 hurrying

> *Exam advice*   *Matching features*
>
> • Scan the passage for the options – A, B, C, etc. – and underline them. (They are always in the same order in the passage as they are in the box, but they may occur more than once.)
> • Underline the key ideas in each question.
> • Read around each option carefully and match it to the question(s).

8 **Work in small groups. Discuss these questions.**

1 Are there other places in the world where tourist numbers are affecting the environment?
2 Should governments in some parts of the world limit tourist numbers? Why? / Why not?

Vocabulary

tourism or *tourist*?

1 **IELTS candidates often confuse the words *tourism* and *tourist*. Read these extracts from the CLD and the examples. Then circle the correct word in sentences 1–4 below from the passage on pages 78–79.**

> tourism *noun* [U] the business of providing services for tourists, including organising their travel, hotels, entertainment, etc.
> ***Tourism** is an important global industry.*

> tourist *noun* [C] someone who visits a place for pleasure and does not live there
> *Millions of **tourists** visit Rome every year.*
>
> NB Both *tourism* and *tourist* are used as adjectives to form a noun phrase. Note these compound nouns: *tourist destination, mass tourism, tourist trade, tourist season, tourism/tourist industry, tourist numbers.*

1 Travel at the North and South Poles has become an expensive leisure activity, suitable for *tourism / tourists* of all ages.

2 Annual figures for the Arctic, where *tourism / tourist* has existed since the 19th century, have increased from about a million in the early 1990s to more than 1.5 million today.
3 In the same period that *tourism / tourist* has exploded, the 'health' of the poles has 'deteriorated'.
4 At the meeting of the Antarctic Treaty in Baltimore, the 28 member nations adopted proposals for limits to *tourism / tourist* numbers.

2 **Read these sentences and correct the mistakes made by IELTS candidates. Sometimes two options are possible. Two of the sentences are correct.**

1 Some ~~tourism harm~~ the environment.
   tourists harm / tourism harms
2 The income from tourism is important for local people.
3 International tourism spends a lot of money.
4 There are many advantages of the tourism.
5 My city attracts a huge number of tourism.
6 Most tourist destinations have lost their identity.
7 After the tourism season, the result is clear.
8 The environment has been damaged by mass tourists.

Listening

Sentence completion, Table completion

1 **You are going to hear a tour guide welcoming visitors to a science museum. Before you listen, work in small groups. Here are some of the things you can see at the museum. Which three would you most like to see? Why?**

Science Museum

Whats on...

TV studio   Find out how a television studio works, through a short programme.

Space academy   Learn how astronauts live, and take a trip to the International Space Station.

Science on stage   Watch fantastic demonstrations and experiments, such as frying an egg with liquid nitrogen.

2 Work in pairs. Read Questions 1–5 and decide what type of information you need for each gap.

Questions 1–5

Complete the sentences below.

Write **NO MORE THAN TWO WORDS AND/OR A NUMBER** *for each answer.*

1 Keep your .... in a safe place throughout your visit.
2 Pass through the .... to enter and leave the museum.
3 You need to buy a .... if you want to use a camera in the museum.
4 Look after your .... and mobile phone.
5 Arrive at the cinema about .... before the start of the show.

3 🔊 (13) Now listen and answer Questions 1–5.

4 🔊 (13) Work in pairs. Look at the key words and phrases below from Questions 1–5. Listen to the recording again and note down the words the speaker uses that have a similar meaning.

1 keep   4 leave   7 look after
2 safe   5 buy   8 arrive at
3 enter   6 use a camera 9 before the start

Exam advice   *Sentence completion*

• Use words in the sentence to help you listen for the answer.
• Check the completed sentences are grammatically correct.

5 Work in pairs. Look at the table below and decide what type of information you need for each gap.

Questions 6–10

Complete the table below.

Write **NO MORE THAN TWO WORDS AND/OR A NUMBER** *for each answer.*

3D Film Choice

name of film	time	what you will see
The Secrets of the Nile	10.00 a.m.	The first **6** .... along the river Nile
7 .... Ocean	11.45 a.m.	Life at the bottom of the sea
Dinosaurs Alive	**8**	A re-creation of a **9** .... of dinosaur
Arabia	2.30 p.m.	A trip across the **10** .... and a dive in the Red Sea

6 🔊 (14) Now listen and answer Questions 6–10.

Exam advice   *Table completion*

• Use the title and headings in the table to focus your listening.
• Check your writing to make sure you have not written unnecessary or incorrect words.

7 Work in pairs.

1 Do you have any museums in your home town? What can you see and do there?
2 What types of museum do you most enjoy visiting? Why?

Climate change   Witness the effects of global warming on plant and animal life.

Three-dimensional cinema   Travel to other times and places in a selection of short 3D films.

Speaking
Parts 1 and 2

1 Work in pairs. Tell your partner about the city, town or village that you come from.

1 Where is it?
2 What does it look like?
3 What do people do there?

2 🔊 Listen to Ulia describing her city and answer these questions.

1 What words does Ulia use to describe her city?
2 What phrases does she use to help her keep going?

3 Read these Part 1 questions and think how you could answer each of them using the prompts below to help you. Then work in pairs and take turns to ask and answer the questions.

> 1 Can you describe your town or village?
> 2 How important is tourism in your town/ village? Why? / Why not?
> 3 What places would you recommend people to visit in your town/village?
> 4 What festivals take place in your local area?

I live in a town/village that … / I live in X, which …

It's very important because … / It's not very important, but …

I would recommend X, which is … / I think X is a good place to visit, because …

We celebrate X, which takes place … / The X festival is held on …

4 Work in pairs. Match the adjectives below (1–12) with their opposites in the box. Then discuss which adjectives describe opinions (O) and which describe facts (F). Some may be both (F/O).

> ~~ancient~~ awful dirty dull noisy
> outdated poor quiet stressful
> unimpressive unpopular urban

1	modern *ancient, F/O*	7	relaxing
2	peaceful	8	impressive
3	clean	9	wealthy
4	busy	10	colourful
5	rural	11	fashionable
6	popular	12	wonderful

▶ page 128 *Fact and opinion adjectives*

5 Work in pairs. Use two adjectives from Exercise 4 to describe each of these scenes. Add an article where appropriate.

1 *an impressive, modern* hotel

2 .... , ... area

3 .... , ... district

4 .... , ... monuments

5 .... , ... landscape

6 .... , ... experience

6 🔊 Read this task, then listen to Ulia giving her talk.

> **Describe a holiday you particularly enjoyed.**
> **You should say:**
>   **where you went**
>   **why you went there**
>   **what you did**
> **and explain why you enjoyed the holiday so much.**

As you listen, note down any adjectives she uses to describe the:

1 Red Sea
2 sea life she saw
3 pyramids and national museum
4 whole holiday.

▶ Pronunciation: *Chunking 2*

7 Work in pairs. Take turns to do the Speaking task in Exercise 6. Before you speak, take a minute to prepare your talk.

8 Now change partners and take turns to do this Speaking task.

> **Describe your idea of a perfect holiday.**
>
> **You should say:**
>
> > **where it would be**
> >
> > **how you would get there**
> >
> > **where you would stay**
>
> **and explain why this would be your perfect holiday.**

Pronunciation
Chunking 2

> Grouping words together in chunks improves your overall fluency.

1 (17) **Listen to this sentence from Ulia's answer to the first Part 1 question (Speaking, Exercise 2). Is it easier to understand with or without a pause?**

I come from Balakovo in Russia.

2 (18) **Listen to these two versions of Ulia's next sentence. Which is easier to understand?**

a It's a / very modern industrial / city / which is / situated / on the / river Volga.
b It's a very modern / industrial city / which is situated / on the river Volga.

3 (19) **Listen to this extract from Ulia's Part 2 talk and mark with / where the speaker pauses.**

I'd like to talk about a holiday which I took in 2005. It's a holiday that I remember very well because we had such a fantastic time. I went with three other girls, who are all friends of mine, and we still talk about this holiday today.

4 Work in pairs. Take turns to read Ulia's answer in Exercise 3 aloud, putting the pauses in the same places.

5 (20) Work in pairs.

1 Read the extract below from Ulia's Part 2 answer and mark where you think she should pause.
2 Listen and check your answer.
3 Take turns to read the answer aloud.

It was funny, because usually I'm a person who's quite scared of things, and I didn't think I would put a mask on my face or go under the water – but I wanted to see the coral so much.

Writing
Task 2

1 Work in pairs. Read this Writing task and <u>underline</u> the key ideas.

> Write about the following topic.
>
> *According to an international travel magazine, many tourists today fly straight to their holiday resort and almost never leave it. Unlike tourists in the 1960s and '70s, they return home with no experience of the local culture.*
>
> *Why do you think this happens? How was tourism different in the past?*
>
> Give reasons for your answer and include any relevant examples from your own experience.

2 How does this photo illustrate the key ideas in the Writing task?

3 Are these statements about the Writing task in Exercise 1 true (T) or false (F)?

1 The main topic is tourism. T
2 I need to give reasons why people did not travel in the past.
3 I have to say whether I agree with the magazine.
4 I need to use present and past tenses.
5 I can just write about my own experience of the topic.
6 I need to explain why tourists do not find out about the local culture.
7 I can answer both questions at the same time.

4 Work in pairs. Discuss the two questions in the Writing task in Exercise 1 and note down some of your ideas in this table.

why tourists almost never leave their resort and have no experience of the local culture	how tourism was different in the past
Flights and transfers take people direct to their hotels.	

5 Read the sample answer below. Which paragraphs/ sentences:

1 deal with the first question?
2 deal with the second question?
3 express the writer's views and experience?

In the last century, air travel had a big impact on tourism. Now we can get to places that were once hard to reach, and I think this has changed many people's holiday experience.

In the past, travellers found their own route to their destination, and this was part of the adventure of travelling. When they got back home, there were many colourful stories that they could tell.

Nowadays, large travel companies sell 'cheap' package deals to tourists. Sometimes this means they are transported from the airport to their hotel, where they stay for the rest of their holiday. I think they lose the opportunity to meet local people and see the real landscape.

Another problem is that today's hotels have many tourist facilities. It is not uncommon to find tourists who never go outside the resort. Although some visitors do, they quickly return to their luxury accommodation, where they feel safe and comfortable.

This is very different from the past, when hotels were more basic and tourists had to find places to eat and beautiful beaches by themselves. I come from an area which is a popular tourist destination. When I was a child, I saw backpackers who talked to local people in our restaurants and streets. In my opinion, this was good for everyone. Today, we seem to have lost these places where tourists and local people can meet.

6 Work in pairs. The sample answer in Exercise 5 has no conclusion. Discuss these questions and tick the answers you think are correct.

1 What is the purpose of a conclusion?
Tick one answer.
A to add some supporting points
B to introduce a new main idea
C to link the points in the essay

2 What can a conclusion contain?
Tick four answers.
A a summary of the arguments
B a new viewpoint
C the writer's view
D concluding words or phrases
E some repetition of the ideas in the essay
F a recommendation

7 Work in small groups. Discuss these three conclusions using the questions in Exercise 6 as a guide. Then choose the best one and give reasons for your choice.

A In conclusion, people look forward to their holidays. They have worked hard all year, so their vacation is important to them and they want to relax and enjoy some good weather. Therefore, I think that it may not be important for these tourists to see the local culture.

B Finally, we don't have as many backpackers these days. This is because people have more money and prefer to fly.

C Unfortunately, tourism has become a global industry and has changed the expectations of holidaymakers. In my view, something should be done about this before we all forget why we travel to new places.

⬤ Key grammar: *Relative pronouns:* who, which, that, where

⑧ Work in small groups. Read this Writing task.

> Write about the following topic.
>
> *Some people say that tourism has many negative effects on the countries that people travel to.*
>
> *How true is this statement? What can tourists do to reduce the harmful effects of tourism on local cultures and environments?*
>
> Give reasons for your answer and include any relevant examples from your own experience.

1 Discuss the two main questions and take some notes.
2 Consider what you will write in your introduction and conclusion.

⑨ Now work alone. Write a plan for the body of your answer, then write your answer to the task in Exercise 8 in at least 250 words.

Key grammar
Relative pronouns: *who, which, that, where*

> Relative clauses add information about a noun by putting a relative pronoun (*who, which, that*) immediately after the noun, followed by a phrase.
>
> noun   relative pronoun   phrase
>
> *I'm staying in a hotel which is full of tourists.*

❶ Read the information in the box above, then <u>underline</u> the relative clauses in these sentences.

1 Now we can get to places <u>that were once hard to reach</u> …
2 … , there were many colourful stories that they could tell.
3 It is not uncommon to find tourists who never go outside the resort.
4 I come from an area which is a popular tourist destination.
5 Today, we seem to have lost these places where tourists and local people can meet.

⬤ page 128 *Relative pronouns*

❷ Complete these sentences using the correct relative pronoun: *who, which, that* or *where*. Sometimes two answers are possible.

1 My city has a shopping festival .... takes place every year.
2 Tourists .... go to Agra in India want to see the Taj Mahal.
3 St Petersburg is the city .... I was born.
4 There is a boat .... leaves the harbour at 10.30 a.m.
5 Thailand is a good place for people .... like sandy beaches.
6 I took the flight .... left at 2.15 p.m.
7 A tourist information office is a place .... you can find out about the local area.

❸ ⊘ IELTS candidates often leave out relative pronouns. Correct the mistakes in each of these sentences by writing *who, which* or *that* in the correct place.

1 It is certainly true that ~~people go~~ abroad for their holidays spend a lot of money on tourist attractions. *people who/that go*

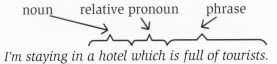

2 People today prefer destinations are less industrialised and exploited.
3 Tourism can be a problem causes local people to worry.
4 The graph shows the number of visitors travel to and from the UK.
5 Children work in their holidays gain some valuable experience.
6 The government has built tourist accommodation is more modern than before.
7 I think there are many people don't like travelling.

Spelling
Introductory and linking phrases

> IELTS candidates often misspell the expressions they use to introduce and link their points.

⊘ Find and correct one mistake in each of these words/phrases taken from the Writing section.

1	in the last centry	6	in my oppinion
2	nowdays	7	therfore
3	sometime	8	in conclucion
4	another probelm	9	finaly
5	although	10	unfortunatly

Vocabulary and grammar review **Unit 7**

Vocabulary

❶ Complete these sentences with the correct form of *raise* or *rise*.

1 My exam results *have raised* my hopes of getting a good job.
2 The government's reading programme is .... literacy levels in rural areas.
3 If the cost of course materials .... , fewer students will buy them.
4 According to the newspaper, last week's concert .... $500 for charity.
5 .... your hand if you would like to listen to the recording again!
6 Even though we have computers and laptops, the amount of paper people use .... over the years.
7 Although the number of people using online English courses .... last year, it did not affect the sale of books.

Grammar

❷ Rewrite these sentences starting with *There* and using a noun phrase.

1 The price of books has risen gradually.
   There has been a gradual rise in the price of books.
2 The amount of study time fell by 20%.
3 Reading speeds improved considerably.
4 Sales of electronic books have dropped slightly this month.
5 The number of lecture hours will increase by 10%.
6 The cost of fees peaked in 2011.
7 As people get older, the number of words they know rises.
8 Literacy levels in rural areas fluctuated during the 1990s.

❸ Study this graph, then complete each gap in the summary below with a preposition from the box. You will need to use one preposition twice.

Proportion of school leavers with no qualifications, 2001–2010

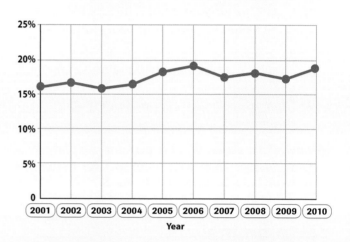

at	between	by	from	~~in~~	of	over	to

The graph shows some changes **1** ...*in*... the percentage of school leavers without a qualification. According to the graph, 16 percent **2** .... school leavers did not have a qualification in 2001. Over the next year, there was a slight rise **3** .... 17 percent, and then the figure dropped back. **4** .... 2004 and 2006, the percentage increased more sharply and it peaked **5** .... 19 percent. After this, it fell again **6** .... 2 percent. Finally, **7** .... 2007 to 2010, the percentage fluctuated, but it rose **8** .... 19 percent in the year 2010. Although there was some variation in the figures **9** .... the ten-year period, the percentage of students leaving school without a qualification remained fairly stable overall.

Vocabulary and grammar review **Unit 8**

Vocabulary

❶ Complete the conversations below with the adjectives in the box.

> dull   fashionable   impressive
> outdated   ~~relaxing~~   stressful

A: What do you usually do on holiday?
B: As I work hard all year, I like to do something
1 <u>relaxing</u>, like sunbathing on a beach.

C: I was amazed when I saw the height of the Burj Khalifa in Dubai.
D: I know, that building is so **2** .... !

E: Let's buy some new luggage for our trip.
F: OK – this suitcase is rather **3** .... now – it was my father's.

G: Why do people say that Hong Kong is a shopper's paradise?
H: Because you can buy **4** .... clothes there at cheap prices.

I: I'm disappointed – there wasn't much to see on the city tour.
J: No – it was a bit **5** ...., wasn't it?

K: Have you seen the awful queues at the check-in desk?
L: Well – this part of the trip is always a bit **6** ...., but we can sleep on the flight.

❷ Correct the order of adjectives in three of these sentences. Write *correct* for the sentences that do not need changing.

1 Eighty percent of people in the US live in ~~urban, crowded~~ areas. *crowded, urban*
2 I've bought a great new rucksack for my holiday.
3 If you want to visit a historical, lively city, I would recommend Cairo in Egypt.
4 We saw some colourful, fascinating birds during our trip to Australia.
5 Because of all the delays, the plane journey was a tiring, disorganised experience!
6 Camping is a healthy, exciting activity for children.
7 I'm afraid I found the museum a rather dull old building.

Grammar

❸ Join the pairs of sentences using *who*, *which*, *that* or *where*. Sometimes two answers are possible.

1 This is a photograph I took. It's of the desert.
This is a photograph *that/which I took of the desert.*
2 Riyadh is a city in Saudi Arabia. I grew up there.
Riyadh is the …
3 We rode horses in the country park. They were very beautiful.
The horses …
4 People travel by train. They can enjoy the passing scenery.
People …
5 Greece is a country. The first Olympic Games took place there.
Greece is the …
6 Some tourists try new activities. More adventurous tourists do this.
Tourists …

❹ Complete this article with *who*, *which*, *that* or *where*. Sometimes two answers are possible.

Space tourism

There are many people **1** <u>who/that</u> dream of going into space, but not many **2** .... can afford it. If you have a spare $20 million, you can spend a week at the International Space Station (ISS) **3** .... orbits the Earth at a distance of around 400 kilometres. However, the ISS is a place **4** .... scientists conduct research. It is not a luxury hotel and it cannot offer the kind of accommodation **5** .... many tourists expect.

In the future, things may change. Companies **6** .... are investing millions of dollars in space tourism believe it is an industry **7** .... will 'take off'. They are planning to build hotels **8** .... guests can enjoy all the luxuries of ordinary hotels and even take space walks!

Unit 9 Every drop counts

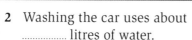
2 Washing the car uses about .... litres of water.

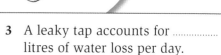
3 A leaky tap accounts for .... litres of water loss per day.

1 It takes .... litres of water to grow enough coffee beans to make one cup of coffee.

4 It takes .... litres of water to produce a laptop.

5 It takes .... litres of water to fill a swimming pool.

Starting off

❶ **Work in small groups. Each of the things in the photos uses an amount of water. Complete the sentences (1–6) by choosing a number from the box (a–f).**

Approximate number of litres
a 15   **b** 45   **c** 250   **d** 675   **e** 6,300   **f** 99,000

❷ **Check your answers to Exercise 1 on page 175. Which figures surprised you, and which figures did you expect?**

❸ **Do people use a lot of water where you live? Why? / Why not?**

Listening
Matching, Flow-chart completion

❶ **Work in pairs. You are going to hear a student talking to a tutor about a talk he is preparing on 'desalination' – the process of making fresh water from seawater.**

1 Why do you think desalination is important?
2 Have you ever given a talk to a group of people? What was it about?
3 How did you prepare for it?
4 How did you feel about it before and afterwards?

6 .... litres of water are used to recycle a newspaper.

❷ Read the task below. <u>Underline</u> the key ideas in the opening question and the box of options (A–C).

Questions 1–5

What comment does the tutor make about each part of the presentation?

*Write the correct letter, **A–C**, next to Questions 1–5.*

NB You may use any letter more than once.

Parts of Presentation

1 the introduction
2 the background
3 the description of the process
4 the advantages/disadvantages
5 the conclusion

┌─────────────────────────────────────┐
│ **Comments**

  A It needs to be shorter.
  B The ideas are difficult to follow.
  C Some information should be added.
└─────────────────────────────────────┘

---

❸ (21) **Now listen to the first part of the conversation and answer Questions 1–5.**

Exam advice *Matching*

• You may have to use the same option more than once.
• Use the key ideas in each question to help you listen for the answers.

❹ Work in pairs. Match these words (1–5) with their correct definition from the *CLD* (a–e).

1 filter *(v)*
2 canal *(n)*
3 pressure *(n)*
4 substance *(n)*
5 marine *(adj)*

a an artificial river built for boats to travel along or to take water where it is needed
b a solid, liquid or gas
c to pass a liquid or gas through a piece of equipment in order to remove solid pieces or other substances
d found in the sea or relating to the sea
e the force that you produce when you push something

---

❺ Work in pairs. Read the flow chart below and decide what type of word you need for each gap.

Questions 6–10

Complete the flow chart below.

*Write **NO MORE THAN TWO WORDS** for each answer.*

The desalination process

Introductory point: a **6** .... can desalinate sea water using its throat.

↓

Collection: sea water passes through a canal into the **7** ....

↓

Treatment: rubbish is removed.

↓

Salt removal: sea water passes through a membrane under high pressure; a very **8** .... process.

↓

Produces fresh water and salty brine – can harm **9** ....

↓

Use: human consumption and irrigating **10** ....

---

❻ (22) **Now listen and answer Questions 6–10.**

Exam advice *Flow-chart completion*

• Read through the flow chart to understand the process.
• Read around the gaps to predict the missing information.

❼ Work in small groups.

1 What disadvantages of desalination were mentioned in the recording? Can you think of any others?
2 Which parts of the world have problems getting fresh water?

Reading

Matching headings, Sentence completion,
Pick from a list

❶ Work in pairs. Discuss these questions about the Reading test.

1 How long is the test?
2 How many sections are there?
3 How much time should you spend on each section?
4 How many questions are there in total in the test?
5 How many marks do you get for each question?
6 Where do you write your answers?
7 What should you check when you write down answers from the passage?

❷ Work in pairs. You are going to read a passage about getting clean water.

1 What problems are there if you don't have running water in your house?
2 What problems are there if you don't have access to clean water?

❸ Quickly read the title and subheading of the passage on your own.

1 What do you think *burden* and *transformed* mean?
2 Which TWO of these topics do you expect to read about?
   a the causes of floods
   b the difficulties of collecting water
   c industrial uses of water
   d building water supplies

❹ Find these words (1–6) in the passage and say what type of word (e.g. noun, verb, etc.) they are. Then match them with their correct definition from the *CLD* (a–f).

1 drought   a   a strong wall built across a river
2 well   to stop the water
3 dam   b   an artificial lake where water is
4 pump   stored before it goes to people's
5 reservoir   houses
6 pipe   c   a long period when there is no
               rain
           d   a piece of equipment which forces
               liquid or gas to move somewhere
          e   a long tube which liquid or gas
               can move through
          f   a deep hole in the ground from
               which you can get water, oil or gas

The burden of thirst

Millions of women carry water long distances. If they had a tap by their door, whole societies would be transformed.

by Tina Rosenberg

A Aylito Binayo's feet know the mountain. Even at four in the morning, she can run down the rocks to the river by starlight alone and climb the steep mountain back up to her village with a container of water on her back. She has made this journey three times a day since she was a small child. So has every other woman in her village of Foro, in the Konso district of south-western Ethiopia in Africa. Binayo left school when she was eight years old, in part because she had to help her mother fetch water from the Toiro River. The water is unsafe to drink; every year that the drought continues, the river carries less water, and its flow is reduced. But it is the only water Foro has ever had.

B In developed parts of the world, people turn on a tap and out pours abundant, clean water. Yet nearly 900 million people in the world have no access to clean water. Furthermore, 2.5 billion people have no safe way to get rid of human waste. Polluted water and lack of proper hygiene cause disease and kill 3.3 million people around the world annually, most of them children. In southern Ethiopia and in northern Kenya, a lack of rain over the past few years has made even dirty water hard to find. But soon, for the first time, things are going to change.

C Bringing clean water close to villagers' homes is the key to the problem. Communities where clean water becomes accessible and plentiful are transformed. All the hours previously spent hauling water can be used to cultivate more crops, raise more animals or even start a business. Families spend less time sick or caring for family members who are unwell. Most important, not having to collect water means girls can go to school and get jobs. The need to fetch water for the family, or to take care of younger siblings while their mother goes, usually prevents them ever having this experience.

D But the challenges of bringing water to remote villages like those in Konso are overwhelming. Locating water underground and then reaching it by means of deep wells requires geological expertise and expensive, heavy machines. Abandoned wells and water projects litter the villages of Konso. In similar villages around the developing world, the biggest problem with water schemes is that about half of them break down soon after the groups that built them move on. Sometimes technology is used that can't be repaired locally, or spare parts are available only in the capital.

E Today, a UK-based international non-profit organisation called WaterAid is tackling the job of bringing water to the most remote villages of Konso. Their approach combines technologies proven to last – such as building a sand dam to capture and filter rainwater that would otherwise drain away. But the real innovation is that WaterAid believes technology is only part of the solution. Just as important is involving the local community in designing, building and maintaining new water projects. Before beginning any project, WaterAid asks the community to create a WASH (water, sanitation, hygiene) committee of seven people. The committee works with WaterAid to plan projects and involve the village in construction. Then it maintains and runs the project.

F The people of Konso, who grow their crops on terraces they have dug into the sides of mountains, are famous for hard work. In the village of Orbesho, residents even constructed a road themselves so that drilling machinery could

come in. Last summer, their pump, installed by the river, was being motorised to push its water to a newly built reservoir on top of a nearby mountain. From there, gravity will carry it down in pipes to villages on the other side of the mountain. Residents of those villages have each given some money to help fund the project. They have made concrete and collected stones for the structures. Now they are digging trenches to lay pipes. If all goes well, Aylito Binayo will have a tap with safe water just a three-minute walk from her front door.

adapted from *National Geographic* magazine

❺ Look at Questions 1–6. Read paragraph headings i–viii and <u>underline</u> the key ideas in each. Then read each paragraph carefully and match it to the correct heading.

Questions 1–6

The reading passage has six paragraphs, **A–F**.

Choose the correct heading for each paragraph from the list of headings below.

List of Headings	
i	Why some plans have failed
ii	A rural and urban problem
iii	A possible success
iv	Explaining a new management style
v	Some relevant statistics
vi	A regular trip for some people
vii	Treating people for disease
viii	How water can change people's lives

1 Paragraph A ....   4 Paragraph D ....

2 Paragraph B ....   5 Paragraph E ....

3 Paragraph C ....   6 Paragraph F ....

Exam advice   *Matching headings*

• Read the headings very carefully, <u>underlining</u> the key ideas.

• Each paragraph heading will cover the main idea of the paragraph.

• Write your answer clearly or you will be marked wrong.

6 Read Questions 7–11. Underline the key ideas and decide what type of information is missing. Then answer Questions 7–11.

Questions 7–11

Complete the sentences below.

*Choose **NO MORE THAN ONE WORD AND/OR A NUMBER** from the passage for each answer.*

7 The water levels in the Toiro River are falling because of ....

8 Globally, the number of people who die each year as a result of using dirty water is ....

9 When families have clean water, they can spend more time growing ....

10 Specialist knowledge and equipment are needed to dig ....

11 WaterAid uses a dam made of .... to capture rainwater.

Exam advice   *Sentence completion*

• Check how many words (or numbers) you can use for each gap.

• You will find the answers in the passage in the same order as the questions.

• Copy the words onto the answer sheet exactly.

7 Underline the key ideas in Questions 12–13 and use these to find the right place in the passage. Then answer Questions 12–13.

Questions 12–13

*Choose **TWO** letters, A–E.*

*Which **TWO** of these activities were performed by the villagers of Orbesho?*

A building a transport route

B digging a reservoir

C gathering building materials

D making pipes

E fitting taps

Exam advice   *Pick from a list*

• The answers may come from one section of the passage or from several paragraphs.

• It does not matter which order you write the two answers in.

8 Work in small groups.

1 Aylito's village needs running water. What other things do you think her village needs? Why?

2 Do you think people should stay in villages without running water, or should they move to cities?

3 What are the good things about living in a village like Aylito's?

Spelling
Some common mistakes

1 ⊙ IELTS candidates often make mistakes when spelling these words from the reading passage. Correct the mistakes.

1 becaus *because*   6 mashines ....
2 furthemor ....   7 availble ....
3 diseas ....   8 belive ....
4 busyness ....   9 creat ....
5 experince ....   10 involv ....

2 When you have finished, check your answers in the passage.

Vocabulary
effect, benefit, advantage and *disadvantage*

IELTS candidates often make mistakes using the nouns *effect, benefit, advantage* and *disadvantage* in a phrase.

1 Read these sentences (a–d), then complete sentences (1–5) below by writing one word in each gap.

a Village life has **many advantages** for people.

b Access to running water **has huge benefits** for everyone.

c The article about Foro **had a powerful effect on** its readers.

d **The main disadvantage** of living in a modern city is the noise.

1 Living by the sea ......*has*...... many advantages.

2 A lack of running water can .... a serious effect .... people's health.

3 The most significant disadvantage .... desalination is the cost of the plant.

4 The projects that were run by WaterAid had numerous benefits .... local people.

5 Some people say that recycling water .... a negative effect .... people's health.

2 ⊙ These sentences contain a mistake made by IELTS candidates. Find and correct the mistakes. One sentence is correct.

1 Technology ~~hands us~~ many benefits. *has/brings*
2 One advantage for tourism is that it improves a country's economy.
3 Air travel has the greatest effect to air pollution.
4 The benefits of drinking water every day are well known.
5 International tourism has not given a bad effect on the environment.
6 The advantages and disadvantages in the water supply are easy to see.
7 In conclusion, there is a major effect quality of life.
8 To sum up, computers give a lot of advantages to us.

Speaking
Parts 2 and 3

1 Work in pairs. What do you remember about Speaking Parts 2 and 3? Circle the correct answer for each statement.

1 You have *one minute / two minutes* to prepare your talk.
2 Your talk should last up to *two / three* minutes.
3 The examiner *will / will not* tell you when to stop talking.
4 You *can / cannot* look at the task as you talk.
5 Part 3 questions are about *personal / general* topics.
6 You *can / cannot* ask the examiner to repeat a question.

2 Work alone. Read this Speaking Part 2 task, then think of an activity that you would find easy to talk about and make notes.

> **Describe an activity that you enjoy that takes place in or near water.**
>
> **You should say:**
>
> > **how you prepare for the activity**
> >
> > **where it takes place**
> >
> > **what the activity involves**
>
> **and explain why you enjoy this activity.**

3 🔊23 Listen to Carlos doing the Speaking task in Exercise 2 and complete the phrases he uses by writing one word in each gap.

1 I'm going to ......*talk*...... about …
2 So how do I .... ready?
3 There are lots of .... where you can go fishing.
4 Fishing is really quite ....
5 All in ...., it's a wonderful activity.

4 🔊23 Listen again and check your answers. What is the purpose of each phrase?

5 Work in pairs. Take turns to give your talks and speak for two minutes.

▶ page 94 Pronunciation: *Intonation 2*

6 Work in pairs. Look at these Speaking Part 3 questions.

> **Water sports**
>
> 1 What water sports are popular among young people?
> 2 How are sports like surfing and swimming different?
> 3 Why do some people not enjoy water sports?

Which question is asking the candidate to:
a compare some water sports?
b name some water sports?
c explain something about water sports?

7 (24) **Listen to Carlos and complete his answers by writing one word in each gap.**

A I think there are **1** ...*many*... water sports that are popular. Near beach resorts, for example, the popular sports **2** .... things like surfing, sailing, waterskiing … **3** .... sports that young people enjoy are – let me think – canoeing, rowing, perhaps, and, well, the **4** .... one's swimming because you can do that in a pool anywhere.

B Well, there are several ways. For a start, you need a lot of waves to surf, **5** .... swimmers usually prefer calm water. Also, you need **6** .... equipment to surf – you know, a board and maybe a wet suit. Yeah, and lastly, swimming's **7** .... than surfing!

C I think it **8** .... on the person, but, um, the most important **9** .... is probably that they can't swim! They don't like it if it's deep and their feet don't touch the bottom. Even some people who can swim are afraid of water. Another **10** .... is that, these days, the sea can be very polluted, and they may be afraid of getting ill.

8 **Work in pairs. Take turns to ask and answer the questions in Exercise 6 using some of the words and phrases in this section.**

9 **Work alone. Prepare some ideas for these questions, then ask and answer them in pairs.**

Attitudes to water

1 What activities do children enjoy in or around water?

2 How does a child's attitude to water differ from an adult's?

3 Why do some adults take part in dangerous water sports?

Pronunciation
Intonation 2

Speakers' voices rise to show that information is new or interesting, but fall to show that they are finishing their point.

1 (25) **Listen to this sentence from Carlos's answer. Notice how the speaker's voice changes on the words with arrows above them. In pairs, take turns to repeat what he says.**

… the main one's swimming, because you can do that in a pool anywhere.

2 **Look at these sentences. Mark with arrows where you think Carlos's voice should rise and fall.**

1 For a start, you need a lot of waves to surf, whereas swimmers usually prefer calm water.

2 Yeah, and lastly, swimming's cheaper than surfing!

3 Even some people who can swim are afraid of water.

4 Another possibility is that, these days, the sea can be very polluted, and they may be afraid of getting ill.

3 (26) **Listen to the sentences and check your answers.**

4 **Take turns to read the sentences to each other using the same intonation.**

5 **Write three sentences you could use to answer the questions in Speaking Exercise 9. Mark the intonation in your sentences with arrows and then read them to your partner.**

Writing
Task 1

1 **Work in pairs. Read the Writing task on page 95 and look at the diagram. Then discuss these questions.**

1 What equipment is needed for the water filter?

2 What materials are used in the filter?

3 Where does the dirty water enter the system?

4 Where does the clean water come out?

5 What is the pipe used for?

The diagram below shows a simple system that turns dirty water into clean water.

Summarise the information by selecting and reporting the main features, and make comparisons where relevant.

Water-Filter Assembly

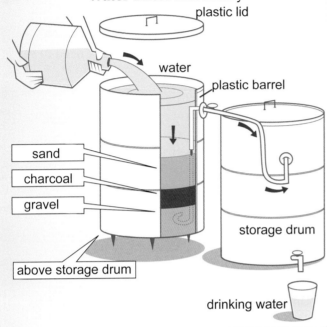

plastic lid

water

plastic barrel

sand

charcoal

gravel

above storage drum

storage drum

drinking water

❷ Read this sample answer to the Writing task above, then complete the plan in the next column by writing a word from the box in each gap.

The diagram shows a method for filtering dirty water using a barrel and a drum, a pipe and two taps.

First, the drum and barrel are placed next to each other so that the top of the barrel is higher than the drum. These items are linked by a pipe that runs from the bottom of the barrel into the side of the drum. Next, the filter is made by adding sand, charcoal and gravel to the barrel. Finally, a tap is fixed to the bottom of the drum and the top of the pipe.

The process begins when dirty water is poured into the barrel. After that, the water goes through the filter and up the pipe into the drum, where it is stored. Then, when the tap in the drum is turned on, clean drinking water comes out.

The system shows how natural materials and basic equipment can be used to produce drinking water in just a few simple stages.

build	list	operate	overview

para. 1	Explain what the diagram shows and a .... the equipment.
para. 2	Explain how to b .... the water-filter system.
para. 3	Explain how to c .... the system.
para. 4	Write an d .... of the diagram.

▶ page 96 Key grammar: *The passive*

❸ The writer uses words and phrases to mark the order in which things happen.

1 Circle the words/phrases that he uses to do this.
2 Which of these words/phrases are used to mark:
   a the start?
   b the end?
   c two things that happen together?
   d one thing that follows another?

▶ page 129 *Sequencers*

❹ ⊙ Find and correct the mistakes made by IELTS candidates in these sentences.

1 The first, they build the filter.
2 Than we add the dirty water.
3 Finaly, the clean water comes out.
4 At last, there is clean water to drink.
5 If they don't raise the barrel, it is too low, when the water goes in, it doesn't go anywhere.

❺ Work in pairs. Look at the Writing task on page 96 and for each picture, A and B, discuss these questions.

1 How deep is the water source?
2 Who or what is collecting the water?
3 What equipment is used?
4 What is the water being used for?

❻ Work in pairs. Each describe briefly how one of the systems works.

❼ Work in pairs. Decide how you should write your answer. You should think about:

1 what to describe and compare in the two diagrams;
2 how many paragraphs you will write, and what you will write in each one;
3 how you will begin and end your answer, and what you will include in the overview.

The diagrams below show two methods of collecting water for irrigation purposes.

Summarise the information by selecting and reporting the main features, and make comparisons where relevant.

A Swing basket

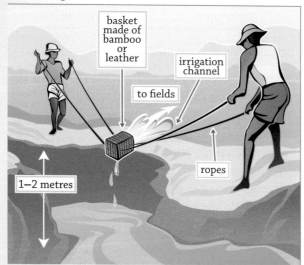

B Rope and bucket

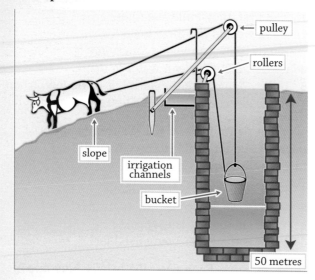

8 Now work alone and write your answer. Write at least 150 words.

Exam advice Writing Task 1

- Look carefully at the diagram(s) and decide what is included and how it works.
- Decide what you will write in each paragraph.
- Remember to make comparisons (if relevant) and include an overview.

Key grammar

The passive

1 Work in pairs. Read the information in the box, then answer questions 1–3 about examples a–d.

> The passive is formed by the verb *to be* + the past participle (*collected, eaten, done*, etc.).
>
> We use the passive when we don't know who or what does/did the action or we don't need to say who does/did it.

a Villagers pour dirty water into the barrel.
b Dirty water is poured into the barrel.
c People built the water filter.
d The water filter was built.

1 Which two sentences are passive?
2 Which two sentences do not say who does/did the action?
3 Which tense is each sentence in?

▶ page 129 *The passive*

2 <u>Underline</u> the eight passive verb forms in the sample answer on page 95.

3 Complete these sentences with a suitable form of the verb in brackets.

1 Salt *is removed* (*remove*) from seawater in a desalination plant.
2 The wells .... (*dig*) ten years ago.
3 Over the past ten years, local people .... (*involve*) in WaterAid projects.
4 Last summer, a reservoir .... (*construct*).
5 Aylito Binayo .... (*believe*) she will have safe water soon.

4 ⊙ IELTS candidates often make mistakes with the passive. Find and correct the mistakes in these sentences.

1 ~~Water used~~ mostly in agriculture in Australia.
   Water is used
2 From the information which shows in the charts, water use has increased.
3 We did not affect by the water shortage last year.
4 A substantial increase in rainfall was occurred during the year.
5 Safe water should be provide for everyone.
6 Water that is came from the dam is reused.

Unit 10 Building design

An Hui Province, China

2 — Prague, Czech Republic

3 Kansas City, US

4 Paris, France

5 Dubai, UAE

6 Tokyo, Japan

Starting off

❶ Read these quotes (a–f). Match each one to a building (1–6).

a Is that an escalator going up the side of the building?
b It's fun, and the roof's an incredible colour and shape – it really stands out!
c It's a very modern block, but it looks like it's falling down!
d Wow, musical instruments – it's so unusual, particularly the part that's made of glass.
e The pyramid shape fits in well with the surroundings.
f It's impressive – but where are the windows?

❷ Work in small groups. What do you think the purpose of each building is? When you've finished, look at the answers on page 175.

❸ Which building design do you like best/least? Why?

Reading

Multiple choice, Matching sentence endings, Yes / No / Not Given

❶ Work in small groups. You are going to read a passage about the Pompidou Centre in Paris. Before you read, discuss these questions.

1 Why do many cities have large, impressive buildings?
2 Who should organise and pay for the construction of city buildings?

2 Now read the title, subheading and passage quite quickly to find out:

1 how old the Pompidou Centre is.
2 how the architects were chosen.
3 what effect the building had on their careers.

3 Work in pairs. Look at these phrases from the passage. Use their context and form to choose the correct definition for each of the words in *italics*. Then express each phrase in your own words.

1 the most *outstanding* new building (paragraph 1)
  a popular **b** large and ugly
  c excellent and better than others
2 a *downbeat* moment (paragraph 3)
  a unexciting **b** important **c** expected
3 a *passing* crisis (paragraph 3)
  a unknown **b** real **c** temporary
4 changed their *tune* (paragraph 3)
  a music **b** mind **c** prices

4 Work in pairs. Find these words in the passage and use the same methods to decide what they mean.

1 overcome   4 urban planning
2 enabled   5 landmark projects
3 movable   6 snaking

The Pompidou Centre

More than three decades after it was built, the Pompidou Centre in Paris has survived its moment at the edge of architectural fashion and proved itself to be one of the most remarkable buildings of the 20th century.

It was the most outstanding new building constructed in Paris for two generations. It looked like an explosion of brightly coloured service pipes in the calm of the city centre. However, when in 1977 the architects Richard Rogers and Renzo Piano stood among a large crowd of 5,000 at the opening of the Centre Culturel d'Art Georges Pompidou (known as the Pompidou), no one was really aware of the significance of this unusual building.

Rogers was only 38 when he and Piano won the competition to design a new cultural centre for Paris in the old market site. Young, unknown architects, they had been chosen from a field of nearly 700 to design one of the most prestigious buildings of its day. After six difficult years, with 25,000 drawings, seven lawsuits, battles over budgets, and a desperate last-minute scramble to finish the building, it had finally been done.

Yet the opening was a downbeat moment. The Pompidou Centre had been rubbished by the critics while it was being built, there was no more work in prospect for the architects, and their partnership had effectively broken down. But this was just a passing crisis. The Centre, which combined the national museum of modern art, exhibition space, a public library and a centre for modern music, proved an enormous success. It attracted six million visitors in its first year, and with its success, the critics swiftly changed their tune.

The architects had been driven by the desire for ultimate flexibility, for a building that would not limit the movement of its users. All the different parts were approached through the same enormous entrance hall and served by the same escalator, which was free to anyone to ride, whether they wanted to visit an exhibition or just admire the view. With all the services at one end of the building, escalators and lifts at the other, and the floors hung on giant steel beams providing uninterrupted space the size of two football pitches, their dream had become a reality.

The image of the Pompidou pervaded popular culture in the 1970s, making appearances everywhere – on record-album covers and a table lamp, and even acting as the set for a James Bond film. This did much to overcome the secretive nature of the architectural culture of its time, as it enabled a wider audience to appreciate the style and content of the building and so moved away from the strictly professional view.

The following year, Rogers was commissioned to design a new headquarters for Lloyd's Bank in London, and went on to create one of Britain's most dynamic architectural practices. Piano is now among the world's most respected architects. But what of their shared creation?

It was certainly like no previous museum, with its plans for a flexible interior that not only had movable walls, but floors that could also be adjusted up or down. This second feature did not in the end survive when the competition drawings were turned into a real building. In other ways, however, the finished building demonstrated a remarkable degree of refinement – of craftsmanship even – in the way the original diagram was transformed into a superbly detailed structure. It was this quality which, according to some critics, suggested that the Pompidou should be seen as closer to the 19th-century engineering tradition than the space age.

Nevertheless, as a model for urban planning, it has proved immensely influential. The Guggenheim in Bilbao* and the many other major landmark projects that were built in the belief that innovatively designed cultural buildings can bring about urban renewal are all following the lead of the Pompidou Centre.

Other buildings may now challenge it for the title of Europe's most outlandish work of architecture. However, more than a quarter of a century later, this construction – it is hard to call it a building when there is no façade, just a lattice of steel beams and pipes and a long external escalator snaking up the outside – still seems extreme.

Today, the Pompidou Centre itself still looks much as it did when it opened. The shock value of its colour-coded plumbing and its structure has not faded with the years. But while traditionalists regarded it as an ugly attack on Paris when it was built, they now see it for what it is – an enormous achievement, technically and conceptually.

* a modern-art museum in Spain designed by the North American architect, Frank O. Gehry

adapted from http://designmuseum.org

❺ <u>Underline</u> the key ideas in Questions 1–4. Then answer the questions.

> **Questions 1–4**
>
> *Choose the correct letter, **A**, **B**, **C** or **D**.*
>
> 1 What does the <u>writer say</u> in the <u>first paragraph</u> about the <u>opening</u> of the Pompidou Centre?
>   A The elderly did not like it.
>   B The architects were not present.
>   C The atmosphere was very noisy.
>   D The people did not realise its importance.
>
> 2 What does the writer say in the second paragraph about the construction of the Pompidou?
>   A There was a hurry to complete it.
>   B It cost less than expected.
>   C Other experts helped draw the plans.
>   D The market location was criticised.
>
> 3 What is the writer's main purpose in the third paragraph?
>   A to explain the multi-functional role of the centre
>   B to praise the architects for their design ideas
>   C to say why some people's opinions quickly altered
>   D to show how the media benefited from its success
>
> 4 What was the architects' 'dream', referred to in the fourth paragraph?
>   A to become famous
>   B to provide entertainment
>   C to allow visitors to use it freely
>   D to build the biggest museum in the world

Exam advice   *Multiple choice*
- The answers to these questions are in the same order in the passage.
- When you have chosen your answer, quickly check that the other options are wrong.

6 Read Questions 5–8 and the box of endings A–F.

1 <u>Underline</u> the key ideas in the questions and use these to find the right place in the passage.

2 Read that part of the passage carefully and match the information to the key ideas in the endings.

Questions 5–8

Complete each sentence with the correct ending, A–F, below.

5 The escalators and lifts inside the Pompidou

6 In the 1970s, pictures of the Pompidou

7 The original plans for the floors of the Pompidou

8 The detailed structure of the finished building

> A reminded some people of past building styles.
>
> B were used to decorate everyday objects.
>
> C fitted in well with the external surroundings.
>
> D were situated on one side of the building.
>
> E showed people which area to visit.
>
> F were changed during the construction process.

Exam advice   Matching sentence endings

• <u>Underline</u> the key ideas in the questions and use these to find the right place in the passage. (You will find them in the same order.)

• <u>Underline</u> the key ideas in the sentence endings and match one to each question.

• Read the completed sentences to check they say the same as the passage.

7 <u>Underline</u> the key ideas in Questions 9–14 and use them to find the right place in the passage. Then read each part of the passage carefully in order to answer the questions.

Questions 9–14

Do the following statements agree with the views of the writer in the reading passage?

Write

YES   *if the statement agrees with the views of the writer*

NO   *if the statement contradicts the views of the writer*

NOT GIVEN   *if it is impossible to say what the writer thinks about this*

9 The Pompidou has influenced the way cities are designed.

10 The Guggenheim has been more popular than the Pompidou.

11 The word *building* fits the Pompidou better than the word *construction*.

12 The Pompidou's appearance has changed considerably since it opened.

13 Nowadays, the design of the Pompidou fails to shock people.

14 The traditionalist view of the Pompidou has changed over the years.

Exam advice   Yes / No / Not Given

• Use words in the questions to find the right place in the passage (this applies to 'NOT GIVEN' questions, too).

8 Work in small groups.

1 Is it important for people to like a building in their local area? Why?

2 Are there any buildings that you would recommend to visitors in your country? Why?

Listening
Note completion

Exam information

- You hear one speaker giving a talk on an academic subject.
- Section 4 has no break.

1 **Work in small groups. How much do you remember about the Listening test? Say whether these statements are true (T) or false (F). If you think a statement is false, write what you think is correct.**

1 There are 40 questions in the test: ten in each section.
2 You hear each part twice.
3 You may hear the answers in the recording in a different order from the questions.
4 Section 4 is harder than Section 1.
5 Each question has one mark.
6 You write your answers straight onto the answer sheet.
7 You do not have to spell all words correctly.

2 **Work in pairs. You are going to hear a lecturer giving a talk about traditional house design in Samoa. Before you listen, look at the picture below.**

1 What features of the house does the picture show?
2 What do you think is the purpose of each of these features?
3 How do these features compare with a modern house where you live?

3 **Work in pairs. Look at Questions 1–10 and decide what type(s) of word and what information you need for each gap.**

Questions 1–10

Complete the notes below.

Write **NO MORE THAN TWO WORDS AND/ OR A NUMBER** for each answer.

Traditional Samoan Houses

Overall design

- house: round or **1** ....
- no walls
- **2** .... : to shelter occupants from wind and rain
- floor: **3** .... to control temperature

Roof

- dome-shaped and thatched using **4** .... leaves
- **5** .... sides prevent dampness
- high top permits **6** .... loss

Supporting posts

- made using wood from the **7** .... around the village
- used to show **8** .... of chiefs and speakers at meetings
- attached using rope made by the **9** .... in the village
- rope pulled tightly to form a **10** .... around beams and posts

4 (27) **Now listen to the recording and answer Questions 1–10.**

5 **Work in small groups. Discuss these questions.**

1 Would you like to live in a house like this? Why? / Why not?
2 What does a traditional house in your town/village look like?

Exam advice   *Note completion*

- Use the headings and key ideas in the questions to help you keep your place.
- Read the notes through afterwards to check that they make sense and that words are spelled correctly.

Vocabulary
Word choice

> You can vary and improve your vocabulary by using words that have a similar and sometimes more exact meaning than more common, basic words.

❶ Read these two sentences. Which one is better, and why?

a Old houses in my town have many interesting parts.

b Traditional houses in my town have many interesting features.

❷ Match the words/phrases (1–12) with their synonyms (a–l).

1	high	a	appearance
2	wood	b	apartments
3	(very) important	c	construct
4	build	d	tall
5	make	e	wealthy
6	flats	f	create
7	place	g	enjoyable
8	middle	h	essential
9	look (n)	i	timber
10	rich	j	area
11	nice	k	centre
12	fun	l	attractive

❸ Improve these sentences by replacing the <u>underlined</u> words in each one with an alternative from Exercise 2.

1 There are many ~~high~~ *tall* buildings in the ~~middle~~ *centre* of town.
2 Some modern <u>flats</u> have an amazing <u>look</u>.
3 There are many <u>rich</u> <u>places</u> in Hong Kong.
4 People use <u>wood</u> from the forests to <u>build</u> their homes.
5 It is <u>very important</u> to <u>make</u> parks and gardens in towns.
6 Buying <u>nice</u> furniture for my room was <u>fun</u>.

Speaking
Parts 2 and 3

❶ Work in pairs. Read the Speaking task in the next column and discuss what you could say, making notes as you speak.

> Describe a building that you have enjoyed spending time in.
>
> You should say:
>
> where the building is
>
> what the building looks like
>
> how it feels to be inside the building
>
> and explain why you have enjoyed spending time in this building.

❷ Change partners and take turns to give your talks.

❸ When you have finished your talk, the examiner may ask you a short question. Complete the answers to these questions using one word only.

1 Did you visit this building as a child?
   – Yes, I ....*did*.... . / No I ..*didn't*.. .
2 Have you visited this building recently?
   – Yes, I .... / No, I ....
3 Do your friends like this building?
   – Yes, they .... , actually. / No, they .... really.

❹ Work in pairs. Read the examiner's question and Phillipe's answer below.

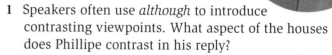

Let's talk about old houses. Do you think old houses should be knocked down so that new homes can be built?

Well, not really. Although some old houses are ugly, others have quite beautiful architecture ... so I don't think we should knock them down.

1 Speakers often use *although* to introduce contrasting viewpoints. What aspect of the houses does Phillipe contrast in his reply?
2 Read Jaeun's answer to the same question and link the ideas together to form an answer using *although* and *so*.

1 .... we need more space to build new homes, some old houses can be turned into flats, **2** .... it's not necessary to knock them down.

◗ Pronunciation: *Sentence stress 3*

❺ ⟨28⟩ **Listen to Jaeun, Billy and Phillipe giving their answers to another question and note down the:**

1 linker they use to introduce a contrast.
2 points that they contrast.

◗ page 129 *Using linkers to contrast or compare*

❻ **Work in pairs.**

1 Read the question and the student's ideas below. How does the student introduce his response?
2 Why does he use *even though*, not *although*, to make a contrast?

In what ways are architects different from builders?

Builders earn less money / architects earn a lot

Well, what they earn is different. Even though builders construct the whole building, architects earn much more money than them. It isn't really fair.

3 Use these contrasting sets of ideas (a–c) to build three more answers to the question above.

	architects	builders
a	design buildings	construct buildings
b	work in an office	work on a building site
c	can become famous	no one knows them

❼ **Work in pairs. Read these questions and brainstorm some ideas for answers. Then change pairs and ask and answer the questions.**

Different types of building

• How is a building such as a school different from a theatre?

• Are modern theatres basically the same as old theatres?

• Which is more important to a town – a sports centre or a museum? Why?

Exam advice   Speaking test

• If the examiner asks you a question on your Part 2 talk, you only need to give a brief reply.

• Use linkers of contrast to show different viewpoints and use sentence stress to help communicate your ideas.

Pronunciation
Sentence stress 3

We use stress to help show a contrast.

❶ ⟨29⟩ **Listen to this sentence from Jaeun's answer and underline the words the speaker stresses. Why does she stress those words?**

Even though some traditional houses looked amazing when they were built, most of them just look old-fashioned now.

❷ **Now work in pairs and take turns to repeat what she says.**

❸ ⟨30⟩ **Underline the words that you think Billy and Phillipe should stress in these sentences, then listen to check your answers.**

1 New houses can look great from the outside, while inside their shape is a bit dull and boring.

2 … whereas some traditional houses in my country have interesting features – like doors and windows – others are just very plain …

❹ **Work in pairs. Take turns to say the sentences in Exercise 3.**

❺ **Take turns to ask and answer these questions, stressing the contrast in your answers.**

Example: *Our hospital is old, while our arts centre is new.*

a What type of buildings are there in your home town or village?

b Which building do you like the most? Why?

c What was your school building like?

d What facilities did your school building have?

Writing
Task 2

❶ Work in pairs. Think about Writing Task 2 and complete the statements below by choosing the correct word from the box.

20	40	fewer	more	notes	paragraphs
parts	plan	punctuation	write		

1 You should spend about .... minutes doing Task 2.
2 You have to write 250 words or ....
3 You should answer all .... of the question.
4 You should not use .... in your answer.
5 It is important to .... your answer quickly first.
6 Leave time to check your grammar and .... at the end.

❷ Work in small groups. Read this Writing task, then answer the questions below.

> Write about the following topic.
>
> *Some people think that buildings such as flats and houses should be designed to last a long time. Others believe that it is more important to provide accommodation quickly and cheaply.*
>
> *Discuss both these views and give your own opinion.*
>
> Give reasons for your answer and include any relevant examples from your own knowledge or experience.

1 How many parts are there to the question? What are they?
2 Why do some buildings last a long time? (building materials? design?)
3 Brainstorm some of the advantages of this. (financial? practical?)
4 Brainstorm reasons why quick, cheap accommodation is sometimes necessary. (People need homes? Disasters happen?)
5 What type of people might have the views in the task?
6 What is your opinion? What types of accommodation are there where you live? Where could you include this in your answer?

❸ Read this sample answer, without paying attention to spelling or punctuation errors, then answer the questions below.

> Most goverments have to build housing for their citizens. As populations grow more homes are needed, and sometimes the demand for accommodation increases rapidly. If people cannot find places to live it is a huge worry for them. They do not care about the quality of their housing – they just need somewhere to live.
>
> In the past, many buildings were carefully designed, and people could see that there external appearance was important. In my contry, some of the most beautiful houses are old ones because they have an interesting shape and the architecture is impressive. Even though they were constructed a long time ago they are still used and they can still cost a lot of mony to buy. For this reason, some people belive that homes today should also be well built, using good materials.
>
> Although I agree with this I also feel that poor people might not think it is fair. Some types of building material are much more expensive then others. Architects are also expensive if you use them. We have a lot of apartment blocks in the area where I live, and people want to live in them. They do not think about how much they cost to build. Unfortunately, these buildings may not last very long, and the occupants may have all sorts of proplems with the building, wich may mean that more homes have to be built.
>
> In conclusion I think that both views are relevant. While city accommodation must be well built so that it does not start to fall down to soon it should also be affordable and availble for people who need it.

1 Where is the writer's answer to the first part of the question?
2 Where is the writer's answer to the second part of the question?
3 Where are the writer's opinions?
4 What words does the writer use to introduce her opinions?
5 Where does the writer give examples of her own knowledge or experience?
6 What examples can you find of linkers used for contrast?

❹ The sample answer contains ten spelling mistakes and is missing six commas. Make the corrections.

▶ page 129 *When to use commas*

❺ Work in small groups. Read this Writing task and discuss the questions below.

> Write about the following topic.
>
> *Some people think that large, impressive buildings are important for a city. Others believe that the money should be spent on improving schools and hospitals.*
>
> *Discuss both these views and give your own opinion.*
>
> Give reasons for your answer and include any relevant examples from your own knowledge or experience.

1 Decide who might have the two opinions in the task, and why.
2 Choose some vocabulary from the unit that might be useful in your answer.
3 Consider how you could include some linkers of contrast.
4 Decide on your own opinion and any personal experience that you could include.
5 Write a plan for your answer.

❻ Now work alone and write an answer to the task. Write at least 250 words.

Key grammar
Modal verbs

> We use modal verbs (*can, could, may, might, must, should* and *have to*) to express possibility, ability and obligation.

❶ Read these sentences (1–8) from the sample answer on page 104 and look at the words in *italics*. Then answer the questions (a–d) in the next column.

1 Most governments *have to* build housing for their citizens.
2 If people *cannot* find places to live, it is a huge worry for them.
3 … people *could* see that their external appearance was important.
4 For this reason, some people believe that homes today *should* also be well built, using good materials.

5 … poor people *might* not think it is fair.
6 Unfortunately, these buildings *may not* last very long …
7 … city accommodation *must* be well built so that it does not start to fall down too soon, …
8 … it *should* also be affordable and available for people who need it.

Which modal verb(s) do we use to:

a say that it is necessary to do something?
....*have to*.... and ....
b express a possibility?
.... and ....
c express ability to do something?
.... and ....
d give strong advice about the right thing to do?
....

▶ page 130 *Modal verbs*

❷ Choose the correct modal in each of these sentences.

1 If a building has thin walls, people (might)/ *have to* hear their neighbours.
2 The museum is free – you *don't have to / mustn't* pay to enter.
3 In my opinion, architects *should / must* be paid less money.
4 Last year, the visitors *can't / couldn't* use the main entrance.
5 Although I *can / may* see the advantages of living in the city, I don't enjoy city life.
6 In my view, city buildings *shouldn't / may not* cost too much money.

❸ ⊙ IELTS candidates often make mistakes using modals. Find and correct the mistakes in the modal verbs in these sentences.

1 Nowadays, we can build a lot of things that we ~~can't~~ in the past.   *couldn't*
2 Some people may are happy to live there.
3 When I was younger, I should to work in my father's building company.
4 Maybe they can't buying a house with their financial problems.
5 Children cannot played in the street now.
6 People have to saved money to buy a home.
7 The police might stops you entering the building.
8 The government must uses the money from taxes for this.

Vocabulary and grammar review **Unit 9**

Vocabulary

❶ Complete these sentences using words connected with water that fit the crossword grid.

1   Lack of rainfall can cause a *drought* .
2   There are various .... methods that you can use to water farmland and crops.
3   Countries that get a lot of rain build .... to collect and store it.
4   Don't go .... if you are afraid of being underwater for long periods.
5   You won't get .... if you take an umbrella!
6   Turn the .... on and fresh water will come out.
7   Exercise can make you very hungry and ....
8   If you .... seawater, you get fresh water.

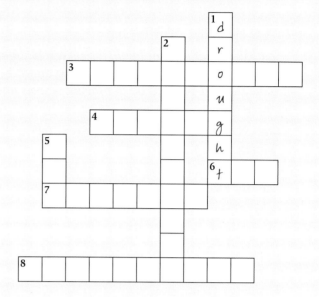

Grammar

❷ Complete each of these sentences with the correct form (active or passive) and tense of the verb in brackets.

1   The first dams *were built* (build) in Middle Eastern countries.
2   Some very early dams .... (destroy) by heavy rain during construction.
3   In the third century, India had a water management system that .... (include) 16 reservoirs and dams.
4   The Romans .... (design) many of the dams still used today.
5   The oldest surviving irrigation system in China includes a dam which .... (make) of earth.
6   Sometimes natural dams .... (create) by animals, such as beavers.
7   Dams .... (classify) according to their height and shape.
8   The word *dam* .... (come) from the Dutch language.
9   Both human and animal life .... (can affect) by the construction of dams.

❸ Complete the short summary of this diagram by choosing a verb from the box and writing it in the correct form (active or passive) and tense.

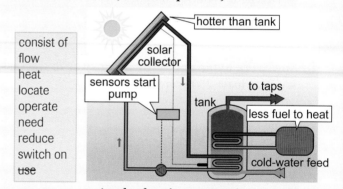

A solar heating system in operation

| consist of |
| flow |
| heat |
| locate |
| operate |
| need |
| reduce |
| switch on |
| ~~use~~ |

Solar water-heating systems **1** .....*use*..... heat from the sun to help produce hot water inside the home. The system **2** .... a solar collector, water pipes, a tank and a pump.
The solar collector **3** .... above the boiler, so a pump **4** .... to move the water around the system. The pump **5** .... by a controller with sensors. If the collector is hotter than the tank, the sensors **6** .... the pump.
The process is very simple. First, cold water **7** .... into the bottom of the boiler. Then it goes up to the roof, where it **8** .... by the solar collector. After that, the water goes back to the tank, and the hot pipes help to heat the water.
This system effectively **9** .... the amount of fuel that the boiler consumes.

Vocabulary and grammar review **Unit 10**

Vocabulary

❶ **Complete the missing letters in the words, then use each word to make a noun phrase (1–7).**

- flexi _ _ _ _ _ _
- _ s c a l _ t o r _
- u _ b _ n
- l a n d _ _ _ _
- e x h i b i t _ _ _
- a r c h _ _ _ _ _ s
- t h a t c h _e_ _d_

1 a _thatched_ roof
2 a .... project
3 lifts and ....
4 the .... hall
5 complete ....
6 .... planning
7 famous ....

❷ **Complete the sentences below with the words in the box.**

| accommodation | appearance | feature | foundations |
| inside | materials | outstanding | surroundings |

1 High-rise buildings can provide more _accommodation_ for people than houses.
2 The rope attachments are an interesting .... of Samoan house design.
3 Wood, concrete and stone are common building ....
4 The architecture outside the building is decorative, but the .... is very plain.
5 Buildings look better if they are designed to fit in with their ....
6 The .... of a tower block must be strong enough to support it.
7 You can still see today that the ancient Greek temples were .... pieces of architecture.
8 The external .... of a new building is very important to local people.

Grammar

❸ **Insert six more missing commas that are necessary in this paragraph.**

Frank Owen Gehry
Frank Owen Gehry lives in Los Angeles⸲California. He has won many prizes for his architecture and many of his buildings are tourist attractions. They include the Guggenheim Museum in Spain the Walt Disney Concert Hall in Los Angeles and the Dancing House in Prague.
As a child Gehry made small buildings out of wood. His mother who was an artist encouraged him to make designs. His father gave him the materials he needed from his shop. He gradually developed an interest in architecture and went to university in southern California.
Although Gehry drew many beautiful designs on paper he didn't become famous straight away. But he built his own home and everything changed. Nowadays he is a celebrity and many people admire his post-modern designs.

❹ **Circle the correct option in *italics* in each sentence.**

1 If the owner agrees, the building (can be)/ has to be decorated.
2 Visitors mustn't *touch / to touch* the exhibits.
3 People have different views on architecture, which is good – they *don't have to / haven't to* agree.
4 In my opinion, the entry fee *shouldn't / mustn't* be so expensive.
5 An unusual design can *encourage / encourages* people to look at a building more closely.
6 The company *had to / must* stop working on the building project last year because of financial problems.
7 You *cannot / can not* tell how old this building is!
8 Many years ago, the government *couldn't / can't* accommodate all its citizens, whereas now it can.

Speaking reference

What to expect in the exam

The Speaking Test is the last part of the IELTS exam and it is normally held on the same day as the other parts.

- The Speaking Test lasts 11–14 minutes and has three parts.
- You do the test on your own.
- There is one examiner in the room, who gives you the instructions, asks the questions and assesses your performance.
- It is recorded for administrative purposes.

Part 1: Introduction and interview

Part 1 lasts between four and five minutes. It consists of:

- a short introduction in which the examiner asks you your name and where you come from, and checks your identification;
- some initial questions about what you do or where you live;
- some questions on topics such as your hobbies and activities, places you know, family celebrations, holidays, etc.

You studied and practised Part 1 in Units 1, 2, 5 and 8.

How to do Part 1

1. Listen carefully to each question the examiner asks you. Think about the topic and the tenses that you need to use.
2. Give relevant replies and try to provide some reasons for your answers.
3. Don't memorise answers, but make sure you know the sort of topics that are often used in Part 1 and learn some vocabulary related to these.
4. Speak clearly so that the examiner can hear and understand you.
5. Try to look confident and relaxed; look at the examiner when you are speaking.
6. If you don't understand a question, ask the examiner to repeat it: *I'm sorry, could you repeat the question, please?*

Part 1 questions

Match each of the questions in the next column (1–9) to an appropriate answer (a–i). Then work with a partner and take turns to ask and give your own answers to the questions.

1. Where do you come from? ....f....
2. Who do you live with? ....
3. How did you get to school when you were a child? ....
4. How often do you use a mobile phone? ....
5. Do you have any pets or animals at home? ....
6. Have you ever written a diary? ....
7. What type of holiday do you prefer? ....
8. Roughly how much water do you drink each day? ....
9. Can you describe the buildings in your town? ....

a. Yes, we have some chickens in our garden, and my uncle has a goat!
b. My brother and I share a flat in the centre of town.
c. Only when I was a little girl. These days, I'm too busy to write something every day.
d. Oh, definitely something active like skiing or camping – I don't like sunbathing very much.
e. Well, I only have it in tea or coffee – I know it's good for you, but I prefer cola or lemonade.
f. I was born in Guangdong province in southern China.
g. They're very old – some of the architecture is quite beautiful, and tourists enjoy coming to see it.
h. Well, I usually make calls and send texts in the morning or the evening because I switch it off when I'm at work.
i. My father always drove me in his car because it was a five-mile trip.

Part 2: Long turn

Part 2 lasts between three and four minutes. The examiner gives you a topic to talk about. The topic is written down and includes some bullet points to guide you. The examiner also gives you some paper and a pencil. You have one minute to prepare for the talk and two minutes to give the talk. When you have finished, the examiner may ask you a short *yes/no* question about the talk.

You studied and practised Part 2 in Units 3, 4, 5, 7, 8, 9 and 10.

How to do Part 2

1. Listen carefully to the instructions. The examiner will tell you how long you have to prepare and to talk.
2. Read the topic carefully, including all the bullet points, which help give you ideas and a structure for your talk.
3. Use the minute's preparation time to write down some key points.

4   Introduce your talk when you start speaking. As you continue, link your points together and give the talk an ending.

5   Don't memorise a talk; the examiner will know if you do this.

6   Aim to speak for two minutes. You don't need to stop until the examiner says 'Thank you'.

7   If the examiner asks you a short question at the end, you only need to give a very brief answer.

Useful language

Introducing your talk

Well, I'm going to talk about …

I'd like to talk about …

Giving a reason/detail/explanation

Also, …

Because …

So …

For example / For instance, …

Introducing a new point

So how/where/what do I …?

The good/bad things were …

When you don't know a word/phrase

What's the word …

I'm not sure how you say this, but …

I don't know what their name is in English.

How can I say it?

Describing the stages in a story

First, … then …

And what else (did we do)?

I have great memories because …

Ending the talk

To finish the talk, …

In all, I think …

All in all, …

Exercise

In pairs, read the instructions and the sample topic in the next column and discuss your ideas for a couple of minutes. Afterwards, spend a minute making some notes on your own and then take turns to give your talk. Try to talk for about two minutes.

Examiner's instructions

Now I'm going to give you a topic and I'd like you to talk about it for one to two minutes. Before you talk, you'll have one minute to think about what you're going to say. You can make some notes if you wish. Do you understand?

Here's a paper and pencil for making notes and here's your topic.

I'd like you to describe someone you would like to meet.

Describe someone you would like to meet.

You should say:

   who this person is/was

   how you know about this person

   what this person does/did

and explain why you would like to meet this person.

Part 3: Two-way discussion

Part 3 lasts between four and five minutes. The examiner asks you questions that are linked to the Part 2 topic. They are very different from the Part 1 questions. In Part 3, the questions are about general, abstract topics, not personal topics. This means that you should give your opinions, rather than talking about yourself. This is your opportunity to show the examiner the full range of your language.

You studied and practised Part 3 in Units 6, 7, 9 and 10.

How to do Part 3

1   Listen carefully to the instructions and questions. Think about what you need to do, e.g. give reasons, explain something, compare two things, agree or disagree, etc.

2   Make sure your replies are relevant and try to say more than you did in Part 1.

3   Don't use memorised answers, but make sure you know the sorts of topic that you may have to talk about in Part 3 (e.g. environmental issues, language and communications, human relationships, education and learning, etc.) and learn some vocabulary and phrases related to them.

4   Speak clearly so that the examiner can understand you.

5   Remember that there are no right or wrong answers. The examiner is interested in hearing whether you can talk fluently about abstract topics and organise your points in a logical way.

Useful language

Starting your response

I think that …

In my view, …

I would say that …

When you are not sure of your answer

Well, I'm not sure.

I think it depends.

Maybe …

Let me think.

Giving reasons

Because …

One/Another reason is …

The problem is …

Perhaps because …

Naming / Giving a list

Well, there are several (ways) …

For a start, …

Also, …

Lastly, …

Comparing and contrasting

Although … / Even though … / Whereas … / While …

Exercise

In pairs, read these instructions and discuss the sample questions. Think about what sort of reply you need to give and write down some useful vocabulary.

Examiner's instructions

We've been talking about someone you would like to meet and I'd like to ask you one or two more general questions related to this.

Let's consider first of all famous people today.

- *What kinds of activity can make people famous today?*
- *How is someone like an inventor different from a singer?*
- *Why do many famous people earn a lot of money?*

Let's move on to talk about famous people from the past.

- *What types of people were famous in the past?*
- *Why do schools teach children about famous people from the past?*
- *Who is more important to society – a famous artist or a politician?*

Then ask each other the questions.

How are you rated?

The examiner listens carefully to your speech and gives you a Band Score from 1 to 9 for the whole test. This means that the three parts are not rated separately. However, there are things that you need to do in order to achieve a certain band.

As the examiner is talking to you, he or she thinks about these questions:

1 How long are your answers? How well can you link your ideas?

2 How much vocabulary can you use, and how accurate is it?

3 How many grammatical structures can you use, and how accurate are they?

4 How well can you pronounce words?

Exercise

Here are some things you should try to do in the Speaking Test. Match each of them (a–j) to one of the questions above (1–4).

a   Be understood, even though you make grammatical mistakes.

b   Give quite long answers in Part 3.

c   Be understood, even though some words are mispronounced.

d   Use a range of different words and phrases.

e   Use a range of linkers.

f   Use some accurate intonation and stress.

g   Be understood, even though you sometimes use the wrong word.

h   Paraphrase when you cannot find the right word.

i   Use a mix of simple and complex sentences.

j   Pause naturally as you speak.

Preparing for the Speaking Test

Part 1

- Build up a list of vocabulary that you can use to talk about the topics that are often used in this part of the test. Start by looking back at page 108 and <u>underlining</u> the topic vocabulary in the questions.

- Practise making statements about yourself in relation to Part 1 topics, e.g. talk about your likes, dislikes and preferences; your activities and when you do them; what you are studying and why; your favourite shop/animal/place; things you did as a child; where you would like to live/travel in the future, etc.

- Keep a list of topics and useful words and phrases in a Speaking notebook, and add to this list when you can.

Part 2

- Practise talking on your own on a topic for two minutes. There are plenty of examples of topics in IELTS practice materials. You can also use the topics in Units 3, 4, 5, 7, 8, 9 and 10 of this book, but think of a different idea from the one you used in the classroom.

- Make a collection of topics. Think of some ideas and vocabulary, and keep a record of them under a topic heading in your notebook.

- Study the model talks in the units. They will show you how to structure a Part 2 talk and how to link ideas. Make a note of any useful vocabulary and linkers.

- Record yourself and practise using some of the Useful language in this section. Also try to include some of the grammatical structures that you have learned on this course, such as comparisons, conditionals, relative clauses, etc. When you first practise, allow yourself the time you need.

- When the test date is near, use practice tests and try to spend only a minute preparing for your talk. Make sure you have a fairly good idea of how much you need to say to fill two minutes.

Part 3

- Build up a list of Part 3 Speaking topics in your notebook and record some vocabulary that you can use to talk about them. Start by re-reading the articles in this book and checking the relevant Word lists. Topics like transport, education, tourism, architecture, etc. are common Part 3 topics.

- Develop your ideas by reading some articles on international topics such as city life, pollution, nature, the rich and poor, etc.

- Practise expressing views on the issues, using some of the Useful language on page 110. Write a list of questions, with a friend or classmate if possible, and then practise answering them, e.g.:

1 Why do some people want to live in big cities?

   I think one reason is that they want a well-paid job and it's harder to get that in the country. Perhaps another reason is that they prefer a crowded place to a quiet place.

2 How can drivers be encouraged to leave their cars at home?

3 When do people make changes in their lives?

For all parts, record yourself speaking and ask a teacher / native speaker to point out:

- how clearly you speak;

- any individual sounds or words that you don't pronounce clearly;

- how effectively you group words and phrases;

- how well you use stress to emphasise words;

- whether you need to use more or less intonation.

On the test day

Remember these important points because they may affect your mark.

- **Listen carefully to the examiner's questions and instructions**
  Each answer you give should be relevant. If you cannot understand the examiner, ask him/her to repeat the question.

- **Smile at the examiner and look interested**
  Communication works better for everyone if people are interested in what they are saying.

- **Make sure the examiner can hear you**
  If you speak too softly, too quickly or not clearly enough, the examiner may mark you down for pronunciation and may be unable to judge your true language level.

- **Provide enough language for the examiner to assess**
  Examiners can only rate what they hear. Even if you know a lot of English, you won't get a high mark if you don't say enough to demonstrate your true language ability.

- **Use your imagination**
  There are no right or wrong answers to the questions. If you don't have any experience of the Part 2 topic, think about something you have read or seen on television, or make something up. If you don't have a view on a Part 3 question, imagine one that someone else might have.

- **Be prepared and be confident**
  The Speaking Test materials are designed to help you talk as much as possible. During the test, the examiner will cover a number of different topics and will encourage you to speak. If you are well prepared, you should feel confident enough to do your best.

Writing reference

What to expect in the exam

The Writing Test is the third paper in the exam and it takes place after the Reading Test.

You do two tasks in one hour:

- Task 1 is a summary of one or more charts or diagrams on the same subject;
- Task 2 is a discursive essay. (There is only one topic.)

Task 1

In this task, you must summarise and compare information from one or more graphs, charts, tables or diagrams.

Your summary must be at least 150 words long. You may write more than this, but if you write less, you will lose some marks. You should spend about 20 minutes on this task.

You should try to:

- include all the key points;
- include some details or data from the graphs or charts to support the key points;
- compare some of the information;
- include an overview;
- organise your answer in a logical way;
- use relevant vocabulary;
- use your own words where possible, rather than copying from the question;
- write grammatically correct sentences;
- use accurate spelling and punctuation;
- write in a formal academic style (not bullet points or note form).

You studied and practised Writing Task 1 in Units 1, 3, 5, 7 and 9.

How to do Task 1

1 Read the instructions and study the headings and information carefully. Find at least three key points and decide which features you should compare. (Allow between two and three minutes.)

2 Decide how many paragraphs to write and what to put in each one. Decide what will go in your overview. (Allow between two and three minutes.)

3 Write your answer, allowing a couple of minutes to check it through afterwards. (15 minutes)

Graphs, charts and diagrams

There are different types of visual information that you will have to deal with.

1 Pie charts showing how 100% of something is divided up into smaller percentages

Look at the Writing task below.

1 Say what the pie chart shows.

2 Select two key points on the pie chart.

3 What extra information does the table provide?

4 What are the key points in the table?

5 What tense should you use to write about the information?

The pie chart and table below give information on tourist arrivals in Nepal in March 2008.

Summarise the information by selecting and reporting the main features, and make comparisons where relevant.

Tourism in Nepal, South Asia, 2008

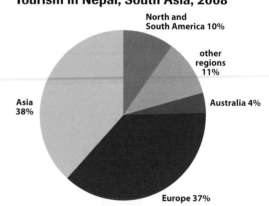

Increase in numbers from March 2007	
Asia	+188
Europe	+3,321
Australia	+426
other regions	+932
North and South America	+1,043
Total	+5,910
Percentage increase 16%	

---

6 Read the sample answer on page 113. <u>Underline</u> the writer's key points.

7 Are the data that support the key points accurate?

8 Read the answer again. <u>Underline</u> the words that the writer uses to contrast information.

Sample answer

The pie chart shows where tourists to Nepal came from in March 2008, while the table shows the increase in tourist numbers from March 2007.

In March 2008, more than three-quarters of the tourists in Nepal were from Asia (38 percent) or Europe (37 percent). On the other hand, the smallest percentage of tourists, four percent, were from Australia. The remaining 21 percent of tourists travelled to Nepal from America or other regions.

The total number of tourists who visited Nepal in March 2008 went up by 5,910. This represented a 16-percent increase from the same month in the previous year. However, the increase in tourists from each region varied. Whereas numbers from Asia increased very slightly, by 188 people, the number of visitors from Europe and America rose considerably.

Thus tourists arrived in Nepal from two main areas of the world, and between March 2007 and 2008, tourist numbers increased from all the areas on the chart. However, the growth from Europe was the biggest.

2 Charts and graphs showing trends over time

Look at the Writing task below.

1 What do the figures represent on the vertical axis?

2 What period of time does the graph cover?

3 What are the key points on the graph?

4 How could you organise the information into paragraphs?

The chart below shows the number of Apple iPhones sold between June 2007 and December 2010.

Summarise the information by selecting and reporting the main features, and make comparisons where relevant.

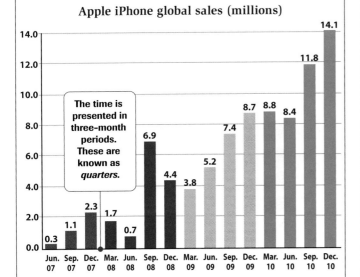

Apple iPhone global sales (millions)

The time is presented in three-month periods. These are known as *quarters*.

5 Read the sample answer below. Underline any words/phrases that the writer uses to describe trends, including prepositions.

Sample answer

The graph gives information on the sale of iPhones around the world over a period of almost four years.

During this period, sales increased enormously, although there was some fluctuation. Between June 2007 and June 2008, the number of iPhones that were sold rose from 0.3 million to 2.3 million in December, but then fell back to 0.7 million. However, in the next quarter, sales increased by more than 6 million units and reached a peak of 6.9 million.

After September 2008, there was another drop in sales to 3.8 million, but then in June 2009, they began to rise again and the figures show a considerable increase, to 8.8 million in March 2010. This was followed by a very slight decrease in June 2010 and then another big increase over the next two quarters, to 14.1 million in December 2010.

Clearly, there has been an upward trend in global sales figures over the period, and the most significant growth was in 2008.

6 Read the answer again. Underline the introduction and the overview.

3 Tables showing information in rows and columns

Look at the Writing task below.

1 What comparisons could you make between the table and the graph?

2 What should you put in your overview?

The table and graph below give information on the weather in Dubai. The graph shows annual rainfall and the table shows annual temperatures.

Summarise the information by selecting and reporting the main features, and make comparisons where relevant.

Month	Average minimum temperature °C	Average maximum temperature °C
Jan–Feb	14	25
Mar–Apr	17	32
May–Jun	24	37
Jul–Aug	29	48
Sep–Oct	27	35
Nov–Dec	19	26

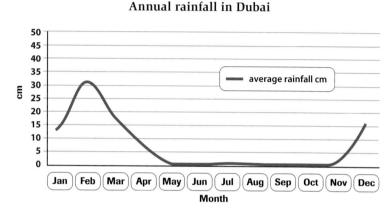

Annual rainfall in Dubai

---

3 Read this sample answer. How has the writer organised the information?

> Note how the writer has changed the words in the task to her own vocabulary.

Sample answer

The table and graph show the average temperatures in Dubai and how much rainfall there is over a year.

The table shows that Dubai is a warm place. The hottest temperatures are between June and September, and the coolest months are from November to March. In July and August, temperatures can range from 29 to 48 degrees. It then gets cooler towards the end of the year. The lowest temperatures are around 14 degrees from January to February, but it can still rise to around 25 or 26 degrees during this season.

According to the graph, there is almost no rain in Dubai between June and October, so this is a dry season. However, there is some rain at other times of the year. In February, annual rainfall peaks at 32 centimetres and then falls gradually to under five centimetres in May. In November, there is a little rain, and this increases to 15 centimetres in December.

Overall, Dubai has rain in the cooler winter months and is dry during the hot summer months.

4 Read the sample answer again. Which figures has the writer included, and why?

4 Diagrams showing a process and/or how something works

Look at the Writing task below.

1 What similarities and differences can you see in the diagrams? (Explain them to a partner.)

2 What vocabulary will you use?

3 What tense and verb forms will you use?

The diagrams on the right show two types of building design that help reduce the effects of earthquakes.

Summarise the information by selecting and reporting the main features, and make comparisons where relevant.

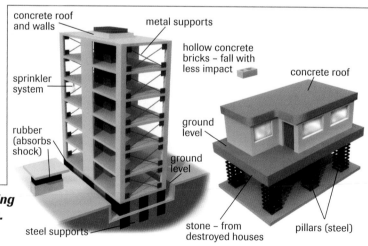

Earthquake-resistant buildings

4 Read the sample answer on the right. How has the writer organised the key information? Where is the overview?

5 Read the answer again and underline the passive verb forms. Why has the writer used the passive?

Sample answer

The diagrams show an apartment block and a house that were built in areas that have earthquakes. Some aspects of the two buildings are similar, but there are also differences.

Both the buildings are rectangular and both have flat roofs that are made of concrete. They also have steel pillars that go deep into the ground. However, the apartment block also has rubber sections that absorb shocks and let the building move.

The apartment block is much taller than the house, so the walls are constructed using concrete. Metal bars are also placed in each wall. The house, on the other hand, is made of hollow bricks, because if they fall, they will cause less damage.

While recycled stone was used for the floor of the house, the high-rise building has modern features, including sprinkler systems to prevent fires.

Overall, the design of each type of building is related to its size and its purpose, but they clearly show how to help a building stand up during an earthquake.

> Note that some words, like *concrete* and *steel*, cannot be changed.

> Use synonyms of key words if you know them, e.g. *build* and *construct*.

> Note the use of the present tense to describe the features of the buildings and the past tense to describe their construction.

Task 2

This task is in the form of a statement and question(s). There may be more than one part to discuss, and you need to give your own opinion.

Your answer must be at least 250 words long. You can write more than this, but if you write less, you will lose some marks. You should spend about 40 minutes on this task. There are twice as many marks for Part 2 as for Part 1.

You should try to:

- discuss all the questions in the task;
- present main ideas and support these with examples;
- include relevant examples from your own experience;
- write a conclusion;
- organise your answer, using paragraphs;
- use linking words and phrases to connect your ideas;
- use your own words where possible and avoid copying from the question;
- write grammatically correct sentences;
- use accurate spelling and punctuation;
- write in a formal academic style – not points or notes.

You studied and practised Writing Task 2 in Units 2, 4, 6, 8 and 10.

How to do Task 2

1   Read the instructions carefully. Decide how many parts there are to the question and underline them. Decide what your view is on the topic. (Allow between two and three minutes.)

2   Quickly think of some ideas and write a plan. Decide how many paragraphs to write and what to put in each one. Decide what you want to put in your conclusion. (Allow between three and four minutes.)

3   Write your answer, allowing up to five minutes to check it through afterwards.

Task 2 questions

There are different types of Task 2 question. Here are some examples.

Advantages and disadvantages

Read the Writing task below.

1   What two points of view are presented in the first sentence? Underline the key words.

2   Which point of view do you agree with most? Why?

> *Some people like to travel to somewhere new and different when they go on holiday, while others prefer familiar places.*
>
> *Do you think there are more advantages or disadvantages to visiting new places?*
>
> Give reasons for your answer and include any relevant examples from your own knowledge or experience.

3   Read the sample answer on the right and complete the lists of advantages and disadvantages in these notes.

Notes

Advantages

• Travel about **1** exploration. – more to **2** ....
• **3** .... , e.g. food, scenery
• Better **4** .... of other cultures, e.g. homes, clothes, music

Disadvantages

• More **5** .... , e.g. making **6** ....
• Can **7** .... , e.g. booking restaurants and **8** ....

Sample answer

Most people take a holiday during the year, and when they book their holiday, they have a choice. They can go somewhere they know well or they can go to a place that they have never visited before. This second option has positive and negative aspects.

> Write a short introduction to the essay.

In my view, travel is really about exploration. Although it is reassuring to go to a place you know, there is less to discover because you have been there before, whereas you can have new experiences in a city or country that you have not visited. For example, you may eat food you have never tried or see scenery that is very unusual.

What is more, I think the most important advantage of visiting a new place is that you develop your understanding of the world. You can read about other cultures, but I think it is better to go where other people live and see the clothes they wear, the music they like and so on.

> Link new paragraphs to previous paragraph using appropriate linkers.

However, there are some disadvantages when you go to new places. Firstly, it is more stressful, as it takes longer to make all the travel arrangements. When I went away last summer, I spent hours booking the holiday. Secondly, it is easy to make mistakes. When you have been to a place before, you know which restaurants and trips to avoid.

All in all, I think there are more advantages if you go somewhere new because it makes a change. If human beings do the same things all the time, they will not develop new interests or find out about the world.

> Sum up your points and give your opinion.

4   Read the answer again. How has the student used her notes to write the answer?

5   Has the student answered the question about advantages and disadvantages?

To what extent do you agree?

Read the Writing task below.

1 Do you agree with the opening statement in the task? Why?

2 Are there any places in the world where people do not need to worry about how much water they use? Why?

> **As water is a valuable resource, governments all over the world should control how much water their citizens use.**
>
> **To what extent do you agree or disagree with this statement?**
>
> *Give reasons for your answer and include any relevant examples from your own knowledge or experience.*

3 Read this sample answer and underline the main and supporting ideas. What examples does the writer use?

Sample answer

Everyone knows that we need water to survive. We also use it for many of our daily activities. However, some countries have access to a lot of water, while others do not. Does this mean that we should all use less? I think it depends on where you live.

The amount of water a country has is linked to its weather. In parts of Europe, for example, people do not worry about water supplies because they have a lot of rainfall. Occasionally their country has a dry period, but it is not long enough to cause any serious problems. In my view, it is not necessary to control water use in these countries.

In other parts of the world, such as Africa, Australia and the Middle East, many people experience drought. Here, people know that they have to conserve water and they cannot use too much. There may be government controls about using water, for things like recreation or washing cars, but sometimes water is so hard to find or collect that controls are not needed.

Sometimes weather patterns change, and in some countries this can cause an unusual situation. A place that usually has rain may have none. I think these governments should tell people to use less water all through the year. Then, if a drought comes, they will be able to deal with it.

In conclusion, different parts of the world have different needs. While it is important to limit water use in some countries, it is impossible or unnecessary to do this in others.

4 Read the answer again and find the writer's views. Does the writer clearly answer the question 'To what extent do you agree or disagree …'?

5 Underline the vocabulary that is linked to the topic of water.

Two questions to answer

Read the Writing task below.

1 What two points does *this* refer back to?

2 Why is the example in brackets?

> Both questions must be covered

> **Animal habitats have been destroyed, and some animal species (e.g. the tiger and the rhino) have become endangered.**
>
> **Why does this happen?**
>
> **What can be done to protect endangered animals?**
>
> *Give reasons for your answer and include any relevant examples from your own knowledge or experience.*

3 Read this sample answer. In which paragraphs are the writer's answers to each question in the task?

Sample answer

> animals

Animals and human beings have to live together. Sometimes, however, we only think about ourselves and we do things that harm animals or the places where they live.

In the past, humans hunted animals for food and clothing. Nowadays, we hunt them for other reasons. In my view, this is wrong. We should not make money by taking away an animal's life. There are so few tigers and whales in the world today that they are protected species. However, it may be too late now to increase their numbers significantly.

Other activities that threaten animals' lives include cutting down forests and building roads and railways on farmland or grassland. This happens in my country and in many other parts of the world, and it destroys animal habitats. If animals cannot produce any young, they will not survive. However, large organisations do not always think about the effects of their activities.

In my opinion, anything that puts animals' lives in danger should be controlled. Governments can fine hunters and put up signs to warn them. If forests are cut down, the organisations that do this should ensure that they do not remove too many trees in one area.

Another way to protect animals is to provide safe areas for them to live and breed. Sometimes special areas are created in bushland, such as game reserves in Africa. Other methods are building animal sanctuaries and taking some animals there to breed. This is what is happening with the giant panda in China.

Overall, I think that there are many ways that we can look after endangered animals. Both governments and individuals have a responsibility to do this.

4 Read the answer again. What do the underlined words refer back to?

Useful language

Giving your opinions

In my view/opinion, …

I think/believe …

Introducing other people's opinions

Some people say/think …

Presenting reasons/examples

For example, …

Because (of) …

As …

Adding information

Also, …

What is more, …

Comparing and contrasting

In the past, … Nowadays, …

However, …

Although / Even though, …

On the other hand, …

While/Whereas …

Giving personal experience

In my country/town/home/family, …

Where I live, …

Concluding

In conclusion, …

Overall, …

All in all, …

Preparing for the Writing Test

For Task 1, practise summarising the information in a range of different charts and diagrams. You can find examples by doing an internet image search or you can use newspaper articles, school science books and some magazine articles.

For Task 2, practise writing arguments on a range of different topics. There are plenty of examples in academic study-skills books and other IELTS practice materials. Make a collection for your IELTS preparation.

Before you write, brainstorm some ideas and then select your main ideas and organise them into paragraphs.

Study the sample answers in the units and in this Writing reference. They have been written to show you how to structure an answer and how to link ideas. Make note of any useful vocabulary that has been used and use it in your own work.

If you are doing a course with a teacher, look back at the corrections in pieces of work that he or she has marked. Try to avoid making the same mistakes again. Aim to use some of the grammatical structures that you have learned on this course, e.g. conditionals and relative clauses.

When you first practise, use as much time as you need. As the test date approaches, use practice tests and try to write each answer in 20 minutes for Task 1 and 40 minutes for Task 2.

On the test day

Remember these points because they affect your mark.

Task 1

- **Make sure you fully understand the data**
  Study the task first and make sure you understand it.

  - If it is a graph or chart, look carefully at the axes. Don't just look at the figures – look at any labels or keys as well.

  - If it is a table, look at all the headings.

  - If it is a diagram, look at all the steps or stages in the process or structure.

- **Include the key points**
  Decide on at least three key points and make sure you highlight these in your answer.

- **Include some data and make sure they are accurate**
  Make sure that the figures or details that you include to illustrate your key points are accurate.

- **Include an overview of the information**
  The overview is like a conclusion and it gives your reader a simple picture of what the graphic shows overall. It is not the same as the introduction, which states what the information is about. The overview usually goes at the end of the answer, but it doesn't have to. As long as it is there, you will get credit for it. If it is not there, you will lose marks.

Task 2

- **Make sure you understand the question**
  Take time to read the question very carefully. <u>Underline</u> the parts you have to write about and ask yourself:

  - What is the main topic?

  - What other points do I need to cover?

  - How many parts are there?

  - Do I need to present arguments for and against?

  - What is my opinion?

- **Introduce your essay**
  The introduction sets the scene for your readers. It tells them what you are going to discuss, what the issues are, and often what your opinion is.

- **Make your opinion on the topic clear to the reader**
  Decide on your view and state this clearly in your essay. Make sure your view is consistent.

- **Include some main ideas**
  Decide on at least three main ideas and some supporting points. Build your paragraphs around your main ideas. Ideas can come from other people's opinions, your own opinions, facts, etc.

- **Include some personal experience**
  Make sure this is relevant to the question. You only need to write a sentence on this, and if you have no personal experience, you do not need to worry. Just say *Although I have no personal experience of this, I think* …

- **Draw a conclusion**
  At the end of your essay, you need to write one or two sentences that summarise your arguments and your point of view.

How are you rated?

The two tasks are rated separately, but Task 2 is worth twice as many marks as Task 1. The marks are combined to produce one Band Score from 1 to 9 for the whole test.

There are levels of performance that you need to reach in order to achieve a certain band.

The examiner considers these questions:

Task 1

- Have you understood the task and the data/diagram(s)?

- Have you included all the key points?

- Is there an overview?

Task 2

- Have you understood the task?

- Have you covered all the parts/questions in the task?

- Is your opinion clear?

- Have you presented relevant ideas?

Both tasks

- How well have you organised the answer? Is there a range of linkers? Can you use referencing?

- How adequate is your vocabulary, and how accurate is it?

- How many different grammatical structures can you use, and how accurate are they?

Language reference

Unit 1

Present simple and present continuous

Present simple

Forms

affirmative	I / You / We / They **come** from Cairo. He / She / It **comes** from Cairo.
negative	I / You / We / They **do not** (**don't**) **come** from Cairo. He / She / It **does not** (**doesn't**) **come** from Cairo.
question	**Do** I / you / we / they **come** from Cairo? **Does** he / she / it **come** from Cairo?

Uses

We use the present simple:

- to describe something that is always true or something that is permanent:
  Children **learn** languages more quickly than adults.
  Hanan **lives** in Muttrah.

- to describe an activity that happens regularly:
  I **do** my homework every Friday evening.

- with thoughts and feelings using these verbs:
  believe, know, remember, think (meaning believe),
  feel (meaning believe), suppose, love, like, want,
  dislike, hate, prefer, etc.:
  I **love** my city.

Present continuous

Forms

affirmative	I **am** (**I'm**) **eating** lunch. He / She / It **is** (**He's** / **She's** / **It's**) **eating** lunch. We / You / They **are** (**We're** / **You're** / **They're**) **eating** lunch.
negative	I **am** (**I'm**) **not studying**. He / She / It **is not** (**isn't**) **studying**. We / You / They **are not** (**aren't**) **studying**.
question	**Am** I **making** too much noise? **Is** he / she / it **making** too much noise? **Are** we / you / they **making** too much noise?

Uses

We use the present continuous to talk about:

- something happening now:
  She**'s making** some notes.

- a situation which is changing or developing:
  Your English **is improving**.

- an activity which is in progress, but not exactly now:
  She**'s studying** chemistry in Wuzan.

- a temporary situation:
  He**'s living** in a student hostel while he's in England.

Spelling changes when we make nouns plural

We make most nouns plural by adding –s:
book → books

However:

- for nouns ending in –ch, –o, –s and –sh, we add –es:
  match → matches; mass → masses

- for nouns ending in –y (e.g. study), we change –y to –i and add –es:
  study → studies

- when the word ends in –ay, –ey or –oy, we don't change –y to –i:
  toy → toys

- when the noun ends in –f or –fe, we often, but not always, change the –f to –v:
  knife → knives

Some nouns are irregular:
man → men; woman → women; child → children;
foot → feet; tooth → teeth

Notes

- Some nouns ending in –ics are singular:
  politics, physics

- These nouns ending in –s may be singular or plural:
  species, series, means:
  The zoo contains one **species** of elephant and two **species** of kangaroo.

Unit 2

Past simple
Forms

1 Verb *to be*

affirmative	I / He / She / It **was** busy. We / You / They **were** busy.
negative	I / He / She / It **was not** (wasn't) busy. We / You / They **were not** (weren't) busy.
question	**Was** I / he / she / it busy? **Were** we / you / they busy?

2 Other verbs

- Regular verbs form the past with *–ed*:
  arrive → *arrived*
- Many verbs have an irregular past form (see *Common irregular verbs* on page 131):
  write → *wrote*

affirmative	I / He / She / It / We / You / They **arrived** *yesterday.*
negative	I / He / She / It / We / You / They **did not** (didn't) **arrive** *yesterday.*
question	**Did** I / he / she / it / we / you / they **arrive** *yesterday?*

Uses

We use the past simple to describe:

- actions or events in the past:
  *I **visited** New Zealand in 2010.*
- things which happened for a long time in the past:
  *Freya **lived** in Italy for many years.*

Some meanings of affixes

Adding syllables before or after a word (affixes) changes or adds meaning to a word. Affixes before a word are called prefixes; after a word, they are called suffixes.

- *–ist* and *–ant* (like *–er*) mean 'someone who does a thing':
  scientist = someone who works in science
  applicant = someone who applies
- *–ment* means 'something which does a thing':
  advertisement = a thing which advertises
- *–ise*, *–ate* and *–ify* mean 'to make or do this thing':
  summarise = make a summary
  solidify = make something solid
- *–able* means 'able to do/be a thing':
  enjoyable = you can enjoy it
- *im-*, *in-*, *dis-* and *un-* give a word a negative meaning:
  impossible = not possible
  unopened = not unopened

- *pre–* means 'before':
  preheated = heated earlier/beforehand.
- *re–* means 'doing the thing again':
  reread = read again

Spelling changes when adding *–ed* to verbs

We double the final consonant* when we add *–ed* to:

- a one-syllable verb which ends in consonant–vowel*–consonant:
  stop → *stopped*
- verbs of two or more syllables which end in consonant–vowel–consonant and the final syllable is stressed:
  admit → *admitted*

We don't double the final consonant when:

- there are two final consonants:
  end → *ended*
- there are two vowels before the final consonant:
  appear → *appeared*
- the verb ends in a vowel:
  save → *saved*
- the stress is not on the final syllable:
  open → *opened*
- the verb ends in *–w*, *–x* or *–y*:
  play → *played*

A final *–y* after a consonant becomes *i*.
carry → *carried*

* Consonants are *b*, *c*, *d*, *f*, *g*, etc. Vowels are *a*, *e*, *i*, *o* and *u*.

Pronunciation of verbs + *–ed*

When we add *–ed* to:

- verbs ending in the sounds /tʃ/, /k/, /p/ and /ʃ/, we pronounce *–ed* as /t/:
  risked
- verbs ending in the sounds /d/ and /t/, we pronounce *–ed* as /ɪd/:
  stated
- all other verbs, we pronounce *–ed* as /d/:
  entered

Also, *and*, *but* and *however*

And

We use *and* to join things.

- We can join the final thing on a list to the rest of the list:
  *I'm studying physics, biology **and** chemistry.*
- We can join two similar adjectives when they don't come before a noun:
  *The journey was long **and** dangerous.*

- We can join two sentences which do not express different ideas:
  *At school, children learn to work hard **and** they learn to study.*

Note: We do not usually join more than two sentences with *and*.

Also

Also means 'and'.

- We use *also* to add extra information or an extra opinion to things we have already said:
  *Children should learn good behaviour from their parents. They should **also** learn to behave well at school.*

- We cannot use *also* to join two sentences, but we can place it at the beginning, in the middle or at the end of the second sentence:
  *A good education is expensive. **Also** it takes a long time. / It **also** takes a long time. / It takes a long time **also**.*

But

We use *but* to join:

- sentences when the information or opinion in the second sentence is different from the first sentence:
  *It is hard work looking after children, **but** it is enjoyable.*

- two adjectives which seem to have opposite meanings:
  *My brother is clever, **but** lazy.*

- We normally use a comma before *but* (see *When to use commas*, page 129).

However

- *However* means 'but'.
- We cannot use it to join sentences.
- We use *however* at the beginning of a sentence to say something different from the sentence before:
  *Many children don't enjoy helping in the house. **However**, it teaches them to be responsible.*

- *However* is usually followed by a comma.

Unit 3

Making comparisons

We can compare information using comparative and superlative adjectives and adverbs.

- We use comparative adjectives (+ *than*) to compare people, things, places or events:
  *Bicycles are **quieter than** cars.*

- We use comparative adverbs (+ *than*) to compare actions:
  *You can get to work **more quickly** by car **than** by bus.*

- We use *the* + a superlative adjective or adverb to compare one person or thing with everyone or everything else in the group:
  *I find trains **the most comfortable** means of transport.*

Forming comparative and superlative adjectives and adverbs

We add –*er* and –*est* to:

- one-syllable adjectives:
  *slow**er** (than), the fast**est***
- two-syllable adjectives ending in –*y* (note that the –*y* changes to *i*):
  *easi**er** (than), the happi**est***
- one-syllable adverbs:
  *fast**er** (than), the **hardest***

We add *more* and *most* to:

- adjectives with two or more syllables (except two-syllable adjectives ending in –*y* – see above):
  ***more** efficient (than), the **most** complicated*
- adverbs with two or more syllables:
  ***more** easily (than), the **most** dangerously*

Some adjectives have irregular comparative and superlative forms:

good, better, best

bad, worse, worst

far, farther/further, farthest/furthest

many, more, most

much, more, most

little, less, least

Some adverbs have irregular comparative and superlative forms:

badly, worse, worst

well, better, best

To say one thing is less than another, use *less* and *least* before the adjective or adverb:
*Travelling by plane is **less** dangerous than travelling by car.*

Spelling changes when adding –er and –est to adjectives

- We double the final consonant when we add –*er* and –*est* to adjectives which end in consonant–vowel–consonant:
  thin, thinner, thinnest
- We don't double the final consonant when:
  - there are two final consonants:
    old, older, oldest
  - there are two vowels before the final consonant:
    clear, clearer, clearest
  - the adjective ends in a vowel:
    safe, safer, safest
  - the adjective ends in –*w* or –*x*:
    slow, slower, slowest
- Change a final –*y* to *i*:
  funny, funnier, funniest

Unit 4

Deciding the type of word

When we don't know the meaning of a word we read, it's helpful to first decide what type of word it is (noun, verb, adjective, etc.). This will help us to:

- get closer to the meaning if we are guessing the meaning from the context;
- choose the correct definition if we are using a dictionary. For example, if you look up *design* in the online version of the *CLD* (at http://dictionaries.cambridge.org), you will find:
  – design *n*
  – design *v*

If you know what type of word it is, you will know which definition to click on.

We can tell what type of word it is by the words near it and its position in the sentence.

Nouns …

- often have *a*, *an* or *the* before them:
  *They produced **a design** for **the house**.*
- usually end in –*s* if they are plural:
  *His **designs** have been very popular with the public.*
- come near the beginning of a sentence before a verb:
  *The **design impressed** us.*
- come after a verb:
  *They **chose** my **design**.*
- often have adjectives before them:
  *It was an **unusual design**.*

Verbs …

- are often in a tense formed by –*ed* or –*ing* and with an auxiliary verb (*is / are / have / has / may / will*, etc.) before them:
  *They **are designing** a new bridge.*
- usually come after a noun or pronoun (*he*, *it*, *they*, etc.):
  ***He designed** the first one in 1904.*
- do not usually come at the beginning of a sentence unless in the –*ing* form:
  ***Designing** the new bridge was his first job.*
- have *to* before them in the infinitive:
  *He decided **to design** it using recycled materials.*

Adjectives …

- usually come before nouns:
  *an **unusual design***
- can come after the verbs *be* (*is*, *was*, etc.), *become*, *feel*, *grow*:
  *The design **was extraordinary**.*
  *The climbers soon **became exhausted**.*

Present perfect

Forms

affirmative	I / You / We / They **have taken** photos. He / She / It **has taken** photos.
negative	I / You / We / They **haven't arrived**. He / She / It **hasn't arrived**.
question	**Have** I / you / we / they **finished**? **Has** he / she / it **finished**?

Uses

We use the present perfect to describe:

* something which started in the past and still continues now:
  I've lived in Guangzhou all my life. (I was born there and I still live there now.)

* things which happened in the past, but no time is given and they have a result in the present:
  *There's no class today because our teacher **has gone** on holiday.* (She went on holiday sometime in the past and the result in the present is that there's no class today.)

For and *since*

For

* We use *for* + a number of hours/days/years, etc. to say how long something has been happening:
  *He has worked here **for 12 years**.*

* We use the present perfect + *for* to say how long something has been happening and is still happening now:
  *I've had this camera **for** six months.*

* We use the past simple + *for* to say how long something happened that started and finished in the past:
  *My piano lesson **lasted for** two hours.*

Since

* We use *since* + a time in the past to say when something started which is still happening now:
  *I've had this car **since January**.*

* We always use *since* with the present perfect because it means 'from [that time in the past] till now':
  *The price of food **has increased since** 2005.*

Unit 5

Directions and prepositions of place

Directions

When we give directions, here are some things we say:

* Continue / Go straight on/ ahead (until you reach ...):
  Go straight on until you reach the lake.

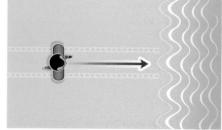

* Go/Continue past ...:
  Continue past the picnic area till you reach the exit.

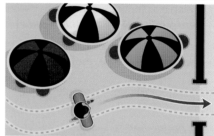

* Go/Turn left/ right at the ...:
  Turn right at the bank.

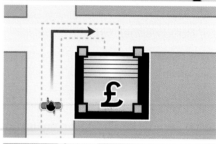

* Take the first/ second/third, etc. turning on your left/ right: *Take the second turning on your left.*

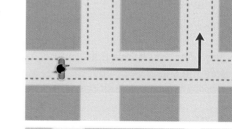

* Cross ...:
  Cross the square, then turn right.

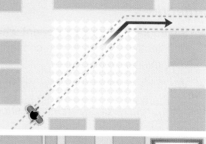

* Follow ...:
  Follow the road until you come to the post office.

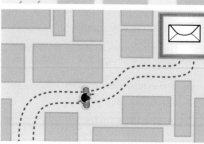

Prepositions of place

We use the following words and phrases to say where things/places are, or where we are.

at

We use *at*:

- when we think of a place as a point:
  at *the traffic lights,* **at** *the crossroads*

- with *the front/back/top/bottom/end of*:
  She stood **at the top of** *the stairs.*
  The house was **at the end of** *the road.*

- with events:
  I met him **at** *the film festival.*

- with the expressions *at home, at work, at school, at university.*

in

We use *in*:

- when we think of a place as an area, or larger than a particular point (see *at* above):
  I live **in** *the centre of London.*

- with *line, queue* and *street*:
  She lives **in** *Saad Zaghlool Street.* (but *She lives* **at** *23 Saad Zaghlool Street.*)

- with the expressions *in bed, in hospital, in class, in prison.*

on

We use *on*:

- when we think of a place as a surface:
  There's a spider **on** *the ceiling.*

- when we think of a place as being part of a line:
  There are three hotels **on** *the road to Perth.*

- with *left* and *right*:
  It's **on** *your* **right** *after the post office.*

- with *corner/bend*:
  The bank is **on** *the* **corner** *of the street.*

above

We use *above* to say something is in a higher position than something else:
The lions live on a hill **above** *the lake.*

over

We use *over* to say something is directly above something else:
They put a roof **over** *the monkeys' enclosure.*

below

We use *below* to say something is in a lower position than something else:
They stayed in a village **below** *the mountains.*

under

We use *under* to say something is directly below something else:
There's a mouse sitting **under** *your chair!*

behind

We use *behind* to say something is at the back of something else:
The giraffes are **behind** *the zebras' enclosure.*

in front of

We use *in front of* to say something is close to the front of something else:
Delia is standing **in front of** *the restaurant.*

opposite

We use *opposite* to say something is in front of something else, but on the other side:
The café is **opposite** *the information centre.* (in front of the information centre, but on the opposite side of the road)

between

We use *between* to say that something is in the space which separates two other things:
My village is **between** *the sea and the mountains.*

next to

We use *next to* to say something is very close to something else with nothing between:
Tasha and Fatma sat **next to** *each other so they could do the crossword together.*

Types of word and word endings

Word endings (or suffixes) often help us to know what type of word it is.

- Words ending in these suffixes are always nouns:
  –ness: heaviness
  –ity: ability

- Words ending in these suffixes are often, but not always nouns:
  –ment: environment
  –ion: information
  –er / –or: doctor
  –ance: entrance

- Words ending in *–ify* are always verbs: *simplify*

- Words ending in these suffixes are often, but not always verbs:
  –ise / –ize: organise
  –ate: rotate

- Words ending in these suffixes are often, but not always adjectives:
  –al: emotional
  –able / –ible: sensible
  –ive: active

- Words ending in *–ly* are often, but not always adverbs: *completely*

Countable and uncountable nouns

Some nouns are countable [C]. Other nouns are uncountable [U].

- A good learner's dictionary will tell you if a noun is countable or uncountable:

  rain *noun* [U] water that falls from the sky in small drops

  zebra *noun* [C] an animal like a horse with black and white lines

- Countable and uncountable nouns have different grammar rules, and we can often tell when a noun is countable or uncountable by looking at the words around it and whether it is singular or plural.

Countable nouns:	Uncountable nouns:
• use *a* or *an* when they are singular: *a zebra, an ant*	• do not use *a* or *an*: *water*
• have a plural form: *zebras, ants*	• do not have a plural form (and so the verb is always singular): *They drink a lot of water.*
• can use *some* and *any* in the plural: *some rivers, any bees*	• can use *some* and *any*: *some rain, any food*
• can use *few* and *many* in the plural: *few trees, many birds*	• can use *little* and *much*: *little food, much grass*
• can use *number* in the plural: *There were a large number of elephants in the forest.*	• can use *amount*: *Elephants eat a large amount of food every day.*

⊙ This is a list of some common uncountable nouns which IELTS candidates often make mistakes with:

advice behaviour education equipment information
knowledge pollution research stuff traffic work

Prepositions in time phrases

- We use *in* for months and years:
  ***in** August,* **in** *2011*

- We use *on* for days:
  on *Monday,* **on** *21st August,* **on** *New Year's Day*

- For periods of time, we use
  - *between ... and:*
    between *August* **and** *October*
  - *from ... to:*
    from *2005* **to** *2010 (= between 2005 and 2010)*
  - *over* + a number of months or years + *period:*
    over *a 20-year* **period**
  - *during* + a word or phrase that represents a period of time*:
    during *the summer holidays / the lesson / the period between September and January / the five-year period*

* *During* means 'for part of the time mentioned'. *Over* means 'for the whole time mentioned':

Faisal stayed at the hotel for two weeks **during** *the summer.*
The graph shows information about hotel staff **over** *a ten-year period.*

Unit 6

Word formation and spelling

We can change the form of words by adding a syllable/syllables to the end of the word (called a suffix):

-ful: success → successful

There are no clear rules – each word and the words which can be formed from it must be learned individually. Some of the most common are listed below.

verb → noun

suffix	verb	noun
-ment	*achieve*	*achievement*
-ation / -tion / -sion	*inform*	*information*
-er / -or	*research* *investigate*	*researcher* *investigator*

adjective → noun

suffix	adjective	noun
-ance / -ence	*important* *absent*	*importance* *absence*
-ness	*lazy*	*laziness*

noun → adjective

suffix	noun	adjective
-y	*sun*	*sunny*
-ful	*success*	*successful*
-ous	*fame*	*famous*
-al	*nature*	*natural*

noun → verb

suffix	noun	verb
-ise / -ize	*critic*	*criticise/criticize*

adjective → verb

suffix	adjective	verb
-ify	*simple*	*simplify*

verb → adjective

suffix	verb	adjective
-ed	*talent*	*talented*
-ing	*work hard*	*hard-working*
-able	*agree*	*agreeable*
-ive	*attract*	*attractive*

adjective → adverb

suffix	adjective	adverb
-ly	*quick*	*quickly*
-ally	*basic*	*basically*

Spelling words with suffixes

- We double the final consonant when we add *-ed*, *-ing*, *-er* and *-est* to:
    - one-syllable words which end in a consonant–vowel–consonant (apart from *-w*, *-x* and *-y*):
    run → running, big → bigger
    - verbs of two or more syllables which end in consonant–vowel–consonant and the final syllable is stressed:
    occur → occurred, forget → forgetting
    (but *happened, developing*)
    - verbs which end in *-l* after one vowel in British English (in American English they may not double):
    travel → traveller

- We don't double the final consonant when:
    - there are two final consonants:
    depend → depending
    - there are two vowels before the final consonant:
    disappear → disappearance
    - the verb ends in a vowel:
    share → shared
    - the stress is not on the final syllable:
    open → opening
    - the word ends in *-w*, *-x* or *-y*:
    slower, relaxed, player

y → i and i → y

- For words ending in *-y* after a consonant, the *y* becomes *i* when a suffix is added (except *-ing* – see below):
happy → happiness, try → tries

    Note this exception:
    day - daily

- *i* becomes *y* with *-ing*; *y* does not change:
lie → lying, study → studying, try → trying

When to drop the final -e

- We drop the final *-e* if there is a consonant before it and the suffix begins with a vowel (*-er, -ed, -ing, -ance, -ation*, etc.):
amaze → amazing, fame → famous

- We do not drop the final *-e* when the suffix begins with a consonant:
safe → safety, manage → management

Adding prefixes

- When we add a syllable like *un-*, *dis-* or *in-* before a word to make it negative, we do not change the spelling:
appoint → disappoint, satisfied → dissatisfied, like → unlike, necessary → unnecessary

- Before words beginning with *r-*, we use *ir-*:
irrelevant

- Before words beginning with *m-* or *p-*, we use *im-*:
immature, impatient

- Before words beginning with *l-*, we use *il-*:
illogical, illiterate

Zero and first conditionals

We use conditional sentences to express a condition (*If …*) and what will or might happen as a result of that condition.

Zero conditional

If/Unless + present tense … present tense:

If people **work** hard, they **are** usually successful in the end.

We use the zero conditional to talk about something which is always or generally true.

First conditional

If/Unless + present tense … future tense / modal verb (*can, should, must,* etc.):

If I **go** to Beijing, I**'ll visit** the Great Wall.

If he **doesn't do** the work, you **should** complain.

We use the first conditional when we're:

- not talking in general

- talking about something which may possibly happen in the future and the likely result of that:
  If I pass my exams, I'll go on holiday. (I may pass my exams, and if that happens, it's likely that I'll go on holiday.)

Unit 7

Prepositions to describe trends and changes

For prepositions in time phrases, see page 126.

- We use a noun + *in* to say what has changed (*a change in, a rise in, a decrease in,* etc.):
  *There has been **a rise in** sales of handheld computers.*

- To say how much something has risen or fallen, we use a:
  - noun + *of*:
    *There has been **an increase of** three percent.*

  - verb + *by*:
    *The number **fell by** three thousand.*

  - verb or noun + *from … to*:
    *The average **rose from** 0.7 **to** 1.3.*

- To express a level, we use a verb + *at*:
  *Sales **peaked at** 55 million.*

- To say the level something reached, we use a verb + *to*:
  *The number **rose to** 21,000.*

Unit 8

Fact and opinion adjectives

- Some adjectives give factual information:
  a **tall** building, a **red** shirt, an **academic** essay

- Other adjectives express the speaker's opinion:
  a **beautiful** building, an **attractive** shirt, an **interesting** essay

- When we use more than one adjective before a noun, we:
  - don't separate the adjectives with *and*, but generally separate them using a comma (see *When to use commas* on page 129)

  - put 'opinion adjectives' before 'fact adjectives':
    a **beautiful**, **tall** building; an **attractive**, **red** shirt; an **interesting**, **academic** essay

- Note: *luxury* is often used as an adjective to describe places to stay and means of transport:
  a luxury hotel, a luxury car

Relative pronouns

We can add information about a noun using a relative clause and in this way put more information in the same sentence:
The plane was full. I travelled on the plane. → *The plane which I travelled on was full.*

In this sentence, the relative clause is *which I travelled on*.

A relative clause consists of a relative pronoun (*who, which, that, where,* etc.) + a phrase.

We place the relative pronoun immediately after the noun:

noun   relative pronoun   phrase

The plane which I travelled on was full.

We use:

- *who* when we use a relative clause to talk about people:
  *We had a tourist guide **who** could speak eight languages.*

- *which* to talk about animals and things:
  *The excursion **which** I want to go on leaves at seven in the morning.*

- *that* to talk about people, animals or things:
  *We arrived at an airport **that** was 50 kilometres from the resort.*
  *The man **that** drove the bus spoke on his telephone during the whole journey.*

- *where* to talk about places:
  *We stayed at a hotel **where** a wedding party was taking place.*

Unit 9

Sequencers

We use words and phrases to show the start, middle and end of a process. We normally put them at the beginning of a sentence and we put a comma after them.

- For the first stage in a process, we use *First / Firstly / First of all / The process begins when* …:
  First of all, they dig a canal.

- For the middle stages in the process, we often start sentences with *Next / Then / After that / Second / Secondly* (for the second stage in a process):
  After that, they put cement on the walls of the canal.

  If there are a number of middle stages, we use different words and phrases to introduce each stage, as this avoids repetition.

- We can also use *when* + a phrase or *after* + a phrase to show the middle stages in a process:
  When they have put cement on the walls, they leave it to get hard.

- For the last stage in a process, we often start sentences with *Lastly* or *Finally*:
  Finally, they pump water into the canal.

- Note that we don't use *at last* to show the end of a process; *at last* suggests we think something has taken more time than it should:
  At last you've done your report. I've been waiting for ages!

The passive

Sometimes we don't know who or what does/did an action, or we don't need to say who does/did it, perhaps because it's obvious. In these situations, we use a passive.

We often use the passive when describing a process, because it is not important to say who does the action.

The passive is formed by *to be* + past participle (*done/ changed/spoken*).

With verbs like *can*, *should*, *must*, etc., the passive is formed by *can/should/must* + *be* + past participle:

The pump **must be placed** next to the well.

Look at these sentences in the active and the passive:

Active	Passive
People pour water into the barrel.	*Water is poured into the barrel.*
People built the water filter.	*The water filter was built.*
They have finished the canal.	*The canal has been finished.*
People can obtain water by digging wells.	*Water can be obtained by digging wells.*

Note: The passive uses a past participle. It is important to know the past participles of irregular verbs (see page 131) in order to form the passive correctly.

Unit 10

Using linkers to contrast or compare

- We can use *although* and *even though* when we want to join two sentences which contrast ideas or facts:
  Although he has a lot of money, he lives in a small, old house.
  He has very little work **even though** he's a talented architect.

- *Even though* and *although* mean the same. *Even though* is a stronger or more emphatic way of saying *although*.

- We can put *although* and *even though* at the beginning of the sentence or in the middle. If we put them at the beginning of the sentence, we use a comma to separate the ideas. If we put them in the middle, we don't have to use a comma, although it's not wrong to use one.

- We can use *while* and *whereas* when we want to join two sentences which compare ideas or facts:
  While Deng Ling lives in a small flat, her brother lives in a large house.
  Architects can become famous **whereas** builders are often unknown.

- *While* and *whereas* mean the same.

- As with *although* and *even though*, we can use *while* and *whereas* at the beginning or in the middle of the sentence. If they begin the sentence, we separate the two ideas or facts with a comma; if they are in the middle, the comma is not necessary.

When to use commas

We use commas (,):

- when we make lists:
  He has designed bridges, towers, museums and theatres.

  Note: We don't use a comma with the final item on the list; we use *and*.

- to separate adjectives when there are a number of adjectives before the noun:
  The tower must be strong enough to resist sudden, violent storms.

  Note: With short common adjectives, commas are not necessary:
  He lives in a new white house.

- after an adverb or a short introductory phrase at the beginning of a sentence such *as first, as a result, consequently, for this reason, all in all, generally, finally, however, in my opinion*, etc.:
  As a result, many buildings are built cheaply and quickly.

  In my opinion, architects should always try to design beautiful buildings.

- after a time phrase at the beginning of a sentence:
  In 2003, the price of building materials rose by 12%.

- after clauses at the beginning of sentences starting with *if, unless, when, while, after, before, although, even though, whereas, as,* etc.:
  If architects use expensive building materials, many people cannot afford to buy the house.
- when we join two sentences with *but*:
  *The tower in the city centre is impressive, **but** most people think it is ugly.*

Modal verbs

Can, could, may, might, must and *should* are followed by the infinitive (without *to*):
*I **can see** the Moon.*

Have to is also followed by the infinitive:
*I **have to do** three assignments this term.*

Forms

1 modal verbs + infinitive (*can, could, may, might, must, should*)

affirmative	He *can drive.*
	She *should get up* earlier.
negative	He *can't / cannot drive.*
	She *shouldn't / should not* get up earlier.
question	*Can* he *drive?*
	Should she *get up* earlier?

Notes:

- Do not add *–s* to modal verbs.
- *Cannot* is one word.
- Do not use *do* or *does* to form questions.

2 *have to* + infinitive

affirmative	He *has to walk* to work.
	We *have to work* today.
negative	She *doesn't have to work* today.
	(not: *She hasn't to work.*)
question	*Do* you *have to work* today?
	(not: *Have you to work?*)

Uses

- To say that something is possible now or in the future, but that we are not sure, we use *may, might* or *could*. They mean the same:
  I may / might / could visit New Zealand next year.
  (It's possible I'll visit New Zealand, but I'm not sure.)

  Note: We use *could* with this meaning to talk about the present or the future.

- To say someone or something is able to do something, we use *can* in the present and *could* in the past:
  *Few people **can** afford to live in expensive flats.*

  *Two hundred years ago, few people **could** afford to have windows in their houses because glass was too expensive.*

  Note: We usually use *can* with these verbs: *see, hear, afford*:
  *I **can hear** the traffic.*

- To say something is a good idea or important, we use *should*:
  *The government **should** build more schools.*

- To say something is necessary or essential, we use *must* or *have to*:
  *If you want to go to university, you **must** get good grades in your school exams.*
  *You **have to** carry a passport when you travel abroad.*

- To say something is not allowed, we use *mustn't* (not *don't have to*):
  *You **mustn't** smoke in class.*

- To say something is not necessary, we use *don't have to*:
  *You **don't have to** use the stairs. You can take the lift.*
  (It's not necessary to use the stairs, although you can if you want to.)

Common irregular verbs

verb	past simple	past participle
arise	arose	arisen
be	was/were	been
become	became	become
begin	began	begun
bend	bent	bent
blow	blew	blown
break	broke	broken
bring	brought	brought
broadcast	broadcast	broadcast
build	built	built
burn	burned/burnt	burned/burnt
burst	burst	burst
buy	bought	bought
catch	caught	caught
choose	chose	chosen
come	came	come
cost	cost	cost
cut	cut	cut
deal	dealt	dealt
dig	dug	dug
do	did	done
draw	drew	drawn
dream	dreamed/dreamt	dreamed/dreamt
drink	drank	drunk
drive	drove	driven
eat	ate	eaten
fall	fell	fallen
feed	fed	fed
feel	felt	felt
fight	fought	fought
find	found	found
fly	flew	flown
forbid	forbade	forbidden
forget	forgot	forgotten
freeze	froze	frozen
get	got	got
give	gave	given
go	went	gone
grow	grew	grown
hang	hung	hung
have	had	had
hear	heard	heard
hide	hid	hidden
hit	hit	hit
hold	held	held
hurt	hurt	hurt
keep	kept	kept
know	knew	known
lay	laid	laid
lead	led	led
lean	leaned/leant	leaned/leant
learn	learned/learnt	learned/learnt
leave	left	left

verb	past simple	past participle
lend	lent	lent
let	let	let
lie	lay	lain
light	lit	lit
lose	lost	lost
make	made	made
mean	meant	meant
meet	met	met
pay	paid	paid
put	put	put
read	read	read
ride	rode	ridden
ring	rang	rung
rise	rose	risen
run	ran	run
say	said	said
see	saw	seen
sell	sold	sold
send	sent	sent
set	set	set
shake	shook	shaken
shine	shone	shone
shoot	shot	shot
show	showed	showed/shown
shut	shut	shut
sing	sang	sung
sink	sank	sunk
sit	sat	sat
sleep	slept	slept
slide	slid	slid
smell	smelled/smelt	smelled/smelt
sow	sowed	sown
speak	spoke	spoken
spell	spelled/spelt	spelled/spelt
spill	spilled/spilt	spilled/spilt
split	split	split
spoil	spoiled/spoilt	spoiled/spoilt
spread	spread	spread
stand	stood	stood
steal	stole	stolen
stick	stuck	stuck
strike	struck	struck
swim	swam	swum
take	took	taken
teach	taught	taught
tear	tore	torn
tell	told	told
think	thought	thought
throw	threw	thrown
understand	understood	understood
wake	woke	woken
wear	wore	worn
win	won	won
write	wrote	written

Word lists

Abbreviations: n/np = noun / noun phrase; v/vp = verb / verb phrase; adj/adjp = adjective / adjective phrase; adv/advp = adverb / adverb phrase; pv = phrasal verb; T/I = transitive / intransitive; C/U = countable / uncountable

The numbers indicate the page in the unit on which the word of phrase first appears. RS indicates that the word or phrase appears in the recording script.

Unit 1

'access *n* [U] (11) when you have the right or opportunity to use or see something

con'clude *v* [I] (9) to decide something after studying all the information about it very carefully

con'duct re'search *vp* (9) to study a subject to find information about it

con'sume *v* [T] (11) to use something such as a product, energy or fuel

crime rate *n* [C] (8) the amount of crime that happens in a place or during a period of time

'culture *n* [C, U] (9) the habits, traditions and beliefs of a country, society or group of people

di'verse *adj* (11) including many different types

en'vironment *n* [C] (9) the situation that you live or work in, and how it influences how you feel

'feature *n* [C] (16) a quality or important part of something

grow up (11) *vp* to become older or an adult

have 'access to 'something *vp* (11) to have the right or opportunity to have, use or see something

ig'nore *v* [T] (9) to pay no attention to something or someone

'impact *n* (11) the effect that a person, event or situation has on someone or something

'income *n* [C, U] (11) money that you earn by working, investing or producing goods

in'dustrial *adj* (12) with a lot of factories

'influence *v* [T] (14) to affect or change how someone or something develops, behaves or thinks

'landscape *n* [C] (11) the appearance of an area of land, especially in the countryside

'lifestyle *n* [C] (8) the way that you live

'local *n* [C] (9) someone who lives in the area you are talking about

'measurement *n* [C, U] (11) a way of measuring something

nu'trition *n* [U] (11) the food that you eat and the way that it affects your health

'outcome *n* [C] (11) the final result of an activity or process

rank *v* [T] (11) to give someone or something a position in a list which shows them in order of importance or quality

re'action *n* [C, U] (9) something you say, feel or do because of something that has happened

repu'tation *n* [C] (9) the opinion that people have about someone or something based on their behaviour or character in the past

re'sources *n plural* (11) things that a country, person or organisation has which they can use

short of *adjp* (9) If you are *short of* something, you do not have enough of it.

'status *n* [U] (11) the position that you have in relation to other people because of your job or social position

su'rround *v* [T] (11) to be or go everywhere around something or someone

tend to be *vp* (9) to often be in a particular state

way of life *np* (9) the manner in which a person lives

Unit 2

a'ccount *n* [C] (18) a written or spoken description of something that has happened

'ancient *adj* (18) from a long time ago

a'ward *v* [T] (18) to officially give someone something such as a prize or an amount of money

'benefit *n* [C, U] (24) something that helps you or gives you an advantage

com'bine *v* [T] (18) to mix or join things together

'commentary *n* [C, U] (18) a description or discussion of an event

co'mmunity *n* [C] (25) the people living in a particular area

'compass *n* [C] (22) a piece of equipment which shows you which direction you are going in

'context *n* [C, U] (23) all the facts, opinions, situations, etc. relating to a particular thing or event

defi'nition *n* [C] (27) an explanation of the meaning of a word or phrase

de'gree *n* [C] (19) a qualification given for completing a university course

es'tablish *v* [T] (18) to make something start to exist or happen

e'ventually *adv* (18) in the end, especially after a long time

expe'dition *n* [C] (19) an organised journey, especially a long one for a particular purpose

ex'periment *n* [C] (20) a test, especially a scientific one, that you do in order to learn something or discover if something is true

ex'tensive *adj* (18) large in amount or size

'formal edu'cation *np* [U] (18) *Formal education* happens in a school, college or university.

gene'ration *n* [C] (24) all the people in a society or family who are approximately the same age

indi'vidual *adj* (24) considered separately from other things in a group

inte'rrupt *v* [T] (18) to stop an action or activity, usually for a short period of time

'memorise *v* (22) to learn something so that you remember it exactly

pre'serve *v* [T] (23) to keep something the same or prevent it from being damaged or destroyed

prove *v* [T] (22) to show that something is true

re'gard as *pv* (18) to think of something in a particular way

save 'money *vp* (18) to keep money so that you can buy something with it in the future

skill *n* [C, U] (19) the ability to do an activity or job well, especially because you have practised it

su'pport *v* [T] (24) to help and be kind to someone when they have problems

tech'nique *n* [C] (27) a particular or special way of doing something

tra'ditional *adj* (22) following the customs or ways of behaving that have continued in a group of people or society for a long time

'voyage *n* [C] (22) a long journey, especially by ship

wave *n* [C] (22) a line of higher water that moves across the surface of a sea or lake

Unit 3

aim to do 'something *vp* (29) to try to achieve something

al'ternative *adj* (33) An *alternative* plan, method, etc. is one that you can use if you do not want to use another one.

at a re'duced price *phrase* (30) for less money than something usually costs

a'void *v* [T] (33) to not do something

'cancel *v* [T] (33) to say that an organised event will not now happen

compe'tition *n* [C] (30) an organised event in which people try to win a prize by being the best, fastest, etc.

con'venience *n* [U] (33) when something is easy to use and suitable for what you want to do

con'vert *v* [T] (29) to change the appearance, form or purpose of something into something else

'data *n plural* (29) information or facts about something

desti'nation *n* [C] (31) the place where someone or something is going

environ'mentalist *n* [C] (33) someone who tries to protect the natural environment from being damaged

fa'cilities *n plural n* (30) buildings, equipment or services that are provided for a particular purpose

'fashion show *np*[C] (30) a show for the public where models wear new styles of clothes

'forward-'thinking *adj* (33) thinking about and planning for the future

'funding *n* [U] (33) money given by a government or organisation for an event or activity

'increase ca'pacity *vp* (33) to increase the amount or number of something that something can hold or deal with

'innovative *adj* (29) using new methods or ideas

insta'llation *n* [U] (29) when equipment or furniture is put into position

on 'average *np* (34) usually, or based on an average

'passenger *n* [C] (30) someone who is travelling in a vehicle but is not controlling it

pe'destrian *n* [C] (34) a person who is walking and not travelling in a vehicle

'privacy *n* [U] (33) when you are alone and people cannot see or hear what you are doing

range *n* [C] (29) a group of different things of the same general type

revo'lutionary *adj* (29) completely different from what was done before

smog *n* [U] (32) air pollution in a city that is a mixture of smoke, gases and chemicals

souve'nir *n* [C] (30) something which you buy or keep to remember a special event or holiday

'structure *n* [C, U] (32) the way that parts of something are arranged or put together

'system *n* [C] (29) a way or method of doing things

u'nique 'feature *np* [C] (31) something that only happens once or does not exist anywhere else

un'willing *adj* (33) not wanting to do something

up'grade *v* [T] (33) to improve something so that it is of a higher quality or a newer model

'vehicle *n* [C] (28) something such as a car, train or aircraft that takes people or goods from one place to another

Unit 4

'atmosphere *n* [U] (47) the feeling which exists in a place or situation

a'ttractive *adj* (39) beautiful or pleasant to look at

cite *v* [T] (37) to mention something as an example or proof of something else

con'sist of *vp* (43) to be formed or made from two or more things

cool *v* [T] (38) to make something become less hot

'demonstrate *v* [I,T] (39) to show someone how to do something or how something works

de'sign *n* [U] (37) the way in which something is planned and made to have a particular appearance

de'vice *n* [C] (37) a piece of equipment that is used for a particular purpose

di'agonally *adv* (43) going from the top corner of a square to the bottom corner on the other side

drop *n* [C] (37) a small, round-shaped amount of liquid

end up with *vp* (43) to finally have something

en'sure *v* [I,T] (43) to make certain that something is done or happens

'entrance *n* [C] (40) a door or other opening which you use to enter a building or place

e'quipment *n* [U] (37) the things that are used for a particular activity or purpose

ex'tent *n* [U] (44) the amount or importance of something

'factor *n* [C] (37) one of the things that has an effect on a particular situation, decision, event, etc.

go on to do 'something *vp* (43) to do something else in the future

hu'midity *n* [U] (38) a measurement of how much water there is in the air

in'terior *n* [C] (43) the inside part of something

in'terior de'sign *np* [U] (43) the job of choosing colours, designs, etc for the inside of a house or room

in'vestigate *v* [I, T] (43) to try to discover all the facts about something, especially a crime or an accident

'moisture *n* [U] (37) very small drops of water in the air or on a surface

'money-conscious *adj* (38) not wanting to spend too much money

per'mit *v* [T] (43) to allow something

per'suade *v* [T] (39) to make someone agree to do something by talking to them a lot about it

'printing *n* [U] (38) when writing or images are produced on paper or other material using a machine

'reasonable a'mount *np* [C] (44) an amount that is not too much and not too little

'smoothly *adv* (43) happening without any sudden movements or changes

'special 'occasion *n* [C] (41) an event that is important and enjoyable, such as a birthday or a wedding

take up 'space *vp* (38) to use an amount of space

three-di'mensional *adj* (43) having length, depth and height

trans'fer *v* [T] (38) to move someone or something from one place to another

twist *v* [T] (43) to turn something using your hand

'widespread *adj* (38) affecting or including a lot of places, people, etc.

world'wide *adv* (43) in all parts of the world

Unit 5

agri'cultural land *np* [U] (49) land which is used for or suitable for farming

'archive *n* [C] (52) a collection of historical documents that provides information about the past, or a place where they are kept

'beehive *n* [C] (49) a special container where people keep bees, or a place where bees live

'brilliant *adj* (49) full of light or colour

'colony *n* [C] (55) a group of the same type of animals, insects or plants living together in a particular place

come u'pon *vp* (49) to discover something by chance

cut off *vp* (49) to stop the supply of something

desti'nation *n* [C] (52) the place where someone or something is going

dis'tinctive 'markings *np* (52) marks on living creatures that make them easy to recognise

e'cology *n* [U] (53) the relationship between living things and the environment, or the scientific study of this

'estimate *v* [T] (52) to guess the cost, size, value, etc. of something

ex'tend *v* [I] (49) to reach, stretch or continue for a particular distance

'farmland *n* [U] (48) land which is used for or suitable for farming

'focus 'efforts on 'something *vp* (53) to give all your attention or effort to something

get rid of *vp* (49) to make something unpleasant go away

'grassland *n* [U/C] (48) a large area of land covered with grass

'harmless *adj* (49) not able or not likely to cause any hurt or damage

'hemisphere *n* [C] (53) one half of the Earth

'hostile en'vironment *np* [C] (53) a place where the weather or conditions make it difficult or dangerous to be

'indicate *v* [T] (52) to show that something exists or is likely to be true

near-ex'tinction *n* [U] (53) the state where a type of creature is so rare that it may soon not exist at all

ob'serve *v* [T] (53) to watch someone or something carefully

'pattern *n* [C] (53) a particular way that something is often done or repeated

'pesticide *n* [C, U] (49) a chemical that is used to kill insects which damage plants

'poison *n* [C, U] (49) a substance that can make you ill or kill you if it gets in your body

'risky *adj* (49) dangerous because something bad might happen

shift *v* [I] (53) to change

soil *n* [U] (49) the top layer of earth that plants grow in

source of food *np* [C] (49) something that is used as food by a person or creature

spot *v* [T] (52) to see or notice something or someone

under'estimate *n* [C] (53) a guess that is lower than the real size or amount of something

a'chievement *n* [C] (63) something good that you achieve

Unit 6

'background n [C] (67) a person's education, family and experience of life

be good at 'something vp (64) to be able to do something well

'charity n [C, U] (58) an official organisation that gives money, food or help to people who need it

de'mand n [U, no plural] (58) a need for something to be sold or supplied

'diary n [C] (61) a book containing spaces for all the days and months of the year, in which you write meetings and other things that you must remember

'elderly 'people np (60) people who are old

en'courage v [T] (57) to make someone more likely to do something, or make something more likely to happen

ex'perience n [C] (58) something that happens to you that affects how you feel

fall a'sleep pv (61) to start sleeping

fa'miliar adj (57) easy to recognise because of being seen, met, heard, etc. before

flood n [C] (67) when a lot of water covers an area of land that is usually dry

'generous adj (57) giving other people a lot of money, presents or time in a kind way

get to the top vp (64) to be very successful in a job or activity

'graduate n [C] (58) someone who has studied for and received a degree from a university

i'dentify v [T] (59) to find a particular thing or all the things of a particular group

'image n [C, U] (57) the way that other people think someone or something is

in con'clusion np (64) finally (used to introduce the last part of a speech or piece of writing)

keen on ('doing) 'something vp (57) very interested in something or wanting (to do) something very much

key to su'ccess np [C] (62) the most important thing that will help you achieve success

'natural a'bility np [C] (64) a skill or quality that someone is born with

plans n plural (58) drawings from which something is made or built

presen'tation n [C] (66) a talk giving information about something

'quality of life np [U] (60) the level of enjoyment, comfort and health in someone's life

re'ject v [T] (60) to refuse to accept or agree with something

'seminar n [C] (63) a meeting of a group of people with a teacher or expert for training, discussion, or study of a subject

try hard vp (64) to do everything you can to do your best at something

unex'pected adj (61) Something that is *unexpected* surprises you because you did not know it was going to happen.

'vital 'element np [C] (60) a necessary part of something

'wealthy adj (RS) rich

'well-paid job np [C] (58) a job in which you earn a lot of money

Unit 7

a'ssignment *n* [C] (68) a piece of work that you are given to do as part of your studies

a'ttend a 'lecture *vp* (68) to go to a formal talk that is given to students to teach them about a subject

be en'gaged in 'something *phrase* (71) to be very interested in something and give it all your attention

'brochure *n* [C] (68) a thin book with pictures and information, usually advertising something

'concentrate *v* [I] (70) to think very carefully about something you are doing and nothing else

de'crease *v* [I, T] (73) to become less, or to make something become less

dra'matically *adv* (70) in a very sudden or noticeable way

'ebook *n* [C] (76) a book that can be read on a computer screen or special device

e'ffectively *adv* (71) in a way that is successful and achieves what you want

en'rol *v* [I] (69) to become an official member of a course, college or group

enrolment *n* [C, U] (73) the process of becoming a member of a course, college, university, etc.

essential *adj* (70) very important and necessary

expectations *n plural* (69) the things that people expect and want to happen or to have

fall down *vp* (76) to break into pieces and drop to the ground

feedback *n* [U] (69) an opinion from someone about something that you have done or made

fill out a form *vp* (RS) to complete the information on a printed document with spaces for you to add information

flow *n* (70) [U] when something moves or seems to move continuously and easily

i'lliterate *adj* (72) not able to read or write

key facts *np* (70) very important facts (things that you know are true or have happened)

on'line *adv* (68) connected to a system of computers, especially the Internet

'outline *n* [C] (70) a short description of the most important ideas or facts about something

'practise *v* [I, T] (71) to repeat something regularly in order to improve your ability

make 'progress *vp* (71) to develop and improve skills, knowledge, etc.

'qualify *v* [I] (70) to succeed in getting into a competition

re'duce *v* [T] (70) to make something less

'structure *n* [C] (70) a building or something that has been built

trend *n* [C] (70) a general development or change in a situation

tu'torial *n* [C] (69) a class (especially at a British university) in which a small group of students talks about a subject with their tutor

'under 'pressure *np* (70) in a difficult situation that makes you feel worried or unhappy

unem'ployment rate *np* [C] (74) the number of people who do not have a job in a place or during a period of time

Unit 8

a'broad *adv* (85) in or to a foreign country

a'ccompany *v* [T] (RS) to go somewhere with someone

'aircraft *n* [C] (78) a vehicle that can fly

'backpacking *n* [U] (77) travelling or camping with your clothes and belongings in a backpack

'breathtaking *adj* (RS) very beautiful or surprising

'capable of ('doing 'something) *phrase* (78) having the ability or qualities to be able to do something

'continent *n* [C] (79) one of the seven main areas of land on the Earth, such as Asia, Africa or Europe

cruise *n* [C] (77) a holiday on a ship, sailing from place to place

de'lay *v* [I/T] (79) to make something happen at a later time than originally planned or expected

'evidence *n* [U] (79) something that makes you believe that something is true or exists

ex'pand *v* [I/T] (78) to increase in size or amount, or to make something increase

'fashionable *adj* (82) popular at a particular time

'global 'warming *np* [U] (79) when the air around the world becomes warmer because of pollution

'impact *n* (79) [C, no plural] the effect that a person, event or situation has on someone or something

im'pressive *adj* (82) Someone or something that is *impressive* makes you admire and respect them.

'leisure ac'tivity *np* [C] (78) something that you do for enjoyment when you are not working

'local 'culture *np* [U] (83) the habits, traditions and beliefs of the area you are in

'magical *adj* (81) special or exciting

'memorable *adj* (RS) If an occasion or experience is *memorable*, you will remember it for a long time because it is so good.

'monument *n* [C] (82) a building or other structure that is built to make people remember an event in history or a famous person

out'dated *adj* (82) old-fashioned and therefore not as good or as fashionable as something modern

'package deal *np* [C] (84) a type of holiday where you pay a fixed price and the travel, accommodation and sometimes food are arranged for you

reco'mmend 'someone to do 'something *phrase* (82) to tell someone that they would probably enjoy doing something

re'sort *n* [C] (83) a place where many people go for a holiday

sa'fari *n* [C] (77) journey, usually to Africa, to see or hunt wild animals

'sightseeing *n* [U] (77) the activity of visiting places which are interesting because they are historical, famous, etc.

'stressful *adj* (82) making you feel worried and nervous

'survey *n* [C] (79) an examination of something to find information about it

tour guide *np* [C] (80) someone whose job is to take tourists around interesting places and tell them about them

'urban *adj* (82) belonging or relating to a town or city

wi'thin reach *phrase* (78) close enough to travel to

va'cation *n* [C, U] (84) a period of time when you are not at home but are staying somewhere else for enjoyment

Unit 9

'**access** n [U] (90) when you have the right or opportunity to use or see something

a'**ccessible** adj (91) easy to find or reach

a'**ccount for 'something** vp (88) to be the reason for something

'**benefit** n [C] (92) something that helps you or gives you an advantage

con'**struct** v [C] (96) something large that is built

con'**struction** n [U] (91) the work of building houses, offices, bridges, etc.

'**cultivate crops** vp (91) to grow plants such as grains, fruit or vegetables in large amounts

the developing world np (91) describes an area of the world which is poorer and has less-advanced industries, especially in Africa, Latin America or Asia

drain away vp (91) If a liquid *drains away*, it flows out of a place.

drought n [C] (90) a long period when there is no rain and people do not have enough water

fetch v [T] (90) to go to another place to get something or someone and bring them back

'**follow** v [I, T] (89) to understand something

geo'**logical** adj (91) relating to geology(= the study of rocks and the structure of the Earth)

'**human 'consumption** np [U] (89) when people eat or use something

'**human waste** np [U] (90) substances that come out of your body after your food has been digested

'**hygiene** n [U] (90) the process of keeping things clean, especially to prevent disease

irri'**gation** n [U] (96) the process of providing water to an area of land so that crops can be grown

the 'natural world np (RS) all the things in the world that were not created by people, especially the countryside, animals, etc.

po'**lluted** adj (90) water, air, soil, etc. that has become dirty or harmful to humans or animals

pour v [T] (90) to make a liquid flow from or into a container

the pros and cons np (RS) the advantages and disadvantages of something

'**rainwater** n [U] (91) water that has fallen as rain, rather than water which has come from a tap

'**running 'water** n [U] (90) water that comes through a system of pipes

'**rural** adj (91) relating to the countryside and not to towns

'**specialist** adj (92) having a lot of experience, knowledge or skill in a particular subject

treat 'someone for a di'sease vp (91) to give medical care to someone to try to cure their illness

turn on a tap vp (90) to turn the part at the end of a pipe to start the flow of water

'**water su'pplies** np (90) amounts of water that are available to be used

water source np [C] (95) a place where water comes from, especially under the ground

water sports np (93) sports which take place on or in water

water purifi'cation np [U] (RS) the process of removing harmful substances from water

wet suit np [C] (94) a piece of clothing covering the whole body that keeps you warm when you are under water

Unit 10

accommo'dation *n* [U] (104) a place where you live or stay

a'ffordable *adj* (104) cheap enough for most people

'architecture *n* [U] (99) the design and style of buildings

a'vailable *adj* (104) If something is *available*, you can use it or get it.

'benefit from *vp* (99) to be helped by something

'building materials *np* (104) the materials, e.g. bricks or wood, that buildings are made of

'citizen *n* [C] (104) someone who lives in a particular town or city

'decorate *v* [T] (100) to make something look more attractive by putting things on it or around it

de'mand *n* [U, no plural] (104) a need for something to be sold or supplied

engi'neer *n* [C] (RS) someone whose job is to design, build or repair machines, engines, roads, bridges, etc.

'escalator *n* [C] (97) moving stairs that take people from one level of a building to another

ex'ternal su'rroundings *np* (100) the things that are around the outside of something

'flexible *adj* (99) able to change or be changed easily according to the situation

foun'dations *n plural n* (107) the part of a building, road, bridge, etc. that is under the ground and supports it

'housing *n* [U] (104) buildings for people to live in

im'prove *v* [I, T] (102) to get better or to make something better

knock down *vp* (102) to destroy a building or part of a building

'landmark *n* [C] (98) a building that you can easily recognise, especially one that helps you to know where you are

ma'terial *n* [C, U] (104) a solid substance from which things can be made

'occupant *n* [C] (101) someone who lives or works in a room or building

old-'fashioned *adj* (103) not modern

stand out *vp* (97) to be very easy to see or notice

steel *n* [U] (98) a very strong metal made from iron, used for making knives, machines, etc.

straight a'way *adv* (107) immediately

thatched *adj* (101) A *thatched* building has a roof that is made of straw (= dried grass-like stems).

'timber *n* [U] (102) wood that is used for building

tower block *np* [C] (107) a very tall building divided into apartments or offices

tra'ditional *adj* (101) following the customs or ways of behaving that have continued in a group of people or society for a long time

-shaped *suffix* (101) made to look like a particular shape

IELTS practice test

LISTENING

SECTION 1
Questions 1–5

Complete the form below.

Write NO MORE THAN TWO WORDS AND/OR A NUMBER for each answer.

HOTEL
Booking Form

Example	*Answer*
Arrival date:	23rd August

Length of stay:	**1** ....
Type of accommodation:	**2** ....
Name:	*Mr and Mrs* **3** .... *and children*
Address:	*29 Tower Heights,*
	Dunbar
	4 ....
Postcode:	*EH41 2GK*
Contact telephone:	**5** ....
Purpose of trip:	*holiday*

Questions 6–10

Complete the form below.

Write NO MORE THAN TWO WORDS AND/OR A NUMBER for each answer.

Tourist Board
Questions for holidaymakers

Favourite activity:	**6** ....
Beaches:	*busy but* **7** ....
Shop staff:	*are sometimes* **8** ....
Waiters:	**9** .... *and quick*
Suggestions:	*need some* **10** .... *for hire*

SECTION 2

Questions 11–15

Complete the notes below.

*Write **NO MORE THAN TWO WORDS AND/OR A NUMBER** for each answer.*

ORANA WILDLIFE PARK

Facts about Orana

- Orana means '11 ....'.

- The park has animals from a total of 12 ....

- The animals come from many parts of the world.

Things to do at Orana

- 13 .... the giraffes at 12 or 3 p.m.

- Touch the animals in the 14 .... (good for children).

- Watch the cheetahs doing their 15 .... at 3.40.

Questions 16–20

Label the plan below.

Write the correct letter, A–I, next to questions 16–20.

16   New Zealand birds   ....
17   African village   ....
18   Picnic area   ....

19   Afternoon walkabout meeting place   ....
20   Jomo's Café   ....

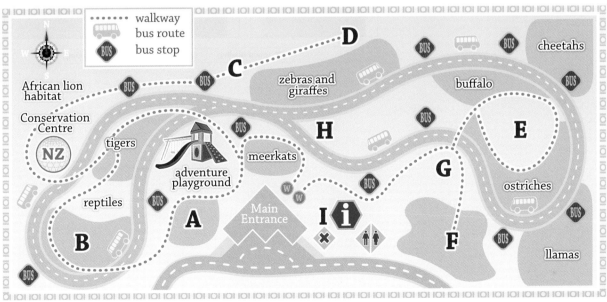

🎧33 **SECTION 3**

Questions 21–27

Choose the correct letter A, B or C.

21 The students did the study skills course because

    A it was part of their syllabus.

    B they needed it to prepare for an exam.

    C their tutor recommended it.

22 Why did Sylvie and Daniel use a questionnaire?

    A Other students preferred the method.

    B It reduced the preparation time.

    C More information could be obtained.

23 How often did the students meet in class for the course?

    A once a week

    B twice a week

    C every weekday

24 Why did Daniel like the course?

    A It improved his confidence.

    B It focused on economics articles.

    C It encouraged him to read more books.

25 What did the students like about Jenny?

    A her homework assignments

    B her choice of study material

    C her style of teaching

26 Which chart below shows how useful students found the course in general?

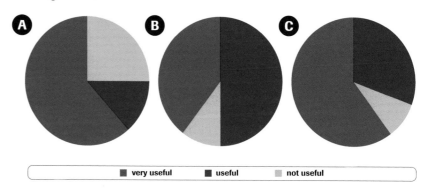

very useful   useful   not useful

27 Which graph below shows how useful students found the different parts of the course?

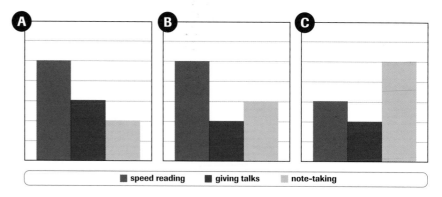

speed reading   giving talks   note-taking

Questions 28–30

Complete the sentences.

Use **NO MORE THAN TWO WORDS** *for each answer.*

28 Good note-taking improves concentration during ....

29 Making notes with the help of a .... is useful.

30 Having a .... on note paper makes notes easier to read.

🎧 **SECTION 4**
Questions 31–40

Complete the notes below.

Write **NO MORE THAN TWO WORDS** *for each answer.*

AIRPORT DESIGN

Can compare a past airport to a **31** ....

Now, can compare an airport to a small **32** ....

Reasons for changes

- Greater passenger numbers because of
  - **33** .... (e.g. package deals)
  - **34** .... (e.g. meetings)
- Need to create a good **35** .... of a country
  - airports called 'gateways'

Types of change

Inside the building

- many big **36** .... provide space and light (e.g. Beijing airport)
- calm atmosphere with easy movement reduces **37** .... for passengers

The exterior of the building

- designed to match the surroundings
  - e.g. – the shape of the **38** .... on the Arctic Circle airport, Norway
    - the **39** .... outside airports in India and Thailand
- structural design reduces **40** .... and costs

---

READING

READING PASSAGE 1

*You should spend about 20 minutes on **Questions 1–13**, which are based on Reading Passage 1 below.*

William Kamkwamba

At only 14 years old, William Kamkwamba built a series of windmills that could generate electricity in his African village, Masitala, in Malawi, south-eastern Africa.

In 2002, William Kamkwamba had to drop out of school, as his father, a maize and tobacco farmer, could no longer afford his school fees. But despite this setback, William was determined to get his education. He began visiting a local library that had just opened in his old primary school, where he discovered a tattered science book. With only a rudimentary grasp of English, he taught himself basic physics – mainly by studying photos and diagrams. Another book he found there featured windmills on the cover and inspired him to try and build his own.

He started by constructing a small model. Then, with the help of a cousin and friend, he spent many weeks searching scrap yards and found old tractor fans, shock absorbers, plastic pipe and bicycle parts, which he used to build the real thing.

For windmill blades, William cut some bath pipe in two lengthwise, then heated the pieces over hot coals to press the curled edges flat. To bore holes into the blades, he stuck a nail through half a corncob, heated the metal red and twisted it through the blades. It took three hours to repeatedly heat the nail and bore the holes. He attached the blades to a tractor fan using proper nuts and bolts and then to the back axle of a bicycle. Electricity was generated through the bicycle dynamo. When the wind blew the blades, the bike chain spun the bike wheel, which charged the dynamo and sent a current through wire to his house.

What he had built was a crude machine that produced 12 volts and powered four lights. When it was all done, the windmill's wingspan measured more than eight feet and sat on top of a rickety tower 15 feet tall that swayed violently in strong gales. He eventually replaced the tower with a sturdier one that stands 39 feet, and built a second machine that watered a family garden.

The windmill brought William Kamkwamba instant local fame, but despite his accomplishment, he was still unable to return to school. However, news of his *magetsi a mphepo* – electric wind – spread beyond Malawi, and eventually things began to change. An education official, who had heard news of the windmill, came to visit his village and was amazed to learn that William had been out of school for five years. He arranged for him to attend secondary school at the government's expense and brought journalists to the farm to see the windmill. Then a story published in the *Malawi Daily Mail* caught the attention of bloggers, which in turn caught the attention of organisers for the Technology Entertainment and Design conference.

In 2007, William spoke at the TED Global conference in Tanzania and got a standing ovation. Businessmen stepped forward with offers to fund his education and projects, and with money donated by them, he was able to put his cousin and several friends back into school and pay for some medical needs of his family. With the donation, he also drilled a borehole for a well and water pump in his village and installed drip irrigation in his father's fields.

The water pump has allowed his family to expand its crops. They have abandoned tobacco and now grow maize, beans, soybeans, potatoes and peanuts. The windmills have also brought big lifestyle and health changes to the other villagers. 'The village has changed a lot,' William says. 'Now, the time that they would have spent going to fetch water, they are using for doing other things. And also the water they are drinking is clean water, so there is less disease.' The villagers have also stopped using kerosene and can use the money previously spent on fuel to buy other things.

William Kamkwamba's example has inspired other children in the village to pursue science. William says they now see that if they put their mind to something, they can achieve it. 'It has changed the way people think,' he says.

Questions 1–5

Complete the flow chart below.

*Choose **NO MORE THAN TWO WORDS** from the passage for each answer.*

Building the Windmill

William learned some **1** .... from a library book.

↓

First, he built a **2** .... of the windmill.

↓

Then he collected materials from **3** .... with a relative.

↓

He made the windmill blades from pieces of **4** ....

↓

He fixed the blades to a **5** .... and then to part of a bicycle .

↓

He raised the blades on a tower.

Questions 6–10

Do the following statements agree with the information given in Reading Passage 1?

Write

TRUE	*if the statement agrees with the information*
FALSE	*if the statement contradicts the information*
NOT GIVEN	*if there is no information on this*

6 William used the electricity he created for village transport.

7 At first, William's achievement was ignored by local people.

8 Journalists from other countries visited William's farm.

9 William used money he received to improve water supplies in his village.

10 The health of the villagers has improved since the windmill was built.

Questions 11–13

Answer the questions below.

*Use **NO MORE THAN ONE WORD** and/or a **NUMBER** from the passage for each answer.*

11 How tall was the final tower that William built?

12 What did the villagers use for fuel before the windmill was built?

13 What school subject has become more popular in William's village?

READING PASSAGE 2

*You should spend about 20 minutes on **Questions 14–26**, which are based on Reading Passage 2 below.*

White mountain, green tourism

The French Alpine town of Chamonix has been a magnet for tourists since the 18th century. But today, tourism and climate change are putting pressure on the surrounding environment. Marc Grainger reports.

A   The town of Chamonix-Mont-Blanc sits in a valley at 1,035 metres above sea level in the Haute-Savoie department in south-eastern France. To the north-west are the red peaks of the Aiguilles Rouges *massif*; to the south-east are the permanently white peaks of Mont Blanc, which at 4,810 metres is the highest mountain in the Alps. It's a typical Alpine environment, but one that is under increasing strain from the hustle and bustle of human activity.

B   Tourism is Chamonix's lifeblood. Visitors have been encouraged to visit the valley ever since it was discovered by explorers in 1741. Over 40 years later, in 1786, Mont Blanc's summit was finally reached by a French doctor and his guide, and this gave birth to the sport of alpinism, with Chamonix at its centre. In 1924, it hosted the first Winter Olympics, and the cable cars and lifts that were built in the years that followed gave everyone access to the ski slopes.

C   Today, Chamonix is a modern town, connected to the outside world via the Mont Blanc Road Tunnel and a busy highway network. It receives up to 60,000 visitors at a time during the ski season, and climbers, hikers and extreme-sports enthusiasts swarm there in the summer in even greater numbers, swelling the town's population to 100,000. It is the third most visited natural site in the world, according to Chamonix's Tourism Office and, last year, it had 5.2 million visitor bed nights – all this in a town with fewer than 10,000 permanent inhabitants.

D   This influx of tourists has put the local environment under severe pressure, and the authorities in the valley have decided to take action. Educating visitors is vital. Tourists are warned not to drop rubbish, and there are now recycling points dotted all around the valley, from the town centre to halfway up the mountains. An internet blog reports environmental news in the town, and the 'green' message is delivered with all the tourist office's activities.

E   Low-carbon initiatives are also important for the region. France is committed to reducing its carbon emissions by a factor of four by 2050. Central to achieving this aim is a strategy that encourages communities to identify their carbon emissions on a local level and make plans to reduce them. Studies have identified that accommodation accounts for half of all carbon emissions in the Chamonix valley. Hotels are known to be inefficient operations, but those around Chamonix are now cleaning up their act. Some are using low-energy lighting, restricting water use and making recycling bins available for guests; others have invested in huge projects such as furnishing and decorating using locally sourced materials, using geothermal energy for heating and installing solar panels.

F   Chamonix's council is encouraging the use of renewable energy in private properties too, by making funds available for green renovations and new constructions. At the same time, public-sector buildings have also undergone improvements to make them more energy efficient and less wasteful. For example, the local ice rink has reduced its annual water consumption from 140,000 cubic metres to 10,000 cubic metres in the space of three years.

G   Improving public transport is another feature of the new policy, as 80 percent of carbon emissions from transport used to come from private vehicles. While the Mont Blanc Express is an ideal way to travel within the valley – and see some incredible scenery along the route – it is much more difficult to arrive in Chamonix from outside by rail. There is no direct line from the closest airport in Geneva, so tourists arriving by air normally transfer by car or bus. However, at a cost of 3.3 million euros a year, Chamonix has introduced a free shuttle service in order to get people out of their cars and into buses fitted with particle filters.

H   If the valley's visitors and residents want to know why they need to reduce their environmental impact, they just have to look up; the effects of climate change are there for everyone to see in the melting glaciers that cling to the mountains. The fragility of the Alpine environment has long been a concern among local people. Today, 70 percent of the 805 square kilometres that comprise Chamonix-Mont-Blanc is protected in some way. But now, the impact of tourism has led the authorities to recognise that more must be done if the valley is to remain prosperous: that they must not only protect the natural environment better, but also manage the numbers of visitors better, so that its residents can happily remain there.

Questions 14–18

Reading Passage 2 has eight paragraphs, A–H.

Which paragraph contains the following information?
You may use any letter more than once.

14 a list of the type of people who enjoy going to Chamonix

15 reference to a system that is changing the way visitors reach Chamonix

16 the geographical location of Chamonix

17 mention of the need to control the large tourist population in Chamonix

18 reference to a national environmental target

Questions 19–20

Choose TWO letters, A–E.

The writer mentions several ways that the authorities aim to educate tourists in Chamonix.
Which **TWO** of the following ways are mentioned?

A   giving instructions about litter

B   imposing fines on people who drop litter

C   handing out leaflets in the town

D   operating a web-based information service

E   having a paper-free tourist office

Questions 21–22

Choose TWO letters, A–E.

The writer mentions several ways that hotels are reducing their carbon emissions.
Which **TWO** of the following ways are mentioned?

A   using natural cleaning materials

B   recycling water

C   limiting guest numbers

D   providing places for rubbish

E   harnessing energy from the sun

Questions 23–26

Complete the sentences below.

Choose NO MORE THAN TWO WORDS from the passage for each answer.

23   The first people to discover the Chamonix valley were ....

24   Chamonix's busiest tourist season is the ....

25   Public areas, such as the .... in Chamonix, are using fewer resources.

26   The .... on the mountains around Chamonix provide visual evidence of global warming.

READING PASSAGE 3

You should spend about 20 minutes on Questions 27–40, which are based on Reading Passage 3 below.

Reading in a whole new way

As technology improves, how does the act of reading change?

Reading and writing, like all technologies, are constantly changing. In ancient times, authors often dictated their books. Dictation sounded like an uninterrupted series of words, so scribes wrote these down in one long continuous string, *justastheyoccurinspeech*. For this reason, text was written without spaces between words until the 11th century. This continuous script made books hard to read, so only a few people were accomplished at reading them aloud to others. Being able to read silently to yourself was considered an amazing talent; writing was an even rarer skill. In fact, in 15th-century Europe, only one in 20 adult males could write.

After Gutenberg's invention of the printing press in about 1440, mass-produced books changed the way people read and wrote. The technology of printing increased the number of words available, and more types of media, such as newspapers and magazines, broadened what was written about. Authors no longer had to produce scholarly works, as was common until then, but could write, for example, inexpensive, heart-rending love stories or publish autobiographies, even if they were unknown.

In time, the power of the written word gave birth to the idea of authority and expertise. Laws were compiled into official documents, contracts were written down and nothing was valid unless it was in this form. Painting, music, architecture, dance were all important, but the heartbeat of many cultures was the turning pages of a book. By the early 19th century, public libraries had been built in many cities.

Today, words are migrating from paper to computers, phones, laptops and game consoles. Some 4.5 billion digital screens illuminate our lives. Letters are no longer fixed in black ink on paper, but flitter on a glass surface in a rainbow of colors as fast as our eyes can blink. Screens fill our pockets, briefcases, cars, living-room walls and the sides of buildings. They sit in front of us when we work – regardless of what we do. And of course, these newly ubiquitous screens have changed how we read and write.

The first screens that overtook culture, several decades ago – the big, fat, warm tubes of television – reduced the time we spent reading to such an extent that it seemed as if reading and writing were over. Educators and parents worried deeply that the TV generation would be unable to write. But the interconnected, cool, thin displays of computer screens launched an epidemic of writing that continues to swell. As a consequence, the amount of time people spend reading has almost tripled since 1980. By 2008, the World Wide Web contained more than a trillion pages, and that total grows rapidly every day.

But it is not book reading or newspaper reading, it is screen reading. Screens are always on, and, unlike books, we never stop staring at them. This new platform is very visual, and it is gradually merging words with moving images. You might think of this new medium as books we watch, or television we read. We also use screens to present data, and this encourages numeracy: visualising data and reading charts, looking at pictures and symbols are all part of this new literacy.

Screens engage our bodies, too. The most we may do while reading a book is to flip the pages or turn over a corner, but when we use a screen, we interact with what we see. In the futuristic movie *Minority Report*, the main character stands in front of a screen and hunts through huge amounts of information as if conducting an orchestra. Just as it seemed strange five centuries ago to see someone read silently, in the future it will seem strange to read without moving your body.

In addition, screens encourage more utilitarian (practical) thinking. A new idea or unfamiliar fact will cause a reflex to do something: to research a word, to question your screen 'friends' for their opinions or to find alternative views. Book reading strengthened our analytical skills, encouraging us to think carefully about how we feel. Screen reading, on the other hand, encourages quick responses, associating this idea with another, equipping us to deal with the thousands of new thoughts expressed every day. For example, we review a movie for our friends while we watch it; we read the owner's manual of a device we see in a shop before we purchase it, rather than after we get home and discover that it can't do what we need it to do.

Screens provoke action instead of persuasion. Propaganda is less effective, and false information is hard to deliver in a world of screens because while misinformation travels fast, corrections do, too. On a screen, it is often easier to correct a falsehood than to tell one in the first place. Wikipedia works so well because it removes an error in a single click. In books, we find a revealed truth; on the screen, we assemble our own truth from pieces. What is more, a screen can reveal the inner nature of things. Waving the camera eye of a smartphone over the bar code of a manufactured product reveals its price, origins and even relevant comments by other owners. It is as if the screen displays the object's intangible essence. A popular children's toy (Webkinz) instills stuffed animals with a virtual character that is 'hidden' inside; a screen enables children to play with this inner character online in a virtual world.

In the near future, screens will be the first place we'll look for answers, for friends, for news, for meaning, for our sense of who we are and who we can be.

Questions 27–31

Choose the correct letter, A, B, C or D.

27 What does the writer say about dictation?

  A It helped people learn to read.

  B It affected the way people wrote.

  C It was not used until the 11th century.

  D It was used mainly for correspondence.

28 According to the writer, what changed after the invention of the printing press?

  A Romance became more popular than serious fiction.

  B Newspapers became more popular than books.

  C Readers asked for more autobiographies.

  D Authors had a wider choice of topics.

29 In the third paragraph, the writer focuses on the

  A legal concerns of authors.

  B rapid changes in public libraries.

  C growing status of the written word.

  D recognition of the book as an art form.

30 What does the writer say about screens in the fourth paragraph?

  A They are hard to read.

  B They are bad for our health.

  C They can improve our work.

  D They can be found everywhere.

31 According to the writer, computers differ from television because they

  A encourage more reading.

  B attract more criticism.

  C take up more of our leisure time.

  D include more educational content.

Questions 32–36

Do the following statements agree with the views of the writer in Reading Passage 3?

Write

YES	*if the statement agrees with the views of the writer*
NO	*if the statement contradicts the views of the writer*
NOT GIVEN	*if it is impossible to say what the writer thinks about this*

32 Screen reading has reduced the number of books and newspapers people read.

33 Screen literacy requires a wider range of visual skills than book-based literacy.

34 Screen reading is more active than book reading.

35 Screens and books produce similar thought patterns in their readers.

36 People are easily persuaded to believe lies on the screen.

Questions 37–40

Complete each sentence with the correct ending, A–F, below.

37 The film *Minority Report* illustrates

38 Our behaviour when we watch a film shows

39 Wikipedia's success relies on

40 Webkinz is an example of

A	the accuracy of its information.
B	people's ability to concentrate.
C	the global use of the Internet.
D	how people behave physically when they read screens.
E	the screen's ability to make an object seem real.
F	how rapidly opinions can be communicated.

WRITING

WRITING TASK 1

You should spend about 20 minutes on this task.

> *The chart below gives information on the global sale of hybrid vehicles* between 2006 and 2009.*
>
> *Summarise the information by selecting and reporting the main features, and make comparisons where relevant.*
>
> ** vehicles that use both fuel and electricity*

Write at least 150 words.

Global hybrid vehicle sales

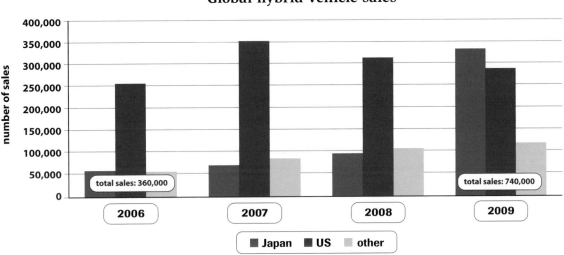

WRITING TASK 2

You should spend about 40 minutes on this task.

Write about the following topic.

> *Inventors are not as important to society as doctors.*
>
> *To what extent do you agree with this statement?*

Give reasons for your answer and include any relevant examples from your own knowledge or experience.

Write at least 250 words.

SPEAKING

PART 1

4–5 minutes

> **Examiner**
>
> *Now, in this first part, I'd like to ask some questions about yourself.*
> *What do you do? Do you work or are you a student?*
>
> - Where are you studying?
> - Who did you meet first on your course?
> - Do you like studying with other people or alone? Why?
> - At what time do your classes finish?
>
> - Where do you work?
> - Who did you meet first in your job?
> - Do you like working with other people or on your own? Why?
> - At what time does your working day end?

> *Let's talk about transport now.*
>
> - What journeys do you make every day?
> - Is public transport expensive in your country? Why? / Why not?
> - Do you prefer to travel by train or by bus? Why?
> - How often do you travel by plane?
> - Have you ever fallen asleep while travelling? When?
>
> *I'd like to talk about animals now.*
>
> - Which animals are well known in your country?
> - Do animals have any special uses in your country? What?
> - Are there any places where tourists can see animals in your country? Where?
> - Have you ever been on a holiday to see animals?
> - Would you like to work with animals? Why? / Why not?

PART 2

2–3 minutes

Examiner

Now I'm going to give you a topic and I'd like you to talk about it for one to two minutes. Before you talk, you'll have one minute to think about what you're going to say. You can make some notes if you wish. Do you understand? Here is some paper and a pencil for making notes and here is your topic. I'd like you to describe a place you enjoyed going to as a child.

Describe a place you enjoyed going to as a child.

You should say:

  where this place is/was

  how you got there

  what you did there

and explain why you enjoyed going to this place.

All right? Remember you have one to two minutes for this, so don't worry if I stop you. I will tell you when the time is up. Can you start speaking now, please?

- Do you still visit this place?
- Do your friends enjoy visiting this place?

PART 3

4–5 minutes

Examiner

We've been talking about a place you enjoyed going to as a child, and I'd like to ask you some more general questions about this.

Let's consider first of all children's activities.

- What sort of activities do children enjoy most?
- Why do many young children like physical activities?
- How have children's activities changed over the last 20 years?

Let's move on to talk about school activities.

- How much of the school day should children spend studying (rather than doing activities like sport or drama)?
- Should subjects like music and art be an important part of school life? Why? / Why not?
- What activities will be important at school in the future?

Thank you. That is the end of the Speaking Test.

Recording scripts

CD1 Track 1

1 R-O-M-N-E-Y

2 C-A-E-R-N-S

3 B-R-A-double G

4 J-I-C-K-E-double L

5 Fawcett, that's F-A-W-C-E-double T.

6 It costs 50 cents.

7 My telephone number is 0726 05791.

8 30 Lovers Road, that's L-O-V-E-R-S.

CD1 Track 2

1 B-R-A-C-K-E-N

2 G-O-W-E-R

3 J-E-R-E-M-Y

4 P-O-double L-A-R-D

5 V-E-R-N-O-N

6 17

7 01950 674236

8 31st

CD1 Track 3

Amanda Dubai Palm Apartments, Amanda speaking. How can I help you?

Leo Oh hi, Amanda. I'm ringing to enquire about a holiday apartment for the month after next.

A OK, no problem. Let me get your details first, then I'll tell you what we've got. Is that all right?

L Fine, go ahead.

A OK. Can I have your name first, please?

L Yes, it's Leo Blucher, that's L-E-O – that's my first name – and my surname is B-L-U-C-H-E-R.

A OK, I've got that. Where are you from, just out of interest, Leo?

L I'm Austrian.

A Right, OK, and what's your address?

L It's number 37 Blumengasse in Vienna.

A Right. Could you just spell *Blumengasse* for me, please, Leo? My German's not too good.

L Sure, it's B-L-U-M-E-N-G-A-double S-E.

A Great, thanks, and what's the weather like in Vienna at the moment?

L It's pretty grey and rainy, I'm afraid. Hope it's better in Dubai.

A Yes, it's lovely at the moment. Sunny and warm, but not too hot. Now, can you give me your phone number?

L Yes, it's 4312 11057.

A Great. So, you're looking for a holiday apartment, Leo. How many people is it for, just yourself?

L No, there'll be four of us, two adults and two children.

A Fine, and when would you like it from?

L Ideally from the 1st of January.

A January the 1st. OK. I'll have a look and see what we've got. How long would you like to stay?

L Well, it depends a little bit on the price, but I think that about nine days would be perfect.

A Fine. And, talking of prices, what would be your maximum, do you think?

L Well, I've looked on the Internet, but I don't know if I'm being realistic if I say 200 euros per day. Things seem to range from 150 to well over 400.

A Well, it depends where, of course, but I think we could probably find something for you at that price.

L Great. There are various other things, though. Our children are quite small, and we don't want to take them to restaurants all the time, so one thing we'd really appreciate is a fully equipped kitchen so we can do some cooking.

A Yes, I completely understand. Do you have any other special requirements?

L Yes, we live in the city centre hundreds of miles from the sea, so we'd really like be able to see it from our apartment.

A OK, I'll note that down. All our apartments come with air conditioning and central heating, by the way.

L Oh dear. One thing I don't like is the noise of air conditioning in the background. Can you make sure it's as quiet as possible?

A Yes, I'll look into that. Anything else?

L Yes, just one more thing. We'd like to hire a car while we're in Dubai, so we'll need to have a parking space, I think – we don't want to have to walk a long way from the car to the apartment.

A I think you're quite right. I'll look into all these things and make a list of possible apartments. Do you have an email address, so I can send them to you?

Examiner Can you tell me what you do, Hanan? Do you work, or are you a student?

Hanan Yes, I'm a student. I'm studying medicine because I want to be a doctor. At the moment, I'm studying English as well because I hope to do part of my degree course in Australia.

E And where do you come from?

H I come from Muttrah in Oman.

E Can you describe Muttrah a little bit for me?

H Yes. It's quite a large city by the sea and also near the mountains. It's very beautiful and very old. It's very hot in the summer, but the winter is usually very pleasant. Also, Muttrah is an important port.

E Can you tell me what you do, Kwan? Do you work, or are you a student?

Kwan I'm a student. I'm studying economics at Chonju University at the moment.

E And where do you come from, Kwan?

K I come from a small village near Chonju in Korea.

E Can you describe your village to me?

K Well, it's in the mountains. The people work as farmers and they are very friendly. It's a good place to live, but not much happens there.

CD1 Track 5

Examiner What do you like about the area where you live?

Hanan Oh, I really like the sea and the part of the city just by the sea because it's very beautiful and there are always lots of people there. I live in the suburbs, but I enjoy going shopping in the city centre. There are plenty of good shops, and I like buying clothes.

E What things in Muttrah do you not like?

H Mm, I'm not very keen on the hot weather, and the hot wind from the desert is something I don't like.

E Mm. How is the area changing?

H They're building more houses and roads. It's getting busier.

E What do you like about the area where you live, Kwan?

Kwan I find walking in the mountains very enjoyable, and another good thing is the people, because they're very friendly and generous. I think people in my village are very happy and relaxed.

E What things in your village do you not like?

K Well, I live by a busy main road and I find the traffic very unpleasant. I really dislike the noise of cars and lorries.

E How is the area changing?

K There's more traffic, so the village is becoming noisier. Also, young people are leaving the village, so it isn't so lively.

CD1 Track 6

Examiner Can you tell me what you do, Hanan? Do you work, or are you a student?

Hanan Yes, I'm a student. I'm studying medicine because I want to be a doctor.

E And where do you come from?

H I come from Muttrah in Oman.

E Can you tell me what you do, Kwan? Do you work, or are you a student?

Kwan I'm a student. I'm studying economics at Chonju University at the moment.

E And where do you come from, Kwan?

K I come from a small village near Chonju in Korea.

Unit 2

CD1 Track 7

Conversation 1

Man Could you give me a contact number, please?

Woman Sure – I'll give you my mobile. It's 07816 038924.

M Thanks – we'll let you know when the glasses are ready.

CD1 Track 8

Conversation 2

Woman How much is the flight to Madrid?

Man It's $349.

W Do you have anything cheaper – say, $300?

M I'm afraid not.

CD1 Track 9

Conversation 3

Man How old are you, Maddy?

Girl I'm 16.

M And what date's your birthday?

G October the 12th.

M Good, so we'll be able to start the driving lessons in the second half of October.

G Yes.

CD1 Track 10

Conversation 4

Man Shall we see each other later in the coffee bar?

Woman OK. What time shall we meet?

M Um, can you get there by four thirty?

W My maths class finishes at four, so … yes … that should be OK.

Clive   Hello?

Debbie   Hi, Clive, is that you?

C   Yes, hi, Debbie.

D   Did you manage to see those candidates for our expedition?

C   Yes, I did, and there was an extra one who was quite a surprise. You know, he hadn't applied and he just turned up out of the blue, so we haven't got any details for him.

D   Really? Tell me about him.

C   OK, and you can take some notes. Then we'll see what we think.

D   Fine.

C   First, he's called Sanjay Dubashi.

D   OK. Sanjay is spelled S-A-N-J-A-Y, right?

C   Correct. And Dubashi is D-U-B-A-S-H-I.

D   D-U-B-A-S-H-I, fine, thanks, I'm just getting that down. And did you find out how old he is?

C   Sure, he's round about our age, you know – well, a couple of years older, he's 27, quite a big man, quite muscular, impressive, with a big moustache.

D   And what does he do?

C   Well, actually, he just says he's an office worker, you know, just one of those people with quite a routine job in an office.

D   Mm, doesn't sound like he finds his job very interesting. Has he got any experience, do you know, of going off to remote places on foot?

C   Yes, he's been all over the place. He was telling me all about a trip he made in a Land Rover across Central Africa from one side to the other, which sounded pretty exciting. And dangerous.

D   Great! I think it would be really interesting to cross Central Africa. I'd love to do that. Anything physical? I mean, where he actually had to walk instead of driving – you know, being so muscular, as you say?

C   Mm, I was coming to that. Last year, he went to Russia with some friends in their summer holidays and they went up a mountain. Let's see, um, Mount Elbrus, it's called.

D   Wow, now that's really quite something. By the way, Elbrus is spelled E-L-B-R-O-S, isn't it?

C   Not quite, it's U-S.

D   Ah, OK … What qualifications does he have which would interest us? Has he done any sort of specialist training, for example?

C   Well, he's done a course in first aid, which may be pretty useful. If any of us get injured, he should know what to do.

D   Good. It might be useful to have someone who knows how to do first aid in case someone has an accident. Can he swim?

C   I didn't ask, now you mention it. I forgot. But he did tell me he can hold conversations in five languages. He's not fluent in all of them, but he can get by. He grew up in India, and I suppose that helps, you know, for learning languages, though now he lives over here.

D   Right. What else? Has he been to university, for instance?

C   Yes, he graduated in media studies, though he says he's never worked in the media.

D: OK, and when he's not off on expeditions to remote places, what does he like doing in his spare time?

C   He seems to do all sorts of things. One thing he told me which could be useful is that he likes fishing.

D   Yes, we'd better tell him to bring his fishing rod – that is, if we choose him.

C   And he seems to spend a lot of time at the gym – he says he really likes to keep fit. And when you meet him, you'll believe it's true.

D   Great, another fitness fanatic, like you. Well, sounds like I should meet him, doesn't it? When can you fix that up?

Examiner   So, Hussein, I'm going to ask you some questions about your childhood. Do you come from a large family or a small family?

Hussein   I'm sorry, could you repeat, please?

E   Do you come from a large family or a small family?

H   Well, actually, it's not large or small, what's the word, it's middle … no, no, sorry, it's medium-sized. I am two brothers … sorry, I have two brothers who are both older than me.

E   As a child, who did you spend more time with, your family or your friends?

H   When I was a small child, I spent more time with my family, my mother, who looked after me, and I played a lot with my brothers. Then, when I was a bit older, about ten or 11, I started to play more with friends I made at school because we enjoyed doing the same things, and my mother went back to her job.

E   And when you were a child, how did you spend your free time?

H   I think I watched television quite a lot when I was a small child and I played computer games with my brothers. When I was older, I did a lot of sports with my friends. We went swimming and we played tennis and football because I love doing sports.

E   What did you enjoy most about school?

H   I think I enjoyed doing science subjects most. I liked physics and chemistry especially. We didn't do sports at school, so I did those in my free time.

E And when you were at school, who do you think was your best teacher?

H I think, perhaps, my chemistry teacher because she explained things very clearly. Also, she was very – I'm not sure about the word – uh, interested, no, enthusiastic. She made us do tests, I mean experiments in the laboratories, so we learned a lot. I never missed one of her lessons.

CD1 Track 13

Examiner So, Hussein, I'm going to ask you some questions about your childhood. Do you come from a large family or a small family?

Hussein I'm sorry, could you repeat, please?

E Do you come from a large family or a small family?

H Well, actually, it's not large or small, what's the word, it's middle … no, no, sorry, it's medium-sized. I am two brothers … sorry, I have two brothers who are both older than me.

CD1 Track 14

Examiner As a child, who did you spend more time with, your family or your friends?

Hussein When I was a small child, I spent more time with my family, my mother, who looked after me, and I played a lot with my brothers. Then, when I was a bit older, about ten or 11, I started to play more with friends I made at school because we enjoyed doing the same things, and my mother went back to her job.

E And when you were a child, how did you spend your free time?

H I think I watched television quite a lot when I was a small child and I played computer games with my brothers. When I was older, I did a lot of sports with my friends. We went swimming and we played tennis and football because I love doing sports.

E What did you enjoy most about school?

H I think I enjoyed doing science subjects most. I liked physics and chemistry especially. We didn't do sports at school, so I did those in my free time.

E And when you were at school, who do you think was your best teacher?

H I think, perhaps, my chemistry teacher because she explained things very clearly. Also, she was very – I'm not sure about the word – uh, interested, no, enthusiastic. She made us do tests, I mean experiments in the laboratories, so we learned a lot. I never missed one of her lessons.

CD1 Track 15

1 asked   **2** mended   **3** called

CD1 Track 16

appeared, asked, ended, enjoyed, finished, hoped, improved, invented, liked, looked, needed, occurred, played, remembered, started, wanted, watched, wished

---

Unit 3

CD1 Track 17

Good evening and welcome aboard the Pride of Poole. In this recorded announcement, we'll give you details of some of the facilities available on board this ship.

You're currently standing in the reception area in the centre of B Deck. If you're feeling hungry after a long day's travelling, go up the stairs to A Deck, where you'll find the restaurant. The restaurant caters for all appetites, with anything from a light snack to a full three-course meal. The restaurant will be open from the moment the ship leaves port to half an hour before arrival.

Next to the restaurant on A Deck in the lounge, there are reclining seats with music headphones if you want to relax. The headphones are free, but people using this area are encouraged to keep noise to a minimum so that other passengers can enjoy themselves and sleep or read if they wish.

For those of you who'd like some entertainment, just next door to us on this deck is a 40-seat cinema showing the latest full-length feature films. The cinema programme is available here at reception, but you'll have to buy the tickets themselves at the cinema entrance just before you go in.

Just next to the cinema is the staircase leading down to the cabins on C Deck. To access your cabin, just show your boarding pass to a steward, who will give you the key.

On this deck, that is B Deck, you'll also find an area where you can either play games in our special electronic games arcade or do your shopping.

Just beyond that on the same level, people who want a bit of fresh air or just want to see the sea can go out onto the viewing deck, which is in the open air. Make sure you wear a jacket or coat, as it can be quite cold and windy.

CD1 Track 18

Now for some further details. This voyage is an overnight trip. The ship leaves port at 7 p.m. and the journey takes just over 12 hours and 45 minutes, reaching our destination at about eight tomorrow morning. This is for the convenience of those wishing to catch the nine o'clock train, which leaves from the ferry terminal.

Passengers with children in their party are informed that there is a special section in the restaurant with kids' food and a play area. People with children are encouraged to turn up early to get a place, as the section is very popular.

Make this a trip to remember. Here at the information desk, you can obtain a souvenir ship's key ring for four euros fifty; you can upgrade from a tourist-class cabin to a first-class cabin; and you can get your train tickets here, which will save you time queuing in the station tomorrow morning. If you buy them on the ship, you can get them for 20 percent off.

For those using the lounge and wishing to check their email, there's a wireless connection, but you'll have to bring your own laptop. You can also watch the latest TV programmes there or in the coffee bar next to the restaurant.

Finally, a unique feature on this crossing only: anyone who buys a fashion item from our wonderful range of men's and women's clothes in the shopping area has the chance to win a free holiday. All you have to do is complete a sentence starting 'I like Sealand Ferries because …' and the best sentence wins the prize of a holiday in Switzerland with tickets to a three-day music festival included. Talk to any member of staff for more details.

CD1 Track 19

Kyung-Soon   Well, I'm going to talk about a trip I made across Australia. The transport I used was a motorbike. It wasn't a new bike, it was – what's the word – second-hand, and I bought it because I wanted to see Australia. I didn't want to use public transport because I wanted to be independent. I had a month's holiday before I started my course and I made the trip with a friend, a Chinese girl, because I was frightened of travelling alone. I met her at a language school where we studied English together. We travelled along the south coast and saw some of the desert. The good thing about the journey was that we met a lot of other people who were travelling. We went to places which are difficult to reach on public transport, and the trip was quite cheap. Also, the motorbike had quite a powerful engine, so it was fast and exciting. The bad things were the rain and the heat because they made us tired. I have great memories of the trip because I felt really free. We could go where we liked. Also, we met some very friendly people and we saw a lot of interesting places. I still have friends who I made during that trip. In all, I think it was the best journey I've ever made.

Examiner   Thank you.

CD1 Track 20

motorbike

CD1 Track 21

transport   studying   independent   holiday   university
powerful   exciting   expensive   memories   interesting

Unit 4

CD1 Track 22

Irina   Good morning. Can you tell me about the ticket options, please?

Man   Certainly, we've got various options, depending on whether you want to just visit parts of the exhibition or all of it. It's organised into various different sections, and because it's so large, you may not be interested in everything or have time for everything. You can buy tickets just for the sections you want to visit, and that makes it a lot cheaper.

I   Well, um, I've really come here to see things to do with electronics.

M   Right. Then I think you'll find the first part of the exhibition as you go in is quite relevant. It's all about electronics and how we can use them to protect the world around us – you know, the environment and what we can do to avoid damaging it further.

I   Protecting the environment. That sounds interesting. Anything I should specially look out for there?

M   There are lots of new devices. One which fascinated me when I went round was a new instrument for measuring how the temperature of the ocean changes at different levels, and this can be done from a ship on the surface right down to the bottom.

I   Great, I'll look out for that.

M   OK, and I see you've got your son with you, which is nice because the subject of the next section is all about different things for keeping an eye on your children and looking after their safety. It contains a range of things, from electronic instruments used in medicine to children's electronic games and even a number of new devices to prevent children from having an accident when they're at home.

I   That sounds useful.

M   Yes, there's even an invention for older children – you'll see a demonstration of it while you're there – which helps parents to make sure their kids are going to school. Really useful in families where both parents work. It sort of electronically tells parents about their kids' attendance and sends them a signal via the Internet.

I   Very convenient. But my son is a bit young to worry about that yet. Are there any other sections which feature electronics?

M   Sure. There's another section – it's the third you come to, I think – which should interest everyone. It contains lots of new electronic instruments or devices for looking after and working with money – you know, like that thing you must have heard of which counts what you're putting into your supermarket trolley and adds up the bill as you go around.

I   Right, money – that sounds interesting, too. Well, thanks for the information. I'd like tickets for myself and my son for those three sections, then, please.

CD1 Track 23

Woman   Excuse me.

Irina   Yes?

W   Before you go through, I wonder if you could help us by answering a few questions for a survey. It won't take long.

I   No problem. We're not in any hurry.

W   Fine, thanks. Now, er, let's look at the questions.

I   OK.

W   Here they are. First one. Why are you visiting the exhibition?

I Well, I want to keep up with the latest developments in electronics, you know – I was recommended by a friend to come here and see what new devices and inventions are coming out and learn a bit. I mean, I don't generally go shopping for new electronics. I'm not the sort of person who goes out and buys all the latest gadgets – the prices are too high when they're new. But it interests me, and I thought also there would be things which would interest my son and he'd enjoy it as well, so that's why we're here.

W OK … and here's a question to find out what sort of consumer you are. Have you bought any electronics recently?

I Recently? Sure. I was thinking of buying a new calculator for the office, but I decided it wasn't really necessary because I can do all the calculations just as easily on a computer. Anyway, I got a new laptop recently because, you know, they have so many applications and they don't take up much space either. Better to have lots of things on the same device, I think. The other thing I bought was a present for my husband's birthday. I thought it would be nice to have a record of our holidays, so I bought him a camera and I'm hoping to get him more interested in photography. I'm not very keen on the sort of pictures you can take with a mobile phone, you see. I think it's better to go for higher quality.

W Right … And here's a question about this building. I know you haven't had a chance to look around a lot yet, but at first sight, what do you think of it?

I Oh, it looks pretty good to me. It's got lots of natural light, so you don't have to put up with lots of electric lighting, which can be quite tiring on the eyes. It feels very large and spacious, which is great because although it's full of activity and quite noisy, it doesn't feel too crowded. Also, when you look up at the ceiling near the entrance with the design of stars and planets on it, that's something I really like. I'm not so keen on those revolving doors, though. I always feel I'm going to get stuck in one.

W And did you have any difficulties getting to the exhibition?

I Well, coming at this time of day the roads weren't too busy, so that was all right … and there were plenty of signposts, so the car park was easy to find. The only problem was it was full when I arrived – I guess I should have come earlier – so I had to find another one quite a long walk away, which was a pity. Then we had to stand outside for quite a long time queuing to get in – this exhibition is pretty popular. That was a bit of a problem, because my son gets impatient, but fortunately it wasn't raining, otherwise we might have gone home.

CD1 Track 24

Well, I'm going to talk about my digital camera. Actually, I've got it here, because it's very small and fits in my bag, but it takes great pictures. Everything is automatic, so I just point it and press the button.

I've had this camera for two years. My parents gave it to me for my birthday when I was 18. I didn't ask for a camera, so it was a complete surprise, but it's been really useful.

Since I got the camera, I've carried it with me everywhere I've gone on holiday. For example, in July I went on holiday to Denmark and Sweden. They're lovely places, and in summer it's still light at midnight, so I got some great photos there. Also, I've taken lots of photos of special occasions. For instance, when my grandmother was 70, I took photos of her party.

I use it to remember things, so I put all the photos on my computer. Then I upload them onto Facebook, so my friends can see them.

I've used the camera so often because it's easy to use and I carry it everywhere. I just enjoy taking photos of places which are beautiful and people I'm with, everywhere they're happy. I've taken more than a thousand photos since July. In all, it's been a really great present and I've really enjoyed using it.

CD1 Track 25

I've had this camera for two years. My parents gave it to me for my birthday when I was 18. I didn't ask for a camera, so it was a complete surprise, but it's been really useful.

CD1 Track 26

Since I got the camera, I've carried it with me everywhere I've gone on holiday. For example, in July I went on holiday to Denmark and Sweden. They're lovely places, and in summer it's still light at midnight, so I got some great photos there.

Unit 5

CD1 Track 27

Hi there, everybody, and welcome to Animal World. Before you start your visit, I'd just like to tell you about a few special events happening here today. They're all free, and I'd really encourage you to go to as many of them as you can, as I think you'll learn a lot.

The first event is called The World of Ants, and it's happening this morning quite soon in the Insect House, which is just a short walk from here. The well-known entomologist Dr David Crocker, who many of you will have seen on television, is giving a lecture all about ants – the different types of ants, how they organise themselves, what they eat, their behaviour and so on. It's actually a fascinating subject. So, The World of Ants, a lecture by Dr Crocker, in the Insect House, and it starts at 11 o'clock and lasts for 60 minutes.

At midday, that's 12 o'clock, there's a film which is just as fascinating and it's called *The Great Migration*. This is all about birds and how they migrate across continents and oceans using the Sun, the stars and the Earth's magnetic field. As I said, it's a film – an absolutely spectacular film – which all the family will enjoy, some fabulous photography – and it's on in Theatre C, which you can see here just behind me – so bear that in mind for 12 o'clock.

The next event is a demonstration taking place in the Exhibition Room and given by Monica Chaddha. It's called Encouraging Garden Wildlife. Monica will be showing you ways of encouraging animals, birds and other wildlife to visit and live in your garden, how to place boxes for nests, what food to put out for them and all sorts of practical advice. That's at 2.30, so just after lunch.

The final free event for today is Birds of Prey. Tasha, their keeper, will be giving a display of some of our most magnificent birds and how they fly, and I thoroughly recommend this event. The display includes eagles, vultures and owls and will be starting at 3.45 on the lawn outside. It's an unforgettable experience, so remember, on the front lawn at 3.45 to see the birds flying.

CD1 Track 28

Now, I'll just give you a few directions before you leave, especially for those of you who are feeling a bit hungry. When you leave the main building, you come to an area where the path divides. If you take the right-hand path, you'll see the lake on your right, and exactly opposite the lake on your left is the gift shop. Apart from selling gifts, it sells snacks, sandwiches and light drinks. If you walk on past the lake, on your right you'll also see the penguins. Go past the penguins and you'll come to the restaurant, also on your right. Don't go too far, or you'll come to the aquarium. The aquarium is on your right at the crossroad, and just over the crossroad, also on your right, is the lion enclosure.

If you're thinking of having a picnic, the best place to go is the picnic area, and for this you need to turn left at the crossroad and walk along a few metres. At the end of the path, you'll find the picnic area on your left.

Now, if you have any questions, I'd be happy to answer them and, once again, I really hope you enjoy your visit. Thank you.

CD1 Track 29

Examiner Which are your favourite animals?

Suchin Cats – well, I love my cat, because I've had him for nearly a year now and I love him. He's so beautiful. He's black with a white nose. He sleeps on my bed every night and he – I'm not sure how you say this – but when he's there, I'm not alone. And I'm quite keen on birds – there are lots in the gardens around my house.

E Which animals don't you like?

S I hate insects in the summer. They're horrible!

E Why?

S Well, I live near a large river and there are lots of – I don't know what their name is in English – small insects which bite and come at night. I'm not too keen on flies, either.

E Where are the best places in your country to see wildlife?

S That's a difficult question. I'm not sure. There are so many places with wildlife, but I'm not sure how easy it is to see the animals because it's really a forest, with many trees.

E How popular is watching wildlife in your country?

S It's hard to say. What is the activity called? Hunting is quite popular for some types of animal, but watching wildlife, I don't think I know if it's popular or not. I think people like to go to zoos, but it's not the same.

CD1 Track 30

1 I'm not sure how you say this – but when he's there, I'm not alone.

2 I don't know what their name is in English.

3 That's a difficult question. I'm not sure.

4 It's hard to say.

5 What is the activity called?

CD1 Track 31

1 I've had him for nearly a year now and I love him. He's so beautiful.

2 I hate insects in the summer. They're horrible!

Unit 6

CD2 Track 1

Well, some people use a calendar and others use a diary. But I think if you're really busy, you'll make a list, maybe on your iPhone if you have one. Or sometimes you see a note on the back of someone's hand!

CD2 Track 2

I think birthdays are very easy to forget. You have to write the dates in a diary if you want to remember them! Um – and some older people can't remember where they put their keys or their phone. Oh, and, er, if something unexpected happens, you might forget a lunch date or a meeting – there are lots of things …

CD2 Track 3

You have to write the dates in a diary if you want to remember them.

… you might forget a lunch date or a meeting …

CD2 Track 4

1 Sometimes people forget their dentist or doctor's appointment or things like that.

2 If a friend waits a long time for you, you should say you're sorry and pay next time you go out.

3 People don't usually fall asleep at work unless they're very tired.

4 A boring meeting or a long car journey can make people go to sleep!

CD2 Track 5

Man So we have to do a presentation on a successful person at our next seminar.

Woman Yes, do you have any ideas?

M	Well, I've been on the Internet and picked out a couple.
W	OK – I've got some suggestions, too.
M	Right, well, you start.
W	OK … um, his name's Mahmoud Kaboor and he's a film maker in Dubai in the United Arab Emirates.
M	Sounds good.
W	Yes. He's the managing director of a very big film company.
M	So what made him successful?
W	Apparently his uncle was a film student and because of that, he started making short films when he was only 16.
M	That's quite young … and were they good?
W	Yup. He won a scholarship to go to Canada and study film, and that's how his career developed.
M	Great. Um … here's one of my suggestions. She was a ballet dancer – born in St Petersburg in Russia in 1881.
W	Anna Pavlova. OK – why have you picked her?
M	Well, firstly, because her parents weren't wealthy – they were very poor, in fact – and yet she still went to the School of Imperial Ballet at ten years of age.
W	That's so young! Was she very talented?
M	Yes, she was, but she didn't follow the rules of ballet. She was very individual and did things that were different from other ballerinas at the time.
W	Ah – and that's what made her stand out …
M	Yes.
W	OK. I've got another woman – Marie Curie.
M	She's very famous. Wasn't she Polish?
W	Yeah, born in 1867, but did you know that she was the first woman professor at the University of Paris and the first woman to win a Nobel prize?
M	Yes – amazing!
W	There were many brilliant scientists around when she was working.
M	So why did she do better?
W	Other scientists couldn't get ahead of her because she sensibly published her ideas straight away.
M	What a clever thing to do!
W	Yeah – everyone does it automatically these days, but all those years ago, people often didn't think about it.
M	Great! Well, here's one more.
W	OK – who is it?
M	This is an African-American guy who worked as a chef in the 1850s. His name was George Crum.
W	Did he make a famous dish or something?
M	Not exactly – but without him, we wouldn't have the potato chip. Or crisps, as the British call them.

W	Oh!
M	Yeah. Apparently, he had a customer who was annoyed because his French fries were too fat and soft. So he sliced a new potato as thinly as he could and fried it until it was hard and crunchy. Added lots of salt …
W	… and a new snack was created.
M	Well, I, I think we've got some interesting people here …

CD2 Track 6

Woman	OK, so we have to choose one of these four people.
Man	It's going to be difficult.
W	Well, why don't we agree on some criteria that will help us?
M	Do you mean things like how old they were when they became successful?
W	Yeah – except I'm not sure how old they all were! Um, what about choosing a woman …
M	Is it fair to select someone because of their gender? And look at celebrities – there are lots of women.
W	But it was different in the past.
M	Oh, I see. Yeah, OK, let's pick a woman.
W	Great. Right, well, they're all pretty talented, aren't they? Some have even won awards.
M	Yeah, but maybe their fame won't last for ever.
W	No … so we should pick someone who's done something great on an international level.
M	Yeah, that changed the world … OK, I think that's it. We've got our two criteria. So what do we need to do before we meet again?
W	Well, how much information have we got?
M	Quite a lot of detail about their lives, but not enough about what they did.
W	OK – so before we meet again, let's both find out as much as we can. It's always better to have too much information.
M	Yeah, you're right. What about pictures?
W	Yeah – I don't even know what this person looks like!
M	OK – well, we might get some from the library – but I can look on the Internet as well.
W	Once we've done that, we can get together and talk about the next stage.
M	Yeah – I don't think we can write the presentation for the seminar yet, do you?
W	No – anyway, it'll be fun working together.
M	Yeah! It's been quite an education doing this.
W	Yes – it's made me think about success and what it really means.
M	It isn't about money, is it?

W No – and you don't have to be experienced to achieve it. It can just be luck.

M But perhaps in most cases you need to have some natural ability.

W Yeah – I agree. And I also think you do have to work hard and be determined.

M Yeah – and really want to succeed.

W No matter where you are or what you've done before.

M Mm. It's quite a curious thing.

Unit 7

CD2 Track 7

Advisor Good morning, The Writing School, can I help you?

Caller Oh, hi. I'm ringing about the online writing courses you advertise on the Internet.

A Yes … would you like me to send you a brochure?

C Um, I would, but I also have some questions.

A OK, well, let me take your details first, and then I can deal with the questions after that.

C OK.

A I just need to fill out this form … so, um, can you give me your first name, please?

C Yes, it's Alex.

A That's great, Alex. And what's your last name?

C It's Sachdeva.

A OK – can you spell that for me?

C Yes, it's S-A-C-H-D—

A Is that P?

C No, D-E-V-A.

A OK, I've got that. Now, can you give me your address?

C Well, I'm staying with friends at the moment, but I'll be in my new flat in Preston next week.

A Well, perhaps the Preston address is best.

C OK. So that's Flat 4A, 396 New Valley Road.

A New Valley Road …

C Yes, that's right.

A OK – that's great … and we know the town … that's Preston.

C Yes.

A Do you know what your postcode will be there?

C Oh – I think I've got it somewhere on a piece of paper … let me see … yes, here it is. Er, it's PN6 3BZ.

A BS?

C No, BZ.

A Right. I guess you don't have a phone number yet?

C No, not at the flat. And my mobile's not working right now. I have to take it to the shop and see what's wrong.

A Oh, I hope it's nothing serious.

C Well, it's new, so it should be all right.

A You could give me the number anyway. For the future.

C Yes, OK. Um, it's 0787 345077.

A That's three-five-four-zero-double seven.

C No, three-four-five.

A Oh, thanks. I'll note that your phone is not working right now.

C OK, thanks.

A Now, the last thing I need is an email address.

C OK, it's Alex7@ptu.com. That's my personal address.

A … ptu dot com. Fine. Now, as you're moving, I'll put something in the message box so that the brochure doesn't come too early.

C Yes, could you do that?

A I'll put 'deliver brochure next week'.

C Oh, that's great.

A Now, what would you like to do about …

CD2 Track 8

Advisor Now, you can see on our website that we have a lot of courses … what are you interested in doing?

Caller Well, I don't want to publish anything. I just want to raise the standard of my own writing.

A Yes, it depends on whether you want to, you know, write creatively or for fun. We also have fiction writing – that includes writing children's stories.

C Well, I work in an advertising agency, so … I'd like to write better so that … well, I'd like my salary to rise.

A OK, so we can send you our brochure for business writing and if you think it'll be right for you, then you can enrol.

C Great. What happens after that?

A Then we send you the course pack.

C What does that contain?

A You get some books that will help you with your writing skills, an audio course on CDs and instructional DVDs to watch, and some lesson texts to read.

C OK. What if I change my mind?

A Well, you can send the materials back to us. You have 21 days to decide, and we'll refund your fees within that time.

C Ah, that's quite good. I see. So the enrolment fee includes the course materials?

A Yes, it does – for all our courses.

C So are there different fees for different courses?

A Yes, at the moment, your course is … let me see. They've just raised the prices … it was £340, but I think it's £375 now. Yes, fees rose a month ago, I'm afraid, um, by ten percent – most of our courses are now between three and four hundred pounds.

C OK, that's not bad – so, who will teach me?

A Well, before we decide that, you do your first written assignment. It's like a personal profile.

C So I write about things like my background and where I was brought up?

A No, it's the future we're interested in.

C Oh, OK, so … what I want to get from the course, and how it will help me to achieve my ambitions?

A That's right. We get a picture of who you are and your needs and then we match you to a personal tutor who will teach you and work with you.

C That's a good idea. And how do I get that to you?

A Well, you send it in to us by post or through our website.

C What about lessons?

A There are 15 lessons altogether, and each one has an assignment.

C And what sort of feedback will I get?

A There's continuous online support, and part of that is a web-based facility for all the students on your programme to get together.

C Oh, so we can share ideas and things?

A That's right. With no need to go into a classroom or be tied to weekly schedules.

C OK. Thanks, I think that's all my questions.

A Don't hesitate to call if you have any more.

C OK, thanks. Bye.

CD2 Track 9

Examiner Why do some children stop reading books as they get older?

Pashta Well, I'm not sure … I think it depends. Some children say that they find reading a bit boring … perhaps because they want to do things like play on the computer. Children spend so much time chatting online nowadays. Um, but other children – I think they prefer to read stories about famous people in magazines and newspapers.

E How could teenagers be encouraged to read more?

Haroon Um, I would say that it's important to show them that you can get a lot of knowledge from books. The problem is – we can use computers to look up information, so they forget about books, as they seem less interesting. Maybe writers should make books more attractive to young people.

CD2 Track 10

particularly, relax, activities, imagination, education, illiterate

CD2 Track 11

1 They like to read with their parents, particularly at bedtime.

2 It helps them relax.

3 Small children do a lot of activities during the day.

4 Books are good for children's imagination.

5 It's part of our education.

6 No one wants to be illiterate when they grow up.

CD2 Track 12

parents, secondary, discussing, chatting, important, enjoyed, assignment, computers, attractive, prefer

Unit 8

CD2 Track 13

Good morning, everyone, and welcome to the museum. Um … there are a few points that you need to remember, so, before you go in, I'll just run through them. Then you can all go off and have a good time!

So, first of all, you've all paid and you all have a ticket that allows you to go anywhere in the museum and includes one trip to the 3D cinema. So you need to make sure that you put the ticket somewhere that is secure but easy to find. This is partly because you'll need to show it to our staff if you decide to go out at any time – there are two restaurants which are outdoors, for example – and, um, anyone who does decide to go outside should go and come back through the grey gates. Please don't use the emergency exits unless there really is an emergency!

Now, I'm afraid that if you want to take photographs, you have to purchase a permit at the entrance … we don't allow visitors to take photographs of anything in the museum unless they have a permit. If you'd like a picture of you and your friends at any time, just let us know. We have a number of professional photographers who'll take a photo for you.

Um, another thing is that you must keep everything that belongs to you with you all the time. A lot of people will come to the museum during the day – you'll probably be here for most of the day yourselves – so don't lose your wallet and make sure you don't leave your mobile phone anywhere. It's easily done, and we aren't responsible for any losses while you're here.

Er, as I mentioned earlier, you can go and see any of the films that are on in the 3D cinema. I'll tell you about those in a minute – there's also a schedule on the back of the museum guide.

I suggest you get to the cinema entrance roughly five minutes early … It takes very little time to seat everyone, so you won't be waiting for the show to begin.

Well, I think those are all the instructions I need to give you …

OK … the films which are on today are being shown at different times. They're also about some amazing subjects. Let me tell you a little bit about them.

The first one is called *The Secrets of the Nile* and starts in half an hour at ten o'clock. It's a beautiful film and it tells the story of the journey that was made down the river Nile for the very first time … starting in the mountains of Ethiopia and passing through the Sudan and Egypt before reaching the Mediterranean Sea. You'll accompany the travellers as they explore some of Africa's truly amazing landscapes.

The second film moves off land and into the sea. It's called *Wild Ocean*, and this one begins at 11.45. So you have some time to look round the museum first if you choose this title. In this film, you'll join the huge number of fish and other animals that live far down near the bottom of the sea. You'll see them search for food, migrate and fight for survival.

Dinosaurs Alive is the third film showing today. It starts at 1.45 p.m. and runs for just 30 minutes. This is a film for people who like special effects because there are plenty of them! Scientists now have a lot of evidence to show that some animals from the dinosaur family are still living on Earth. So in this film, you'll live with a new species of dinosaur that has been re-created using computers.

Our final film today is simply titled *Arabia*. It starts at 2.30 and is a little longer than the others, but it's a really wonderful experience. You'll ride through the desert on a camel. You'll also dive among the treasures of the Red Sea where you'll explore the ruins of an amazing lost city.

Well, these are all magical experiences, so I'll let you decide what you want to see. If anyone has any questions …

CD2 Track 15

Examiner Let's talk about tourism in your town or village. Can you describe your town or village?

Ulia I come from Balakovo in Russia. It's a very modern, industrial city, which is situated on the river Volga. What else? A lot of young, professional people who live there work in the offices and industries. Let me think. It's mainly blocks of flats, but we do have some beautiful monuments.

CD2 Track 16

I'd like to talk about a holiday which I took in 2005. It's a holiday that I remember very well, because we had such a fantastic time. I went with three other girls, who are all friends of mine … and we still talk about this holiday today, even though it's so many years later … I mean, we're all married now! But we decided that, er, we wanted to go away together.

So we chose Egypt, which was absolutely … how can I say it? … the Red Sea was so clear and so impressive. You can see everything … you know … It's not dirty like so many seas these days. And it has amazing sea life … the kind of creatures that you can only imagine in your dreams. It was funny because usually I'm a person who's quite scared of things and

I didn't think I would put a mask on my face or go under the water – but I wanted to see the coral so much … it was such a colourful, wonderful experience that I just put the mask on and then, wow, I couldn't believe all the shapes and types of fish. It was absolutely breathtaking. And what else did we do? Yes, we also went to see the ancient pyramids and the national museum, which were all beautiful and also really impressive. I enjoyed this holiday so much because I had my best friends with me. I don't know if I'll ever have another holiday as memorable as this one.

CD2 Track 17

I come from Balakovo in Russia.

I come from Balakovo … in Russia.

CD2 Track 18

a It's a / very modern industrial / city / which is / situated / on the / river Volga.

b It's a very modern / industrial city / which is situated / on the river Volga.

CD2 Track 19

I'd like to talk about a holiday which I took in 2005. It's a holiday that I remember very well because we had such a fantastic time. I went with three other girls, who are all friends of mine, and we still talk about this holiday today.

CD2 Track 20

It was funny, because usually I'm a person who's quite scared of things, and I didn't think I would put a mask on my face or go under the water – but I wanted to see the coral so much.

Unit 9

CD2 Track 21

Tutor So, Fahad, let's talk about your presentation. Um, you've done a rough outline, so, er, let's go over it and then you can go away and write it all up.

Fahad Sure.

T I asked you to choose a topic related to water, and you've chosen desalination – removing salt from seawater. Now, why did you choose that?

F Well, I come from the United Arab Emirates, and we have the world's largest desalination plant.

T Right, that's very relevant, and I think you should include that – you know, your personal, er, reasons – at the start.

F Say why I decided on this topic?

T Yes – just give a sentence or two, that'll do.

F OK – I mean, I thought I should keep the introduction brief …

T Yes, but you can say why you like the topic … it's a good choice of topic – very interesting – and then I can follow the introduction easily.

F	OK.
T	Now, let's go on to the historical background.
F	Mm, I want to make it clear that seawater purification isn't a new idea.
T	No – indeed, that's a good point to make.
F	So I'm going to describe some of the 'older' methods from the past.
T	Mmm. I got a bit lost reading your notes here.
F	Ah-ha. Is it too long?
T	Well, I think the real problem is that the information isn't in any logical order.
F	I see … well, it is just notes.
T	Well, you start in the 18th century, then move to the present day, then go back to the 20th century.
F	So it needs reorganising.
T	Yes, that would help.
F	OK – I'll make it clearer. What about the description of the process?
T	Ah, yes, that looks pretty good to me, but we'll go over it in more detail in a moment.
F	OK. I may need to cut it down.
T	Yes, definitely – it goes on for a long time and gets a bit technical.
F	Sure, er … OK. After the process, I want to talk about the pros and cons of desalination, because that seems to be the big debate.
T	I totally agree. But you need to sort this section out.
F	Yes, it is a bit confusing.
T	I think you should present the main points one at a time.
F	OK – what, er, the advantages and disadvantages?
T	Yes, and talk about each one individually.
F	OK – rather than presenting them all together?
T	Mmm – it's hard for your listeners to take in like that. It's all a bit unclear at the moment.
F	I see.
T	So, lastly, you conclude that we need to look for alternative ways to remove salt from sea water.
F	Well, yes. Do you think that's the wrong conclusion?
T	No, no – not at all. However, you should tell your audience exactly why you think this.
F	I will in the previous section.
T	Mmm, but you need to summarise the reasons again in the final part of your presentation.
F	Oh, I see. Right … I'll mention them briefly, then.
T	Just a list will do. That'll make the conclusion a better length as well.

F	OK – thanks very much, Dr Tyler.

CD2 Track 22

Tutor	OK, so let's have a closer look at the section on the process of desalination.
Fahad	Well, I just need to outline the principle of the process, don't I?
T	Uh-huh. Yes, yes. You need to explain first what desalination means.
F	Well, I want to start by referring to a natural form of desalination … Um, and to say that a sea bird filters salt out of sea water in its throat.
T	OK, that's interesting … so they just spit the salt out, do they?
F	Yes.
T	Right, that's a good introduction. Then you can go on to describe the mechanical process.
F	Yes – well, the first stage is the collection … um … it involves a large plant that collects the water – actually, it goes through a canal and that passes the water into the plant, which treats it, you know …
T	Removes all the rubbish.
F	Yes.
T	So the treatment's the second stage. What happens next?
F	Well, the next stage is that it goes through a lot of pipes until it reaches the point where the salt is removed.
T	OK – so that's the next point on your chart …
F	Yes – I can talk about this quite a lot … the salt's separated from fresh water.
T	Right … the water passes through a membrane …
F	Mmm – not exactly. That's the whole thing. The sea water has to be forced … er, pumped … and a lot of pressure is involved.
T	Mmm – you need to make that point – explain that the water doesn't go freely.
F	No, because the salt is heavy. This is the really expensive part of the process.
T	OK … so after that, what happens?
F	Well, there's some more treatment after the high-pressure filtering process, but eventually the system produces fresh water.
T	OK – it might be good to mention what's left over.
F	Salt, and that's a really big problem …
T	Where does it go?
F	After the desalination process, the substance that remains – it's called brine – it's a very salty substance and it goes back – usually into the sea.
T	Mmm.

F It's not good for fish, though … it damages marine life.

T Well – you can discuss that in the next section of your presentation.

F Yup. So anyway … a lot of the fresh water that's produced is used for human consumption.

T Uh-huh, yes, and …

F It's also used for irrigation … for watering farmland.

T Great! Well, you've mentioned some of the disadvantages …

CD2 Track 23

I'm going to talk about an activity that I enjoy doing, and that's fishing. Actually, I think someone said that fishing's the most popular hobby in the world. So how do I get ready? Well, if you go fishing, then first you have to get up early. Then you need to pack all your equipment and that includes, er, like … a long, thin stick … I think it's called a rod, um, a box or tin to put the fish in and some … er … the little things that you use to attract the fish. Also you need to take some warm clothes perhaps and … and lastly you need something to drink and maybe a sandwich because you can get hungry. There are lots of places where you can go fishing. Some people go to rivers, but I live near the beach, so I fish in a small, yellow, er, a small, er, type of boat. Um … I wear a life jacket, because I usually row the boat out to sea – about a kilometre – so people can't always see me. Fishing is really quite simple … you just sit and wait. I love it because it's so peaceful, it's perfect. But also it's very exciting when you catch something. I usually get these, um, what are they called, um, long, black and white fish. All in all, it's a wonderful activity – it's like a sport, but you're just competing with yourself or with the natural world.

CD2 Track 24

Examiner What water sports are popular among young people?

Carlos I think there are many water sports that are popular. Near beach resorts, for example, the popular sports include things like surfing, sailing, waterskiing … Other sports that young people enjoy are – let me think – canoeing, rowing, perhaps, and, um, well, the main one's swimming because you can do that in a pool anywhere.

E How are sports like surfing and swimming different?

C Well, there are several ways. For a start, you need a lot of waves to surf, whereas swimmers usually prefer calm water. Also, you need more equipment to surf – you know, a board and maybe a wet suit. Yeah, and, and lastly swimming's cheaper than surfing!

E Why do some people not enjoy water sports?

C I think it depends on the person, but, um, the most important reason is probably that they can't swim! They don't like it if it's deep and their feet don't touch the bottom. Even some people who can swim are afraid of water. Another possibility is that, these days, the sea can be very polluted, and they may be afraid of getting ill.

CD2 Track 25

… the main one's swimming, because you can do that in a pool anywhere.

CD2 Track 26

1 For a start, you need a lot of waves to surf, whereas swimmers usually prefer calm water.

2 Yeah, and lastly, swimming's cheaper than surfing!

3 Even some people who can swim are afraid of water.

4 Another possibility is that, these days, the sea can be very polluted, and they may be afraid of getting ill.

Unit 10

CD2 Track 27

Last week, we looked at some of the features of modern houses, and today we're going to turn the clock back and look at traditional house design. I've chosen to start with Samoa, which is part of a group of Polynesian islands in the South Pacific Sea, because the influence of culture and weather on house design is quite clear there.

Um, so let's have a look at, first of all, at the overall design of a traditional Samoan house. Now, these days, houses in Samoa have become more modern and are usually rectangular, but traditional designs were round or sometimes they were oval in shape. Here's a picture. This traditional style is still used – often for guest houses or meeting houses – and most Samoan villages have at least one of these buildings.

As you can see, there are no walls, so the air circulates freely around the house – Samoa is a place that experiences high temperatures … but the open design of the house also reflects the openness of Samoan society. If the occupants want shelter, there are several blinds made of coconut leaves that can be lowered during rainy or windy weather – or indeed the blinds can also be pulled down if people want some privacy.

The foundations of the house – that's the part beneath the floor – are raised slightly. Um, in the past, the height was linked to the importance of the occupants, which we'll talk about another time. However, the floor of the house was usually covered with river stones. Today, we have a range of methods for balancing the temperature inside a building, but the stones on the floor of a Samoan home are ideal for cooling the building on hot days.

Now, let's have a close look at the roof. This, as you can see in the picture, is dome-shaped and traditionally thatched, or covered with leaves from the sugar cane – that's an established crop in Samoa. This was a job for the women, and it involved twisting the leaves and then fastening them with a thin strip of coconut leaf before fixing them to the roof in several layers.

Now, the shape of the roof is important – you can see that the sides are quite steep, and that's done so that the rain falls straight to the ground without moisture going through the leaves and causing leaks or dampness inside the house. Then, you'll notice how high the top of the roof is – this is a way of allowing heat to rise on sunny days and go through the thatching, thereby cooling the house.

So how does the house stay upright? Well, there are a number of evenly spaced posts inside. They, um, they encircle the interior of the building and go up to the roof and support the beams there. They're also buried – er, usually about a metre and a half – in the ground to keep them firm. These posts are produced using local timber from the surrounding forests. They're cut by men from the family or village, and the number varies depending on the size and importance of the house.

Now, these posts were a very significant part of Samoan culture and did much more than hold up the roof. When there were meetings, people sat with their back to certain posts depending on their status in society. So there were posts for chiefs according to their status and posts for speakers and so on – and ordinary people sat around the side on mats.

The last area I want to look at today is the attachment of the beams and posts – what you call 'fixing' the construction. Traditionally, no nails or screws were used anywhere in such a building. Instead, coconut fibres were braided into rope to fix the beams and posts together. The old people of the village usually made and plaited the rope. This was a lengthy process – an ordinary house used about 40,000 feet of this rope – and as you can see in this picture, the rope was pulled very tightly and wound round the beams and posts in a complex pattern. And in fact, the process of tying it to the beams so that it was tight and strong enough to keep them together is one of the great architectural achievements of Polynesia.

CD2 Track 28

Examiner   Are traditional houses more attractive than new houses?

Jaeun   Well, even though some traditional houses looked amazing when they were built, um, most of them just look old-fashioned now. I think people prefer new houses.

Billy   I think so … because they were designed and built separately and people used traditional designs and materials. New houses can look great from the outside, while inside their shape is a bit dull and boring.

Phillipe   I think it depends on the house … you know … whereas some traditional houses in my country have interesting features – like doors and windows – others are just very plain … a new house would be better!

CD2 Track 29

Even though some traditional houses looked amazing when they were built, most of them just look old-fashioned now.

CD2 Track 30

Billy   New houses can look great from the outside, while inside their shape is a bit dull and boring.

Phillipe   … whereas some traditional houses in my country have interesting features – like doors and windows – others are just very plain …

Practice Test

CD2 Track 31

Man   Good morning, Atlas Hotel, can I help you?

Woman   Oh yes – a friend has told me about your hotel, and I'd like to book some rooms, please.

M   OK. When would you like to stay here?

W   Well, we've booked flights on the 23rd of August.

M   OK … I'll just find that date.

(Pause)

M   Good morning, Atlas Hotel, can I help you?

W   Oh yes – a friend has told me about your hotel, and I'd like to book some rooms, please.

M   OK. When would you like to stay here?

W   Well, we've booked flights on the 23rd of August.

M   OK … I'll just find that date. That seems to be fine – we have a few rooms available then.

W   Oh, that's good. I was a bit worried – we've left things rather late.

M   Well, you're lucky – we had two cancellations last week.

W   Oh!

M   Now, how long do you want to stay for?

W   Well, last year we only stayed a week, and it wasn't long enough … so this time we thought two weeks, if it's possible.

M   Mmm, that looks fine … yes, you do need plenty of time here to *really* relax … it'll be getting towards the end of the tourist season as well, so it won't be quite so hot then.

W   Oh good. Um … we've got two children, and I was wondering if you have any rooms that are next to each other?

M   Mmm. Let's see … I'm afraid that isn't possible, but we do have what we call a family room, which is a lot bigger than a double room and can take two adults and two children.

W   Oh, that sounds perfect.

M   OK – I'll book you in for that. So, can I have your name and address, please?

W   Yes, it's Mr and Mrs Shriver.

M   Can you spell that for me?

W   Yes, it's S-H-R-I-V-E-R.

M   Thank you. And you said two children, didn't you?

W   Yes, they're two boys of ten and 12.

M   Fine – and can I have your home address?

W   Yes, we live at flat 29, Tower Heights.

M   OK – is that England?

W	No, it's Scotland, actually. We're from Dunbar. The postcode's EH41 2GK.
M	OK. Great – that's a country *I'd* really like to visit!
W	You'd have to bring a lot of warm clothes!
M	I know … And can I have a contact telephone number?
W	Sure – our home number is 0-1-3-1 double 9-4-6-5-7-2-3.
M	… 7-2-3. Thank you. I hope you don't mind, but we always ask our guests what the purpose of their trip is. I'm guessing yours is a holiday?
W	Yes – we're really looking forward to it!

(*Pause*)

M	As you've been here before, I wonder if you'd mind answering a few short questions for our tourist board?
W	No, not at all.
M	They collect information from tourists, so that they can try to improve the tourism industry here.
W	That's a good idea.
M	OK – um … so what type of holiday activity do you like best?
W	Well, I like a lot of things … I like shopping and sightseeing … but I think as a family, we all enjoy swimming the most.
M	OK … and do you go to the beaches to do that?
W	Well, sometimes we do. We also like to sit around the pool at the hotel.
M	When you go to the beaches, what do you think of them?
W	Well, they're a bit crowded …
M	I know.
W	But then you expect that in the holidays. The main thing is that they're very clean. That's why we come back.
M	I'm glad to hear that. And you said you like shopping …?
W	Yes – it's fun.
M	How are the shop staff? Are they—
W	Well, I don't want to criticise, but sometimes … well, they're a bit *too* helpful.
M	… trying to sell you souvenirs.
W	Yes – I prefer to choose things myself.
M	Uh-huh … What about eating … and the service in the restaurants?
W	Oh, the food is delicious – always. And the waiters – well, they're polite and so fast … Nothing takes very long.
M	That's good news. Sometimes people complain, but …
W	Well, I haven't been to every restaurant – there are rude waiters everywhere, I suppose.

M	Well, we like to avoid it if we can. Do you have suggestions for things which might improve your holiday experience here?
W	Um – not really. Let me think … Oh, yes – I did notice last time I was there that there are local buses, but you don't seem to have any bikes.
M	No, we don't – most people have cars.
W	Mmm – it's just nice to hire one and get some exercise … go at a slower pace so that you can really see the landscape.
M	OK – I'll note that down. Well, thank you very much …

CD2 Track 32

Good morning, everyone. I'm a keeper here at Orana Wildlife Park, and that means that my job is to look after some of the animals that we have here. First, let me tell you a bit about us. Um, the word 'Orana' means 'welcome' in the local Maori language, and we are very pleased to see you all here.

As you probably know, we're run by a charity and we specialise in endangered species of animals, birds and reptiles. The park grounds cover 80 hectares of land, and we have 400 animals altogether, from 70 different species. So that you can see the animals in their natural environment, we've built streams and banks to separate you from the animals and make sure your trip around the park is safe.

Our animals come mainly from here – New Zealand – and from Australia, Africa and South America. There are a lot of animals to see and quite a number of things you can do here, so let me tell you about a few of the exciting encounters before you decide where to go.

One of our most popular animals is a type of giraffe called a Rothschild. It's easy to spot – it has three horns, rather than the usual two. Giraffes are amazing animals close up, and you have an opportunity to hand-feed them here at the park at 12 noon or three in the afternoon. This is one of the most popular activities and will be one that you'll never forget.

In fact, we believe hands-on education is very important. So, you can touch or pat a variety of friendly animals, such as cows and goats, at the farmyard. This experience goes on all day and is designed to help children take an interest in animals and their environment. I can assure you it's not at all dangerous.

Another exciting activity for visitors is watching some of our big cats reach speeds of up to 70 kilometres per hour during their exercise run. The cheetah is the fastest land mammal, and this 'event' takes place at 3.40 every day. You can watch them go down their paddock in under 30 seconds.

(*Pause*)

So here's a plan of the park. As you can see, we're here at the main entrance, and there's an information centre to your right.

Now – it's quite easy to get around the park. We have daily guided walkabout tours, which let you get up close to the animals. Or if you prefer to be at a distance, you can take the safari bus and drive around with a wildlife expert.

If you decide to take the walkabout tour, it leaves at 10.45 – that's in just under an hour – from the meerkats enclosure next to us. From there, the walk passes the adventure playground, and the otters in the first enclosure, and then arrives at the New Zealand birds area in the next enclosure just in time to see them being fed. Then you go on to the reptile house and the tigers and the rest of the animals!

Alternatively, you can wait until the afternoon walk. There are plenty of other things to see in the morning. One of these is the African Village. Just turn to your right from the main entrance, walk past the first bus stop and it's just before the African wild dogs enclosure. It's a wonderful, colourful experience.

You can also go to the shop and buy your souvenirs there. We have beautiful soft toys – giraffe and zebra – for children and a whole range of T-shirts, hats and skin-care products with an African theme. After that, why not have lunch in the picnic area on the far eastern side of the park? I'd recommend this because, while you're eating, you might catch sight of the ostriches on one side of you or buffalo on the other.

For the afternoon walkabout tour, you'll need to find your own way to the African lion habitat, which is on the west side of the park, just past the Conservation Centre. To join the tour, you actually go past the lion habitat. You'll see two bus stops … keep walking, and the meeting place is about half a kilometre after the second one. If you've gone past the zebra, you've gone too far!

For those of you who would prefer to travel on the safari bus, this runs from 10.30 to 4 p.m. There are stations throughout the park, but the first one is at Jomo's Café, which is directly opposite where we're standing – go straight ahead and it's just in front of the giraffes. There are various feeding times for the animals, and the bus stops in time for all of these. So, let me just give you some safety guidelines …

CD2 Track 33

Tutor Right – now it's time for Sylvie and Daniel to give us the results of their survey into the study-skills course that some of you did last term.

Sylvie Thanks, Mr Driver. Um – shall I start, Daniel?

Daniel Sure, go ahead.

S OK. Well, as you know, some students in our year did the study-skills course run by the English department last term.

D Um, it was interesting because it was completely voluntary … it wasn't a compulsory component of the exam course or anything that we need in that way … but Mr Driver thought it would be a good idea … that it would help with our other work.

S Yeah, so after the course finished, Daniel and I decided to review it … ask students what they thought about it … as part of our education assignment.

D Yeah.

S So … this is how we did it … our study method. At first, we thought about interviewing students face to face. But we have so much other work and we knew it'd be quicker to use email and just send out a questionnaire.

D Though we also had to write that!

S Yes, and this method does rely on students filling it in and sending it back … but the response rate was pretty good.

D Yeah – 70 percent, I think.

S OK – so, first of all, 33 students signed up for the course.

D And we did 12 sessions over the term, and they took place every Monday morning.

S A good start to the week, I thought.

D Yeah – and the rest of the week, we could put things into practice.

S Mmm. So what did we expect?

D For me … I expected it to be useful for all my subjects … things like philosophy—

S Yeah – that's what Mr Driver had said.

D —and I was right … I feel more able to deal with difficult texts now – you know, like the ones we have in economics.

S You feel you can do it. Yeah, I think other people found that it actually made them want to read more frequently … and read books outside the course list.

D If you've got time! Um – as for our teacher on the course – Jenny – everyone felt she was really good. We learned a lot from her. Not because she set a lot of homework or anything like that …

S … the thing people said was that she gave us fascinating articles and ideas to work with … some of them … well, we were quite happy to carry on looking at them at home.

D Yeah – that's so important. It's really easy to get bored in class, but that didn't happen.

(*Pause*)

D OK – so, we've done a couple of charts … let's have a look at the findings. I'll put up the first chart …

S This is your overall view of the usefulness of the course.

D … and as you can see, only a small percentage of students didn't feel it was useful.

S Which is good …

D Yeah – everyone else had a positive view of the course, and more than half of us – that's about 60 percent – thought it was very useful.

S Which … well, as this is the first time the course has been run, I guess this is a strong recommendation for it to take place again next year.

D The next chart shows how useful you felt each part of the course was.

S So just to remind you … there was the speed-reading component – that came out top.

D No surprise there, really.

S Mmm. On the other hand, giving talks was … well, we all like talking, but it's not something we have to do that often.

D Yeah – so that was the least useful. Then the note-taking component you found to be quite useful – and you had a lot of comments about that.

S OK, so let's have a look at some of your comments. You said a lot about the activities, but the main comment seemed to be that the techniques we learned on the note-taking course helped us focus more in lectures.

D Several people said that they daydream much less.

S Yeah … have a longer attention span.

D So that's the first benefit. The second is that students said they really appreciated the instruction on when to use a diagram to take notes.

S Mmm, like many people, I'd never thought of this technique, but now I find it really helpful.

D … and it's much more fun!

S Yeah. And then the last comment we wanted to mention was about the type of paper that we used in the note-taking sessions.

D It seems obvious now that a wide margin down the side of the paper provides another area where you can add points that you've missed.

S And that makes it a lot easier to read the notes afterwards.

D OK, so now we'll look at the results …

CD2 Track 34

Good morning, everyone. Well, last week, we looked at some of the architectural features of modern house design and today we're going to move on to look at airport design and how this has changed over the years.

So, if we start by going back to … um … the 1960s and '70s, when there were a lot fewer airports than there are today … well, check-in desks, customs and waiting areas were all very basic. They were rather like a bus station – er, designed to allow air traffic in and out of the terminal, but not very welcoming for passengers. Even though passengers spent a lot of time there, the important features were related to the flights, rather than the people who took them … or indeed the places where the airports were built.

But that all changed in the next few decades, and if you look at any big airport now, it's more like a mini city. It combines a transport centre with a mall full of shops and facilities designed to make passengers feel more comfortable. So, airports have been transformed. And as with any city building, their design now takes into account features outside the airport terminal as well.

So why did this change happen? Well, there are two main reasons. The first was the huge increase in passenger numbers … in the number of people travelling by plane. And this was a direct result of mass tourism, with things like, um, cheap holiday packages and low-cost airlines … with the construction of high-rise hotels and hotel complexes. And then people started travelling more regularly from one country to another for things like meetings, and so the growth in international business also pushed numbers up. In fact, passenger growth has been so significant over the past 30 years that it's estimated that some 21st-century airports will need to handle up to 50 million passengers a year by 2020.

The second reason for the change is – and this is a key aspect of airport design – people have realised that the airport is the first place you see when you visit another country. This means it forms your first impression of that country and that impression has to be good. Airports are now called 'gateways' to the cities they serve, and that raises visitor expectations.

Now, what are the changes that have taken place in airport design? Well, the interior design – the inside of most airports – is now completely different. First, the dark, enclosed airports of the past have been replaced by large, open areas that look out onto the surroundings. Look at this picture of Beijing airport – there's a huge amount of space and light, and this is typical of many airports today.

Second … well, in the past, you had to go outside the airport to get trains to terminals, but now these are integrated into the design. Also, airport walkways are wide and can cope with the large volume of people … people who want to feel calm and relaxed – who want to get around the airport easily. In this way, the stress of modern travel has been minimised.

Outside, the buildings have changed, too. Airports were once ugly buildings with large towers and concrete boxes around them. Now they're designed to fit into their surroundings. Look at this picture of the Arctic Circle airport in Norway. The airport itself is surrounded by mountains. So, as you can see, the roof of the airport has been designed so that it's shaped like a range of mountains. There are peaks at the top and then steep sides that touch the ground.

In the same way, these airports in Thailand and India have beautiful shaded gardens all around them that reflect the landscape of the country. They also provide a connection with local tradition and art … another feature that is important inside airports, too.

And there's one final but very important issue. It's been said that airports are a 'new building type'. They're often light, steel structures with what looks to the passenger like a lot of glass. But this is special glass that can maximise daylight and comfort and cut down on energy use. Bangkok's main airport is flooded with controlled daylight in a tropical climate … and this is achieved through the use of new materials and modern technology, which have also allowed engineers to come up with methods of reducing costs. So let's take a closer look at some of these …

Additional material

Unit 2, Starting off, Exercise 2, page 17

Student A
- Kenneth Hale (United States): linguist at Massachusetts Institute of Technology; spoke about 50 languages
- Junko Tabei (Japan): first woman to climb Mount Everest, in 1975; nearly died in an avalanche
- Kiran Mazumdar-Shaw (India): started Biocon, India's largest biotechnology company; richest woman in India in 2004

Unit 5, Reading 2, Exercise 1, page 52

2 T 3 T 4 F (All whales come to the surface to breathe.)
5 T 6 F (There are at least 78 species, and some species have only been discovered recently.) 7 T

Unit 9, Starting off, Exercise 2, page 88

1 c 2 d 3 b 4 e 5 f 6 a

Unit 5, Vocabulary, Exercise 4, page 52

a when a type of animal no longer exists
b to guess the cost, size, value, etc. of something
c the place where someone or something is going
d show that something exists or is likely to be true
e scientist who studies the sea
f scientist who studies biology
g relating to or involving two or more countries
h regularly or often
i large in amount or size
j to return to the way it was before
k existing or happening before something else
l easy to recognise because it is different from other things

Unit 2, Starting off, Exercise 2, page 17

Student B
- Nelson Mandela (South Africa): President of South Africa 1994–1999; 27 years in prison
- Naguib Mahfouz (Egypt): Nobel Prize for Literature 1988; wrote *The Cairo Trilogy*
- Yang Liwei (China): first Chinese astronaut in space, October 2003; circled the planet 14 times

Unit 10, Starting off, Exercise 3, page 97

building and date built	purpose	interesting facts
1 **'Piano and violin' building** (2007)	exhibition hall	• Inside the violin is an escalator to the building. • It is considered by locals to be the most romantic building in China. • Wedding couples have pictures taken here.
2 **Dancing House** (1992–96)	apartment block	• Local people say that it looks 'terrible' and 'like a crushed can of Coke'.
3 **Kansas City Public Library** (2004)	the south wall of the library's car park	• It has 22 books – nearly 30 feet tall. • Library visitors selected their 22 favourite books.
4 **Pompidou Centre**	You will read about the Pompidou Centre in the reading passage which follows.	
5 **Raffles Hotel** (2007)	five-star hotel	• The pyramid design is based on those in ancient Egypt. • Botanical gardens on the third floor contain 129,000 different types of plant.
6 **Strawberry House** (1984)	children's themed shopping centre	• It contains many items that look like strawberries, e.g. lights, mirrors and pillows. • Staff sing and tell stories.

Acknowledgements

Author acknowledgements

We would like to give our warmest thanks to the editors and production staff for all their support, feedback and hard work during this project: Dilys Silva, Catriona Watson-Brown, Andrew Reid, Diane Jones, Sophie Clarke, Julie Sontag and Sarah Salter; also to John Green (audio producer), Tim Woolf (audio editor), Elizabeth Walter (wordlists), Louise Edgeworth (photo research), Barry Tadman (audio supervisor) and Kevin Doherty (proof reader). Thanks also to the team at Wild Apple: Tracey Cox, Steve Crabtree and Rebecca Crabtree.

The authors and publishers are grateful to the following for reviewing the material:
Phil Biggerton, Taiwan; Michelle Czajkowski, China; John Langille, UAE; Simon Feros, South Korea; Shida Lee, Hong Kong; Nick Moore, New Zealand; Wayne Rimmer, Russia; James Terrett, UK.

Guy Brook-Hart dedicates his part in this book to his daughter, Elena, with love.

Vanessa Jakeman dedicates her part in this book to her dear friend and colleague, Morgan Terry.

Text and photo acknowledgements

The authors and publishers acknowledge the following sources of copyright material and are grateful for the permissions granted. While every effort has been made, it has not always been possible to identify the sources of all the material used, or to trace all copyright holders. If any omissions are brought to our notice, we will be happy to include the appropriate acknowledgements on reprinting.

The publisher has used its best endeavours to ensure that the URLs for external websites referred to in this book are correct and active at the time of going to press. However, the publisher has no responsibility for the websites and can make no guarantee that a site will remain live or that the content is or will remain appropriate.

p. 9 text adapted from 'Rio is "world's friendliest city"'. Copyright © news.bbc.co.uk; p. 11 Yes Magazine: text adapted from 'Why is Costa Rica smiling?' by Lisa Gale Garrigues, *Yes Magazine* 15.12.09. Reproduced with permission; pp. 14–16 charts copyright © 2002–2010 Tourism Strategy Group, Ministry of Economic Development, New Zealand; p. 18 Cengage Learning: text adapted from *Science and its Times* 1st edition, Neil Schlager (Editor), Josh Lauer (Editor) © 2000 Gale, a part of Cengage Learning, Inc. Reproduced by permission. www.cengage.com/permissions; p. 29 Cosmos: text adapted from 'The electric revolution' by Tim Thwaites, *Cosmos* October 2009. Reproduced with permission; p. 33 The Environmental Magazine: text adapted from 'Sick of traffic jams?' *The Environmental Magazine*. Copyright © 2011 E – The Environmental Magazine. Earthtalk ® is written and edited by Roddy Scheer and Doug Moss and is a registered trademark of E – The Environmental Magazine (http://www.emagazine.com); pp. 33–34 Central Houston Inc.: tables and bar chart adapted from Downtown Houston Commute Survey Report, August 2009. Reproduced with permission; p. 49 National Geographic: text adapted from 'Painting the sky' by Bruce Barcott, *National Geographic* 2008/10. Copyright © Bruce Barcott/ National Geographic Stock; pp. 90–91 text adapted from 'The burden of thirst' by Tina Rosenberg, *National Geographic* 2010/04. Copyright Tina Rosenberg/National Geographic Stock; pp. 52–53 Nature Publishing Group: text adapted from 'Humpback whale breaks migration record' by Janelle Weaver. Copyright © 2010 Nature Publishing Group; p. 60 Michigan State University: text adapted from 'Sleep helps reduce errors in memory, MSU research suggests' by Kimberley Fenn, *Michigan State University News*, http://news.msu.edu/story/6804; pp. 68–69: Oxford Open Learning: listening exercise and text adapted from *The Joy of Writing*. © 2009 The Writing School at Oxford Open Learning; pp. 70–71 text adapted from www.speed-reading-techniques.com; p. 74 graph A on 'World illiteracy' by James Lundberg; p. 74 graph B from Australian Government Department of Education, Employment and Workplace Relations, © 2011 Commonwealth of Australia; p. 74 graph on Unemployment rate for adults from the US Bureau of Labor Statistics; p. 76(2) graph from Wistatutor.com; pp. 78–79 Geographical Magazine Ltd: text adapted from 'Here today, gone tomorrow (get the T-shirt)' by Christian Amodeo, *Geographical Magazine* November 2009 and for pp. 149–150 text adapted from 'White mountain, green tourism' by Marc Grainger *Geographical Magazine* October 2009. Copyright © Geographical Magazine Ltd; pp. 98–99 text adapted from http://designmuseum.org. Copyright © Design Museum. Reproduced with permission; p. 112 chart and table Copyright © 2001–2009 Nepal Vista.com; p. 113 chart from http://4.bp.blogspot.com; p. 114 table and graph adapted from www. wildexpeditions.co.za; p. 143 Orana Wildlife Trust for the listening test. Reproduced with permission. www.oranawildlifepark.co.nz; pp. 147–148 text adapted from 'Teen's DIY energy hacking gives African village new hope' by Kim Zetter. Copyright © 2009 Condé Nast Publications. All rights reserved. Originally published in Wired.com.

Reprinted with permission and Bryan Mealer 'The boy who harnessed the wind' http://www.bryanmealer.com; p. 152 text adapted from 'From print to pixel' by Kevin Kelly. Originally published in Smithsonian, August 2010. Reproduced with permission of Kevin Kelly; p. 155 chart adapted from © Polk. Reprinted with permission.

Photos
p. 8(1): Shutterstock/Emin Kuliyev; p. 8(2): Thinkstock/istockphoto; p. 8(3): Shutterstock/Hainaultphoto; p. 8(4): photolibrary.com/Martin Moxter; p. 8(5): Thinkstock/Digital Vision; p. 8(6): Shutterstock/Chee-Onn Leong; p. 9: Press Association/John Birdsall; p. 10: Press Association/AP Photo/Nakheel Development, HO; p. 11R: Spectrum Photofile; p.11L: P.J Heller/PhotoReporters; p. 12TL: Rex Features/DeeDee DeGelia & Brent Winebrenner & DeGelia/Mood Board; p. 12TC: Shutterstock/Daniel Loretto; p. 12TR: Thinkstock/Hemera; p. 12BL: Shutterstock/Iakov Filimonov; p. 12BC: Art Directors & TRIP/Helene Rogers; p. 12BR: Alamy/Edd Westmacott; p. 13R: Alamy/Anna Yu; p. 13L: Alamy/Gino's Premium Images; p. 16: Alamy/Daniel Kerek; p. 17(1): MIT/Donna Coveney; p. 17(2): Corbis/John Van Hasselt; p. 17(3): Press Association/WEITZ/AP; p. 17(4): Rex Features/Sipa Press; p. 17(5): Science Photo Library/Volker Steger; p. 17(6): Rex Features/Sipa Press; p. 18: Getty Images/Popperfoto; p. 19: Robert Harding/age footstock; p. 20: Alamy/itanistock; p. 22R: Corbis/Anders Ryman; p. 22L: PhotoResourceHawaii; p. 23: Alamy/Alvey & Towers Picture Library; p. 24: Alamy/Ace Stock Ltd; p. 28TL: Shutterstock/Oleksiy Mark; p. 28TC: Shutterstock/bubamarac; p. 28TR: Shutterstock/Ilja Masik; p. 28BL: Shutterstock/Vibrant Image Studio; p. 28BC: Shutterstock/Isaak; p. 28BR: Shutterstock/Philip Lange; p. 31: Alamy/Directphoto.org; p. 33: Alamy/Iain Masterton; p. 37(1): Press Association/All Action/EMPICS Entertainment; p. 37(2): Alamy/permian creations; p. 37(3): Alamy/Imagestate Media Partners Ltd-Impact Photos; p. 37(4): Rex Features/Courtesy Everett Collection; p. 37(5): Press Association/Topham Picturepoint; p. 37(6): Alamy/Vintage Image; p. 38B: Press Association/AP; p. 38T: Art Directors & TRIP/Eric Pelham; p. 39: Corbis/Ken Seet; p. 40: Alamy/Turkey; p. 42(a): photolibrary.com/Bridge; p. 42(b): Art Directors & TRIP/Helene Rogers; p. 42(c): Thinkstock/Hemera; p. 44TL: Corbis/Clarissa Leahy/cultura; p. 44BL: Press Association/Shea Walsh/AP; p. 44R: Rex Features/Etienne Ansotte; p. 45L: Robert Harding/age footstock; p. 45R: Alamy/David J.Green-lifestyle themes; p. 48(1): Thinkstock/istockphoto; p. 48(2): Shutterstock/idreamphoto; p. 48(3): Shutterstock/aleks.k; p. 48(4): Shutterstock/Tom C Amon; p. 48(5): Shutterstock/efendy; p. 48(6): Thinkstock/Stockbyte; p. 48(7): Thinkstock/Photodisc; p. 49: Getty Images/Joe Petersburger/National Geographic; p. 50L: Robert Harding/Image Broker; p. 50R: Corbis/Rungroj Yongrit/epa; p. 51: Shutterstock/Pius Lee; p. 53: Thinkstock/istockphoto; p. 54: Shutterstock/Uryadnikov Sergey; p. 55L: Shutterstock/Serg64; p. 55R: Thinkstock/Photos.com; p. 58: Shutterstock/Gorilla; p. 60: Thinkstock/istockphoto; p. 61T: Shutterstock/Konstantin Sutyagin; p. 61B: Alamy/Anna Yu; p. 62L: photolibrary.com/EPA/Tibor Illyes; p. 62CL: Getty Images/Redferns/Nigel Crane; p. 62CR: Rex Features/Micha Theiner/City AM; p. 62R: Shutterstock/stefanolunardi; p. 63: Alamy/new photo service; p. 64BL: Rex Features/Sipa Press; p. 64BR: Rex Features/CSU Archv/Everett; p. 64TC: Rex Features/Sipa Press; p. 64TR: Rex Features/Sipa Press;

p. 64TL: Rex Features/Aflo; p. 68(1): Thinkstock/Pixland; p. 68(2): Corbis/Oliver Berg/dpa; p. 68(3): Shutterstock/ARENA Creative; p. 68(4): Thinkstock/Digital Vision; p. 68(5): Alamy/H.Mark Weidman Photography; p. 68(6): Alamy/Radius Images; p. 70: Corbis/Ocean; p. 71: www.CartoonStock.com; p. 72T: Alamy/Purestock; p. 72B: Alamy/Yuri Arcurs; p. 77(1): Alamy/StockShot; p. 77(2): Thinkstock/istockphoto; p. 77(3): Art Directors & TRIP/Douglas Houghton; p. 77(4): Corbis/Frank May/dpa; p. 77(5): Thinkstock/istockphoto; p. 77(6): Shutterstock/kkaplin; p. 79: Corbis/Ralph Lee Hopkins/National Geographic Society; p. 81: Alamy/Stocktrek Images Inc; p. 82(1): Shutterstock/Joseph Calev; p. 82(2): Alamy/philipus; p. 82(3): photolibrary.com/Imagebroker.net; p. 82(4): Shutterstock/N Mrtgh; p. 82(5): Shutterstock/Patryk Kosmider; p. 82(6): Shutterstock/Jan Kranendonk; p. 83: Shutterstock/Natalia Barsukova; p. 88(1): Shutterstock/Yuri Arcurs; p. 88(2): Shutterstock/lovu4ever; p. 88(3): Shutterstock/Colourstripe; p. 88(4): Thinkstock/istockphoto; p. 88(5): Alamy/James Schutte; p. 88(6): Thinkstock/Hemera; p. 90: Corbis/Lynn Johnson/National Geographic Society; p. 93T: Shutterstock/eAlisa; p. 93R: Thinkstock/Ryan McVay; p. 93BL: Alamy/Jeff Greenberg; p. 94: Alamy/UpperCut Images; p. 97(1): Press Association/Xinhua/Landov; p. 97(2): Robert Harding/age footstock; p. 97(3): Emy Smith Photography; p. 97(4): Getty Images/Arnaud Chicurel/hemis.fr; p. 97(5); Corbis/G Bowater; p. 97(6): Lebrecht Music & Arts/Haga; p. 98: Alamy/David Noton Photography; p. 100: Rex Features/Rick Colls; p. 101: Harry Pidgeon Collection, UCR/California Museum of Photography, University of California, Riverside; p. 102B: istockphoto/PhotoTalk; p. 102T: Alamy/Robert Fried; p. 103: Alamy/Robert Fried; p. 146: Lucas Oleniuk/GetStock.com; p. 149: Robert Harding/age footstock; p. 152: Rex Features/CSU Archives/Everett Collection.

Illustrations:
Kveta pp. 30, 61, 96, 124, 143; Peter Marriage pp. 14, 15, 16, 29, 35, 54, 55, 73, 74, 75, 76, 86, 112, 113, 114, 144, 155; Andrew Painter pp. 95, 106; Martin Saunders pp. 29, 50, 52; Mark Turner p. 114; David Whamond p. 73; Gary Wing p. 57

Corpus
Development of this publication has made use of the Cambridge English Corpus (CEC). The CEC is a computer database of contemporary spoken and written English, which currently stands at over one billion words. It includes British English, American English and other varieties of English. It also includes the Cambridge Learner Corpus, developed in collaboration with the University of Cambridge ESOL Examinations. Cambridge University Press has built up the CEC to provide evidence about language use that helps to produce better language teaching materials.

CALD
The *Cambridge Advanced Learner's Dictionary* is the world's most widely used dictionary for learners of English. Including all the words and phrases that learners are likely to come across, it also has easy-to-understand definitions and example sentences to show how the word is used in context. The *Cambridge Advanced Learner's Dictionary* is available online at dictionary.cambridge.org. © Cambridge University Press, 3rd edition, 2008, reproduced with permission.